THE
LIVING
LANDSCAPE

THE LIVING LANDSCAPE

DESIGNING FOR BEAUTY AND BIODIVERSITY IN THE HOME GARDEN

RICK DARKE & DOUG TALLAMY

PRINCIPAL PHOTOGRAPHY BY RICK DARKE

TIMBER PRESS Portland · London

Page 1: Umbrella magnolia and two-winged silverbells flower in early May in the understory below a pin oak in a Pennsylvania garden. Pages 2-3: The layered landscape in late April in the Darke-Zoehrer garden

Published in 2014 by Timber Press, Inc.

The Haseltine Building
133 S.W. Second Avenue, Suite 450
Portland, Oregon 97204-3527
timberpress.com

6a Lonsdale Road
London NW6 6RD
timberpress.co.uk

Printed in China
Book design by Susan Applegate

Library of Congress Cataloging-
in-Publication Data

Darke, Rick.
   The living landscape: designing for beauty and biodiversity in the home garden/Rick Darke and Doug Tallamy; principal photography by Rick Darke.—1st ed.
       p. cm.
   Designing for beauty and biodiversity in the home garden
   Includes bibliographical references and index.
ISBN 978-1-60469-408-6
   1. Natural landscaping—United States. 2. Ecological landscape design—United States. I. Tallamy, Douglas W. II. Title. III. Title: Designing for beauty and biodiversity in the home garden.
   SB439.D37 2014
   712′.2—dc23   2013040141

A catalog record for this book is also available from the British Library.

Contents

Watching the woods from a tree house at Longwood Gardens.

Preface
by Rick Darke

My gardening life really began more than four decades ago when I joined the staff of Pennsylvania's Longwood Gardens. Fresh out of school with a degree in botany, I had the good fortune to be hired as assistant to Longwood's Ph.D. plant taxonomist, Donald "Dutch" Huttleston.

Dutch grew up in rural upstate New York with a pet crow trained to perch on his shoulder. Hoping to make his career as a naturalist, he taught himself to know both the local flora and fauna: the wildflowers, trees, shrubs, ferns, mushrooms, and lichens as well as the birds, insects, and other animals. As we began working together, frequently on foot through the great woodlands and meadows surrounding Longwood's formal gardens, his ability to put a name on virtually any plant we encountered and to identify unseen birds by their song delighted me. Along the way, we hunted for morels rising through the leafy woods floor after spring rains. In the course of our work, we observed bees and butterflies engaged in myriad pollinating and nectar-gathering activities.

I was in awe of the breadth of his knowledge, which made life in Longwood's landscapes all seem connected, and I asked how he'd come to focus on plant taxonomy. Dutch explained that in his era the dream of earning a living as a naturalist proved an unlikely prospect, and for economic reasons he accepted the need to specialize. In time, I too specialized professionally, though I've held on to the belief that our definition of the garden could be broadened to include a wondrous array of vital connections. Over the years, I've looked for opportunities to promote this idea in projects, lectures, and publications.

The chapter-long study of life along the Red Clay Creek that forms the ethical core of my book *The American Woodland Garden: Capturing the Spirit of the Deciduous Forest* draws directly from observations of local natural process, and from both floral and faunal associations. My earlier submission of the study in preliminary form to a garden magazine was nearly rejected by a horticulturally oriented editor who first dismissed it as "nature study, not gardening!" I'm grateful to the editors at Timber Press for taking the chance that the gardening community's recognition of the relevance of such an ecological work might be growing.

Despite this, the fact that the book's over 700 photos include only one bird and one bee (and those are both in the Red Clay Creek chapter) is a reflection of the then-current separation of non-plant diversity from garden design.

Doug Tallamy and his wife, Cindy, are friends and neighbors with my wife, Melinda Zoehrer, and me. We all share personal and professional interests in supporting biological diversity, and we each garden in our own way. In recent years, Doug and I have been on the programs of various conferences together, and these events have revealed both the overlap in our work and the insights that result from combining our respective disciplines. My perspective is primarily that of a plant ecologist, horticulturist, and landscape designer, and Doug's is primarily that of an entomologist, behavioral ecologist, and ornithologist.

Many conversations with professional friends and with conference attendees encouraging us to collaborate led inevitably to the idea of producing a book together. Our goal has been to focus on the common ground in our approaches and methods without losing the varied perspective that results from preserving individual voices. In keeping with this, the majority of the text is written in a combined voice with both authors contributing. Following our respective introductions, individually written material is identified with abbreviated bylines: —RD (Rick Darke) or —DT (Doug Tallamy).

Is this book only about gardening with native plants? No. It's a book about how native plants can play essential roles in gardens designed for multiple purposes, with a focus on proven functionality. For better and worse, the native plant movement in North America has evolved in the last decade. Increased interest in natives has resulted in a greater diversity of commercially available locally and regionally indigenous plant species, and this is for the better, even if it is still only a fraction of the whole. Unfortunately, the focus has remained primarily on decorative qualities such as colorful flowers rather than suitability for a variety of roles in which plants make gardens truly alive and livable. Providing beauty is a valuable function; however, other equally important functions include screening, organizing spaces, cooling, groundwater recharge, and providing food and shelter for both humans and diverse wildlife.

One of the most important functionalities is durability: the capacity to thrive over a long time without dependence on resource-consuming maintenance regimes. Claims that natives are *always* better adapted than exotics fail to take into account radically altered environmental conditions in many suburban landscapes. Claims that a palette primarily of exotic plants has no negative impact on relational biodiversity are equally flawed, as Doug discusses in depth in chapter two. In most cases and most places, the design of broadly functional, ecologically sound, resource-conserving residential gardens requires a carefully balanced mix of native and non-native plants. It's time to stop worrying about where plants come from and instead focus on how they function in today's ecology. After all, it's the only one we have.

Since writing *The American Woodland Garden,* I've worked on, visited, and revisited a broad array of gardens and habitats, documenting observations I believe are relevant to modern landscape design and management. Melinda and I have now had the uncommon experience of tending the same garden for more than 20 years. It's been both our home and our living laboratory, and has provided a wealth of first-hand experience and lessons that I've made extensive use of in this book.

One of those lessons has been a deeper appreciation of the vital role of wildness in designed landscapes. Although *The Wild Garden: Expanded Edition* gave me the chance to frame this concept and point to its promise for modern gardeners, the present book provides the opportunity to illustrate the practical application of wild gardening in much greater detail.

It isn't easy to write a book about combining beauty and biodiversity in garden design without constantly referencing Nature (with a capital "N"), but we've done our best. Why? Because the traditional idea of Nature is rooted in separatism—in the dichotomy of Man and Nature—and this book is about connection.

British philosopher Raymond Williams suggested the word *Nature* is a "singular term for the multiplicity of things and living processes," and I can live by that definition. However, popular culture defines Nature as an "other," a near-sentient force operating beyond the bounds of human community. I was raised with that notion and can empathize with the nostalgia often accompanying it, but I can't accept the idea of a separate Nature any more than I believe digital data resides in "The Cloud" (the data resides in machinery that is typically plugged into a wall socket).

No other species on Earth is as influential as ours is, yet we are part of it all, connected to it all. Our actions have far-reaching consequences, and if we're thoughtful, most of them can be good ones. Making a garden and living in it is a great way to practice the art of ethical, functional design. A well-made garden should be full of life, human and otherwise, providing infinite, daily opportunities to experience that glorious multiplicity of things and living processes.

Preface
by Doug Tallamy

A blue grosbeak male stakes out his breeding territory.

A grosbeak nest built with shed snake skins within alternate-leaf dogwood (*Cornus alternifolia*).

Three summers ago my wife, Cindy, and I were privileged—but not accidental—participants in one of nature's special performances. A pair of birds nested in our yard. I know: that doesn't sound very special, but when you think about what it took for that avian couple to reproduce successfully in our suburban setting, it becomes very special indeed.

I still remember the first time I saw the male blue grosbeak. I thought it was one of our many indigo buntings, but it was larger, had a beautiful streak of red on its wings, and produced a different song. At first, he spent all day singing. From his perch on one of our ironwood trees, he would flex his azure crest and sing his heart out. His goal was not to entertain me, but to stake his claim to a breeding territory. He chose our property to raise his young because it is dotted with the small trees and shrubs that are perfect for concealing his nest. Even more important, the insects he needed to feed his nestlings are plentiful here.

The male grosbeak sings for two reasons: to warn off intruding males and to attract a mate. It didn't take him long to find romance; a chocolate-colored female, lured by his melodies, found him and the quality of the territory he was guarding to her liking. Soon she started to construct a nest deep within an alternate-leaf dogwood tree.

Blue grosbeaks are among the few birds that use snakeskins as nesting material. The task of locating a suitable skin typically falls to the male, and at our house, he was in luck: a black rat snake had left a 4-foot skin near a groundhog hole in our meadow. Soon the grosbeak and his mate had woven the skin among grass blades and sticks to form the nest that would become home for three nestlings. This was his only successful bout of reproduction that year, but he sang in celebration every morning at seven sharp from midsummer until early autumn when he and his family departed for their overwintering grounds in southern Mexico.

Please remember that what I have described did not take place in a national park, or even in a small county preserve. It happened in our yard. It happened there because we have built our landscape with all of the bits of nature that blue grosbeaks require to make more blue grosbeaks. Once mowed for hay, our property is now a mix of young oaks, birches, and viburnums; gray, flowering, and alternate-leaf dogwoods; eastern red cedars, winterberries, and inkberries; American elms, plums, chestnuts, and beeches; silverbells, fringe trees, black cherries, red maples, and other productive native species. We have planted our yard with a diversity of plants that, not coincidentally, makes the food necessary for grosbeak reproduction. Our woody natives alone support well over a thousand species of caterpillars, as well as myriad other insects that are the sole source of nutrition for young grosbeaks. After the fledglings leave the nest, these same plants supply the grosbeak family with seeds and berries to supplement their continued diet of insects.

We have the snakeskins our grosbeaks use to build their nest because we have black rat snakes, black racers, milk snakes, dainty little DeKay's snakes, ring-necked snakes, garter snakes, and ribbon garter snakes in our yard. We have these harmless reptiles because we have the mice, voles, shrews, salamanders, pollywogs, frogs, and toads that they eat, and because we have groundhog dens that are perfect places for snakes to avoid the weather extremes of winter and summer. In addition, we have snake food because we have the plants that supply the insects and seeds eaten by mice, voles, shrews, and toads, and because we leave refuges for them so they can avoid being decapitated during Saturday mowings.

We have nesting blue grosbeaks in our yard, as well as chipping sparrows, field sparrows, song sparrows, yellowthroats, willow flycatchers, chickadees, cedar waxwings, robins, cardinals, mockingbirds, bluebirds, brown thrashers, titmice, woodpeckers, wrens, and 40 other species of breeding birds because we have redundancy in each of their ecological requirements. If a mockingbird has already built a nest in a suitable dogwood, our grosbeaks can find an unoccupied dogwood—because we have many. If our black cherry trees do not produce enough larvae of the promethea moth, white furcula, and small-eyed sphinx to satiate the baby grosbeaks, our oak trees will fill the void with unicorn caterpillars, red-humped oak worms, confused woodgrains, variable oak leaf caterpillars, and white-dotted prominents. If our black rat snakes shed their skins within a mole tunnel where the grosbeaks can't find them, our black racers will leave their sheds in plain view on one of our mowed paths.

In short, we have built a landscape that guarantees a steady supply of all of the resources needed by blue grosbeaks to reproduce successfully—a landscape with enough complexity to promote long-term balance and stability in the food webs it creates. We have lawn, but only in the areas we typically walk. At our house, grass carpet is not the default landscape, something we do with the land when we don't know what else to do. Rather, it is a mechanism for formalizing plant communities and for guiding us through our dense plantings. Cindy and I have built a landscape that emphasizes ecological function because we so much appreciate the added value that wild things bring to our lives.

I am an entomologist and ecologist by training, a behavioral ecologist by choice of specialty, and a citizen of this planet by circumstance. My academic experiences have taught me to observe what is happening around me and relate it to the ecological processes that keep water in my bathtub, food on my plate, air in my lungs, and birds at my feeder. I wrote *Bringing Nature Home* to introduce the idea that not only can our residential landscapes make valuable contributions to preserving earth's biodiversity and ecosystems, they must make such contributions to meet the rising human demand for ecosystem services. But I was also motivated to share what Cindy and I have discovered at home; suburban restoration really works! None of my academic training had prepared me for how well and how fast it can work. I needed to tell the world!

Building upon the message in *Bringing Nature Home*, the present book, written in collaboration with Rick Darke, focuses on creating landscapes that support life without sacrificing traditional aesthetic values. This is why Rick, with his sense of aesthetics and skill in conveying the beauty inherent in natural landscapes, and I, with my interest in ecosystem function, are collaborating. We hope our collaboration will be the personification of the new balance between humans and nature that will happen right in our gardens.

Creating beautiful landscapes that are also functional is the point of this book. With just a little thought and knowledge, and a different perspective about what our gardens could be, we can build such landscapes. We can choose plants that inspire us with their own beauty, as well as the loveliness, interest, and yes, excitement that comes from the life around us. We can simultaneously appreciate how landscapes look and how their interconnected parts create the vital ecosystem services that sustain us all.

Introduction

No matter how much any individual garden may seem like a separate place, a refuge, or an island, it is in truth part of the larger landscape, and that in turn is made of many layers. The layering of the larger landscape varies over place and time, and is profoundly influenced by the life within it.

Some landscapes have more layers than others, and some layers are more apparent than others. The richness of life in any given landscape is generally linked to the richness and intricacy in its layering.

OPPOSITE AND BELOW Suburban landscapes in southeastern Pennsylvania in May and November.

A bird's-eye view of typical urban and suburban landscapes reveals that they lack many of the living layers characteristic of broadly functional ecosystems. In addition, many of the layers that are present have been stripped of much of their complexity, and because of this, the biological diversity and ecological functions of these landscapes are greatly diminished.

Since we spend so much of our time in such landscapes, it's easy to adjust to their simplicity and unconsciously to accept it as the norm. However, if our intent is to create beautiful, livable landscapes that are also highly functional in environmental terms, integrating

meaningfully detailed layers has to be a primary design goal.

Many suburban residential landscapes already include a few or many of the literal layers that have made traditional habitats and other long-evolved ecosystems so full of life. Existing layers can be enhanced and missing layers can be appropriately created. The key is to develop a familiarity with the basic functions, inter-relationships and living dynamics of layered landscapes, and then to use horticultural skills to reprise and maintain them. Learning to read and draw lessons from the structure, composition, and processes of functional

A suburban residential development in northern Maryland.

ecosystems will be increasingly essential to good gardening and the making of broadly functional landscapes for life.

The lack of biological layers is especially evident in many commercial landscapes and in the majority of urban landscapes since so much of their available area is dedicated to buildings and to the extensive paving necessary to accommodate cars and other motorized vehicles. Although there are opportunities to reintroduce layers to such landscapes, the greatest opportunity lies in the suburbs, which are now home to approximately half of the United States' population.

Despite frequent remnant patches of layered woodlands, grasslands, and wetlands within the broad suburban landscape, they are just that: patches. These isolated fragments are typically surrounded by highly altered expanses with minimal habitat functionality. Their separation and relatively small size is insufficient to sustain the great diversity of wildlife that requires larger, continuous habitat. Reintroducing layers to residential landscapes is the best strategy for restoring biological function on a vast scale, contributing to habitat and to a wide range of ecosystem services that are broadly beneficial, including replenishment of atmospheric

An urban landscape in northern Delaware.

oxygen, carbon sequestration, groundwater recharge and filtration, soil conservation, and moderation of weather extremes.

The first chapter of this book examines the patterns and processes in wild, unmanaged systems. Using a woodland as example, the chapter unpacks the components of the literal vertical and horizontal layers in a wild landscape. It also addresses cultural and temporal layers, edges (transitional areas), and wildness (the ability of a natural habitat to perpetuate itself).

Chapter 2 looks at relational biodiversity—the interactions of plants and wildlife in a regional ecosystem. Although we often measure biodiversity in terms of the numbers of different species present in an area, this chapter makes the case that biodiversity encompassing long-evolved interrelationships is more meaningful, more functional, and worthy of conservation and enhancement.

The third chapter answers the question, "What does your garden do for you and for the environment?" Some of the human-oriented functions that might be asked of a home landscape include the following:

- create living spaces suitable for play, meals, entertaining
- add beauty and sensual pleasure including color and fragrance, framing, and order
- offer shelter and refuge, privacy and screening
- yield sustenance through edible plantings
- produce opportunities for storytelling and other artistic expression
- inspire and educate by providing exposure to or immersion in natural phenomena including seasonal cycles, cycles of plant and animal growth and migration

Likewise, a home garden can be designed to serve a variety of environmental functions:

- recharge groundwater
- replenish atmospheric oxygen

- sequester carbon
- furnish shelter/cover for wildlife
- promote a stable food web for wildlife
- support pollinator communities
- provide the right conditions for natural hybridization and the continuing development of biodiversity

Because many gardeners confess to an inability to see the life present in local habitats and in their gardens, chapter 4 provides examples and illustrates strategies for developing one's visual acuity and capacity to observe and recognize local biological diversity.

Chapter 5 applies the concepts and strategies of wild landscapes to a home garden. Drawing on personal experience, the authors look at the composition, content, functionality, and maintenance of the literal layers described in chapter 1, starting from below ground and moving up. Other themes such as managed wildness and edge dynamics (primarily a function of lateral spatial design) are addressed as appropriate within each layer, as are varying site conditions such as moisture gradients (dry, average, moist, wet), drainage (sharp well-drained to nearly anaerobic and poorly drained), pH (acidic to alkaline), and available light (full sun to dense shade). Authentically related plants and animals are shown in various settings.

Although the concepts and strategies discussed and illustrated in the book are applicable to many parts of the world, the book's specific examples are drawn from temperate eastern North America. They integrate Rick's conservation-based planting design and management strategies, with Doug's vision of the roles residential gardens can play in sustaining local and regional insect and animal biodiversity. A chart at the back of the book lists selected plants and the functions they support by region, giving home gardeners ideas for getting started wherever they live.

In sum, this book addresses both the practical and ecological functions of the home landscape. It is not a how-to book. Rather it aims to provide readers with inspiration and strategies for making and maintaining truly living landscapes—gardens that are full of life and truly vital to both human needs and the needs of local and regional wildlife communities. Such gardens offer homeowners beauty at multiple scales, outdoor rooms for a variety of social functions, turf areas for kids and dogs to run and play, fragrance, and edible plants, while simultaneously meeting various ecological functions and providing cover, shelter, and sustenance for wildlife.

CHAPTER ONE

Layers in Wild Landscapes

What does a richly layered landscape look like? This chapter reflects upon the layers often found in natural habitats and other landscapes beyond the deliberate influence of human activity, illustrating patterns and processes that can serve as models and inspiration for making and maintaining ecologically healthy residential gardens.

Learning to recognize and read the layers in any landscape is enjoyable and useful. As the layered organization of a landscape becomes apparent, it provides a framework for more detailed observation and understanding. This framework helps us to appreciate the richness and complexity without being overwhelmed by it.

Knowing where to look for elements and events in the life of any layer is an enduring pleasure. An increasing ability to comprehend interactions between elements in the layers makes it ever more possible to recognize stability or to anticipate change, and to perceive the influence of internal and external forces on living systems. Gardens have layers, too, and an appreciation of patterns and processes in unmanaged systems is a powerful tool for deciding how and when to emulate or intervene in the landscape each of us calls home.

Adopt the perspective of landscapes being comprised of layers and it quickly becomes obvious that some layers are more literal than others. Layers that accumulate through the influence of human culture—the cultural layers—are often more conceptual in nature, and can't always be identified by defined spaces or discrete structures. The layering that accrues over time—the temporal layers—are perhaps the most conceptual because they consist of interwoven patterns that are by their nature ephemeral. Though their boundaries aren't often rigidly defined, the vertical or horizontal layers of things and processes—the literal layers—are the most obvious.

THE LITERAL LAYERS

The grand scale, inherent organization, and common presence of the deciduous forest make it an excellent model for beginning an exploration of literal layers. The deciduous forest offers the most dramatic and easily readable example of vertical layering. Starting at the top with the canopy and moving earthward through the understory trees, the shrub layer, herbaceous layer, and ground layer, the forest is comprised of habitat zones distinguished most obviously by elevation.

OPPOSITE A richly layered deciduous woodland in Pennsylvania.

Literal Layers in a Landscape

VERTICAL LAYERS	HORIZONTAL (LATERAL) LAYERS
Canopy	Dynamic edge
Understory trees	Wet edge
Shrubs	Wetlands
Herbaceous plants	Meadows and grasslands
Ground layer	

CANOPY

Formed by the heavily branched tops—the crowns—of the tallest trees, the canopy is the forest layer that literally brushes the sky. The canopy crowns are the first to catch sunlight, and because of this, photosynthetic productivity is higher in this layer than anywhere else in the forest. The direct sunlight captured by the canopy is also responsible for the prolific flowering, fruiting, and seed production that takes place in the canopy.

Lower layers compete for light filtered by the canopy and for light streaming through openings in the canopy. The quantity and quality of light passing through the canopy varies with the growth forms and patterns of canopy trees and with the optical properties of their foliage, which vary among tree species.

Leaf arrangement, size, thickness, color, translucency, reflectivity and other characteristics of internal anatomy all influence the intensity and spectral quality of light traveling through, and this influences the growth of plants growing below. Light in the red and blue ranges of the spectrum is generally most important for plant growth and flowering, and green light is least important. During the

LEFT The mid-October color peak in this western Pennsylvania forest canopy precedes the impending leaf drop, which will enrich the ground layer's organic matter while once again allowing unfiltered sunlight to energize the lower layers.

RIGHT The canopy of this deciduous forest in Pennsylvania is dormant and leafless in early February (top), allowing the majority of available sunlight to pass through to the ground below. By mid-April (center), new leaves are opening and the canopy's photosynthetic activity begins another year. The window of opportunity for plants in the understory, shrub and ground layers to benefit from relatively unfiltered sunlight is about to close. By April's end (bottom), canopy foliage is nearly full-sized, dramatically changing the intensity of light reaching the lower layers until leaves are shed in autumn.

Prolific flowering of red oaks (*Quercus rubra*) near the top of the canopy in early April.

growing season, we see most foliage as green in color because most plants reflect green light.

In addition to influencing light passing through it, the canopy also affects air quality in the forest and sometimes well beyond. When dormant and leafless, the branched crowns of deciduous trees reduce air movement below while allowing sunlight to pass through barely diminished. Consequently, air temperatures inside the forest are often higher than outside of it in late autumn, winter, and early spring. The reverse is true when the canopy is in full

summer leaf. Temperatures within the forest are then noticeably cooler.

As the forest's primary photosynthetic engine, the canopy takes in huge amounts of carbon dioxide and releases a great quantity of oxygen as a photosynthetic byproduct. A single acre of productive forest uses tons of carbon dioxide gas each year, storing or "sequestering" it in the form of carbon as the major component of woody tree tissue. This isn't the end of the story, however: the processes of respiration and decay reverse the equation. These oxidation processes consume oxygen and release carbon dioxide.

Mature, healthy, functioning forests recycle oxygen and carbon dioxide in roughly equivalent quantities, affecting no net change but helping to maintain the Earth's atmospheric oxygen component at approximately 20 percent. The equation changes when forests are felled by human activity, which eliminates oxygen production while accelerating carbon dioxide release through the eventual oxidation of woody material.

A quick look at any forest canopy reveals that no two trees are identical, and there are many reasons for this. Genetic diversity plays a strong role. The common genetic traits of a particular tree species produce an outward appearance that is reliably distinguishable from other species. For example, the flowers, fruits and seeds, leaf shape and color, bark color and texture, branching pattern, and ultimate height of a white oak (*Quercus alba*) make it easy to tell from a beech (*Fagus grandifolia*).

Genetic variability within a species also results in varied appearance. For example, although they will both exhibit all the features that qualify them as white oaks, no two seed-grown, genetically individual white oaks will be exactly the same. Even when growing in identical circumstances, they may grow at different rates to different heights, flower or set seed at slightly different times, or turn different colors at different times in autumn.

Appearance is not the only realm in which genetics plays a role. Genetic variation affects the way tree species and individuals of a species respond to local site conditions. For example, just as some species are more capable than others of thriving in normally dry conditions or of tolerating extended droughty periods, individuals within a species may also respond differently to the same set of conditions.

Over time, the genetic makeup a given population of a tree species may change in response to growing conditions in a local or regional habitat. Although the changes are often quite subtle and may not be expressed in outward appearance, they can significantly affect the trees' response to site conditions. Such genetically distinct populations are called ecotypes.

The structure and form of the canopy reflect long-term conditions far below on the ground. Consistently favorable ground conditions capable of sustaining tall-growing forest species contribute to the formation of an evenly dense canopy. Woodland streams, seeps, ponds, and other constantly saturated areas on the ground can create effective voids within the forest's tall tree growth, resulting in openings or separations in the canopy. Topography, exposure, and underlying geology are also profoundly influential. Tree species vary considerably in their ability to grow on different degrees of slope, and on slopes at different angles to the sun. Rock outcrops within the forest can so strongly influence the type of soil forming over them or the soil's relative moisture that the trees species able to establish there will be dramatically different from adjacent areas.

Contrary to popular belief, trees rarely have

Red oak acorns mature at the top of the canopy in late August.

Used by small mammals, birds, and other wildlife for nesting, perching, foraging, and food storage, dead trees, or snags, often contribute more to functional habitat than when they were alive. Insects that recycle dead wood provide critical sustenance for others higher up in the food chain.

taproots beyond the seedling stage. The root systems of most deciduous trees extend out from the trunk at least as far as the canopy branches, yet they rarely grow deeper than 2 or 3 feet into the ground. This is partly because roots require oxygen, which is increasingly scarce in the lower soil horizons.

Wind and other weather-related events play regular and important roles in shaping the canopy and, consequently, the layers below. Constant winds often influence the form of canopy trees. Canopy openings are often the result of wind bursts or strong storm winds, especially if they are accompanied by rain and saturated soils. Though large-scale fires are uncommon in today's deciduous forests, lightning strikes to trees occur frequently, and are responsible for many openings in the canopy. Standing dead trees, known as snags, make important contributions to the canopy as a functional habitat, providing sustenance and shelter for countless insects, small mammals, and birds. Living trees with hollow trunks, cavities, and dead limbs are similarly essential to wildlife.

Trees make up the canopy, but they're not the only form of life in this layer. The canopy provides habitat for many different plants and animals. Canopy plant life includes vines, which climb up from the distant ground layer by twining stems, tendrils, or adhesive pads. Epiphytes are uncommon in temperate forest canopies, but there are a few including mistletoe (*Phoradendron serotinum*) and rock polypody fern (*Polypodium virginianum*). Lichens are plentiful on the trunks and branches of canopy trees.

Animals that spend much of their time in the canopy layer include squirrels, raccoons, numerous birds, micro-invertebrates, spiders, and a multitude of insects such as katydids, walkingsticks, acorn weevils, and sawflies. Tree squirrels, which include eastern gray squirrels, red squirrels, and fox squirrels, find shelter in the canopy in leaf nests and tree cavity dens.

The leaf nests, which are called dreys, are typically constructed high up in tree crotches or on strong limbs. Dreys are built of a framework of interwoven twigs and occasional vines covered by an outer shell of leaves, moss, and fine twigs. The inner space is often lined with leaves, grass, and strips of bark. Sturdier than they appear, leaf nests offer protection from predators and precipitation.

Katydids also reside in the canopy. Their green color makes them hard to distinguish from foliage; however, their loud mating call, produced by rubbing their forewings together, is impossible to miss. Katydids are primarily active at night, filling the forest with their song. They reach adulthood by mid to late summer, and then spend the rest of their short lives mating and laying eggs. Females glue the flat eggs to twigs in double overlapping rows. These weather the winter months and hatch into tiny wingless replicas of their parents in late spring.

ABOVE Life in the canopy is often obscured from view by foliage. This mid-May photo of a Delaware woodland shows a blue-gray gnatcatcher nest atop a beech branch, effectively hidden from view.

ABOVE RIGHT The greater anglewing katydid (*Microcentrum rhombifolium*), pictured here, is rarely seen because it lives primarily in the upper canopy. Like other katydids, it gets its sustenance by eating the leaves of deciduous trees.

TOP AND ABOVE An eastern gray squirrel peers from a canopy den. Squirrels rely on leaf nests in woodlands where natural cavities are scarce; however, cavity dens offer better protection, especially from cold. Squirrels don't hibernate—they're active all year—and the use of cavity dens means less energy must be expended maintaining body temperature in winter. This squirrel leaf nest, or drey, was built in a river birch tree that has lost its top.

UNDERSTORY TREES

In broad terms, the forest understory includes all plant growth and associated animal species that exist below the canopy; however, a more detailed look at forest structure reveals a layer of understory trees. It consists of two groups: young specimens of canopy species and other inherently shorter-growing species that never attain canopy height. Both are important to the forest's viability. The shorter-growing trees contribute to mid-story habitat and the young tall-growing trees are essential to the ongoing replacement of canopy trees lost to disease, old age, or weather-related events.

Many canopy species are capable of growing for indefinite periods in relatively low light, and they manage this in part by modifying the internal anatomy of their leaves. The majority of forest species can produce shade leaves or sun leaves to suit conditions. Shade leaves are typically thinner, with a thin epidermis and reduced numbers of palisade mesophyll cells (the specialized chloroplast-rich cells that convert sun energy to chemical energy through photosynthesis). Sun leaves have much thicker mesophyll layers and have a thicker, often waxy epidermis that protects from moisture loss and makes them appear glossier. Many canopy tree species growing in shade conditions flower less and produce fewer fruits and seeds to conserve their energy for vegetative growth.

Minimum light requirements vary with species. For example, pines (*Pinus* species), hickories (*Carya* species), and tulip tree (*Liriodendron tulipifera*) require nearly full sunlight to grow and reproduce. Beech (*Fagus grandifolia*), maples (*Acer* species), and basswood (*Tilia americana*) can complete their life cycles in shade or semi-shade conditions. Shorter-growing tree species that are tolerant of the reduced light levels below the canopy include dogwoods (*Cornus* species), ironwood (*Carpinus caroliniana*), and American hop hornbeam (*Ostrya virginiana*).

OPPOSITE Ironwood (*Carpinus caroliniana*) almost exclusively inhabits the understory, rarely attaining canopy height. Like many understory species, it has foliage that opens early, taking advantage of available sunlight before the canopy closes.

ABOVE A flowering dogwood provides cover for a nesting robin.

ABOVE A young black-gum (*Nyssa sylvatica*) makes its way upward through the understory in autumn in a West Virginia woodland. It will eventually join other canopy species, but at this stage, it seeks available light, stretching away from the year-round shade of pines.

RIGHT Sun streaming through the early spring canopy in a Virginia forest illuminates the thin, translucent foliage of a young umbrella magnolia (*Magnolia trip-etala*) in the understory.

Pawpaws together with zebra swallowtail butterflies present a classic example of relational biodiversity. Though pawpaws are capable of growing as single-trunked trees over 30 feet tall with a caliper up to 12 inches, they more commonly form multistemmed thickets or patches. The closely spaced stems are produced as suckers from an extensive root system. Pawpaw patches help reduce woodland soil erosion in times of heavy rains or flooding.

Up to 2 inches wide, the wine-colored flowers of pawpaws are produced in early spring before the foliage of pawpaws or the forest canopy has fully expanded. Pawpaws produce the largest edible fruit of any indigenous North American species. Often difficult to spot in the low light of the understory, pawpaw fruits are technically berries. The thin outer skin encloses a soft edible pulp containing large reddish-brown seeds. The fruits are eaten by a variety of mammals including squirrels, raccoons, opossums, foxes, black bears, and humans.

Zebra swallowtail larvae feed exclusively on the new leaves of pawpaws, ingesting acetogenins, which are present in pawpaw leaves, fruits, and bark. Acetogenins are phytochemicals that make the caterpillars and the mature butterflies unpalatable to birds, protecting zebra swallowtails from predation throughout their life cycle.

Redbud (*Cercis canadensis*) blooms in early May in a Virginia forest. Though they flower best in openings, edges, or full sun habitats, redbuds are tolerant of interior conditions and will bloom even in the shade of a high canopy.

ABOVE Pawpaw (*Asimina triloba*) dominates the shrub layer in an oak-maple forest in western Pennsylvania.

OPPOSITE TOP In this early May image, taken in a Maryland woodland near the Susquehanna River, a female zebra swallowtail deposits eggs on a pawpaw leaf.

RIGHT A zebra swallowtail larva about to feed on the emerging new leaves of pawpaw.

FAR RIGHT An adult zebra swallowtail alights on a sugar maple seedling not far from a pawpaw patch.

SHRUBS

A healthy shrub layer contributes significantly to habitat richness and biodiversity by providing cover and shelter and by adding to the variety of foliage, seeds, berries, and other fruits available to sustain wildlife. Woodland shrub layers inhabit the vertical space from the ground layer to a maximum 15 to 20 feet in height. Shrubs are generally defined as multistemmed plants growing no taller than this, and in most cases this is sufficient to distinguish shrubs from trees, which by definition grow taller and produce single stems of significant diameter. The stem diameter of woody plants is referred to as caliper.

As with so many instances in which we attempt to put living things into rigid categories, there are many exceptions. Some tree species produce tall single trunks over much of their range but grow shorter with multiple trunks as they reach the northern limits of their cold hardiness. Similarly, some shrub species are capable of reaching exceptional heights and developing stems many inches in diameter under ideal conditions. Genetic variability within a species can also determine whether individual plants or individual populations (ecotypes) are likely to be more shrublike or treelike.

Even in healthy shrub layers, it's common for one or just a few species to dominate large areas.

Close observation of the composition and structure within layers often reveals that a given species will often occupy a particular niche, or

LEFT Roseshell azalea (*Rhododendron prinophyllum*) adds color and sweet fragrance to the shrub layer of a West Virginia woodland in May, growing nearly 8 feet tall under a canopy primarily comprised of chestnut oak (*Quercus montana*). The canopy is not completely closed—it has regular openings—and the light reaching the understory is sufficient for the azalea to bloom. Evergreen mountain laurels (*Kalmia latifolia*) join the azaleas at about the same height in the shrub layer, and black huckleberry (*Gaylussacia baccata*) creates its own sub-layer below both of them.

TOP Although there is sufficient light for limited flowering and seed production, the structure and form of oakleaf hydrangea (*Hydrangea quercifolia*) is open and irregular as it grows in the shaded understory of an Alabama oak-maple woodland. As is common with many woodland shrubs, this shade-tolerant species is more dense and rounded when growing in stronger sunlight.

ABOVE The extensive growth of mountain clethra (*Clethra acuminata*) dominates a mature forest in North Carolina. Young trees of Fraser's magnolia (*Magnolia fraseri*) can be seen making their way through the shrub layer to join the canopy eventually.

set of conditions and circumstances. Although witch hazel (*Hamamelis virginiana*) is a broadly adaptable shrub species, it is especially capable of establishing and thriving on steep slopes and rocky ledges. Although in common usage, anthropomorphic statements such as "witch hazel likes steep slopes and rocky ledges" obscure the factual truth, which is that witch hazel's unique physiology gives it a competitive advantage over other species under the same conditions, allowing it to thrive where others fail.

Broadly adapted spicebush (*Lindera benzoin*) is another common plant in the shrub layer of many North American deciduous woodlands. Spicebush is dioecious, meaning individual plants are either male or female. The bright red berrylike fruits, which are technically drupes, are only produced on female plants which have been pollinated by nearby male plants. Spicebush swallowtail larvae feed primarily on plants in the laurel family (*Lauraceae*), with *Lindera benzoin* and closely related sassafras (*Sassafras albidum*) being the two most commonly preferred species.

In some cases a shrub layer dominated by a single species is an indication that the relationships between plant and animal populations have changed dramatically. For example, the near monoculture of spicebush in the shrub layer of a woods may be the result of selective grazing by an unsustainably high white-tailed deer population. In many regions deer populations have skyrocketed as human land development has reduced and concentrated deer habitats while eliminating natural predators. Deer will eat the spicy-fragrant leaves and stems of spicebush, but usually only after they've exhausted the supply of plants they find more palatable. In this new balance, spicebush has a competitive advantage over other shrub species, and it becomes more plentiful. Unfortunately, overall biological diversity is reduced. If deer populations reach extreme levels, they virtually eliminate the regeneration of many plant species that are essential to the functional biodiversity of living landscapes.

TOP LEFT Highly shade tolerant arrowwood viburnum (*Viburnum dentatum*) adds vivid autumn color to the shrub layer of a Maryland forest, competing for light under the canopy with evergreen American holly (*Ilex opaca*).

LEFT Woodthrushes make their nests in a variety of woodland shrubs including arrowwood viburnum (*Viburnum dentatum*), black haw (*Viburnum*

prunifolium), spicebush (*Lindera benzoin*), and sweet pepperbush (*Clethra alnifolia*).

RIGHT Witch hazels dominate the shrub layer on a rocky slope below the canopy of an upper New York state forest. The multiple stems of *Hamamelis virginiana* typically arc and extend outward to create a space below that is often tall enough to stand under.

ABOVE Highly shade tolerant *Hamamelis virginiana* blooms profusely in the shrub layer of a West Virginia forest comprised of oaks, maples, blackgums, and pines.

OPPOSITE TOP The sweetly fragrant flowers of *Lindera benzoin* appear before those of almost any other woody species in the canopy or understory, making them conspicuous as late winter to early spring sunlight floods through the landscape.

RIGHT The lipid-rich fruits of *Lindera benzoin* are important food for birds.

RIGHT CENTER The cartoonlike markings of a spicebush swallowtail larva, seen here on *Lindera benzoin* foliage, are intended to make it appear like a green tree snake. Such mimicry is a defense against being eaten by birds.

FAR RIGHT Though specialists are dependent on specific host plants during their larval stage, the adult butterflies can feed on nectar from a variety of flowering plants, as illustrated here by an adult spicebush swallowtail nectaring on a plant in the laurel family (*Lauraceae*).

These three photographs illustrate the varied effects of out-of-balance white-tailed deer populations.

ABOVE The simplicity of the golden layer of *Lindera benzoin* in this Pennsylvania woodland has immense visual appeal; however, in this landscape, spicebush is dominant because the deer have removed most of its competition.

TOP RIGHT Look closely at the vegetation surrounding two white-tailed deer in this Pennsylvania woodland preserve and you'll see that other than a few older trees, the vegetation consists almost entirely of dormant stems of spicebush, the red stems of introduced brambles (*Rubus* species), and on the ground, only last year's tawny patches of Japanese stiltgrass (*Microstegium vimineum*), along with locally native Christmas ferns (*Polystichum acrostichoides*). A search on foot at the time this photo was taken revealed that seedlings of canopy tree species were almost entirely absent.

RIGHT Created and maintained by the Pennsylvania Department of Conservation and Natural Resources, this deer enclosure on western Pennsylvania's Ferncliff Peninsula demonstrates the effect of deer grazing on woodland regeneration. In just a few years since installation, a naturally regenerated mix of woody and herbaceous species has established itself within the protective fencing. Outside and still vulnerable to deer, only a few seedlings are evident among a carpet of native ferns, which the deer find unpalatable.

HERBACEOUS PLANTS

Plant species diversity is typically much higher in the herbaceous layer than in the shrub layer, understory trees, or canopy, though there are many instances where one or only a few herbaceous species will dominate large areas. When imagining woodland wildflowers, this layer usually comes first to mind simply because this is where the greatest variety of flower color and form is found; however, the herbaceous layer contributes to functional woodland systems long after flowers have faded. Often overlooked are the interactions between plants in the herbaceous layer, which profoundly influence both floral and faunal biodiversity and can significantly influence the regeneration of the woody upper layers.

For the purposes of this book, the herbaceous layer occupies the vertical space from the ground surface to just under 4 feet, which is the approximate maximum height of non-woody plants. The herbaceous layer includes herbaceous plants plus young seedlings and suckers of trees, shrubs, and vines. Plant species in any layer compete for sunlight, moisture, and nutrients; however, competition in the earliest stages of growth has the most profound effect on the eventual species composition and structure of the woods. Interactions between plants and animals in the herbaceous layer dramatically affect the look and function of the entire woodland landscape.

Functional interactions between species in different layers aren't always obvious. For

LEFT In late April, large populations of Virginia bluebells (*Mertensia virginica*) and ostrich fern (*Matteuccia struthiopteris* var. *pensylvanica*) comingle in the herbaceous layer of a Susquehanna River floodplain woodland in northern Maryland.

ABOVE RIGHT Yellow trout lily (*Erythronium americanum*) easily pushes up through decomposing leaves to bloom in mid-April in a Pennsylvania woodland.

ABOVE Diversity is often very high in the herbaceous layer, and species sharing the same "footprint" also share resources, typically taking turns emerging, blooming, seeding, and subsiding. Species visible in the herbaceous layer of this northern Maryland woods in early May include woodland phlox (*Phlox divaricata*), trillium (*Trillium flexipes*), Dutchman's-breeches (*Dicentra cucullaria*), squirrel-corn (*Dicentra canadensis*), and spring beauty (*Claytonia virginica*).

ABOVE In this April photo, Virginia bluebells create a continuous carpet in-between young pawpaws on a wooded floodplain in Maryland.

RIGHT A view into the interior of a skunk cabbage inflorescence, revealing ball-like spadix made up of many individual florets. A pungent odor emitted by this flowering structure attracts pollinators including multiple fly species and occasional bees. Skunk cabbage (*Symplocarpus foetidus*) is often the first to bloom in deciduous woodlands, reaching flowering peak in February or even in late January. Utilizing energy reserves in the large underground stem and roots, the plant uses cellular respiration to raise its temperature sufficiently to melt snow and ice.

example, trout lily is a true spring ephemeral, sprouting and blooming while the majority of deciduous forest plants are still dormant. It soon produces seed and then goes into dormancy while others are just becoming active. While growing it takes up nitrogen, but when it decomposes, this nitrogen is released back into the soil in time to be used by shrubs and trees through the remainder of the growing season. Although plants in the herbaceous layer account for only a tiny fraction of the biomass of the forest, their relative productivity in terms of conversion of sunlight into plant tissue and their role in the recycling of nutrients is disproportionately higher.

Virginia bluebell (*Mertensia virginica*) is an example of a true spring ephemeral: it flowers, sets seed, then its aboveground portions wither and begin decomposing before summer begins.

A West Virginia slope is almost completely clothed in twinleaf (*Jeffersonia diphylla*) in this May photo (below). Scenes like this are a reminder that in wild habitats, the majority of plants propagate themselves by seed. Conditions that allow for continual seed production and seedling establishment are essential to the long-term survival of the population. Closer inspection revealed the presence of maturing seed capsules on most of the twinleaf plants on the slope (above).

The conspicuously colorful flowers attract a wide range of bee species, bee flies, butterflies, skippers, moths, and hummingbirds. Other true spring ephemerals include trout lilies, Dutchman's-breeches, and squirrel-corn. Look for them in the summer woods and you'll find no trace of the plants that bloomed in early spring. The seeds will have been dispersed but won't germinate until the following spring. Many other species in the woodland herbaceous layer bloom in spring, but have foliage that remains and carries on photosynthesis through summer and sometimes even through winter.

Berries of false Solomon's-seal (*Smilacina racemosa*) add color to the herbaceous layer of a Pennsylvania woods in August.

LEFT AND ABOVE Close observation of the processes of flowering and seed production reveals a world of beautiful detail. The snowflake-shaped flowers of miterwort (*Mitella diphylla*) morph into cuplike capsules dispersing glossy jet-black seeds. Miterwort self-sows prolifically but only on sloping ground or other niches that provide sharp drainage.

Mayapple (*Podophyllum peltatum*) and woodland stonecrop (*Sedum ternatum*) spread vegetatively and by seed. Stems of the sedum trail over the ground, and even small sections when separated quickly root and form new plants. Mayapples spread extensively by rhizomes, which also form new plants if separated. This combination in a Delaware woods illustrates how the two species share the same space. The mayapples will be dormant by midsummer, but the sedum will persist through winter.

Nearby in the same Delaware woodland, mayapple, woodland stonecrop, and wild ginger (*Asarum canadense*) share the same space. The ginger is deciduous and will be dormant by late autumn, but its foliage will long outlast the mayapples.

THIS PAGE Mayapple flowers (below left) are often unseen because they are positioned below the umbrella-like leaves. Each flower produces one fruit, which looks like a small apple but is botanically a berry (below right). The fruits are edible but not especially palatable except to eastern box turtles, which are the only known dispersal agent (right) other than gravity, wind, and water.

OPPOSITE TOP In healthy, functioning woodland ecosystems, the herbaceous layer includes seedlings of woody species that are essential to the continual regeneration of the upper layers. In this June photo, oak seedlings make their way through the herbaceous layer in Bear Run Preserve surrounding Frank Lloyd Wright's Fallingwater.

RIGHT Green false hellebore (*Veratrum viride*) takes advantage of plentiful moisture in a shallow drainage slope in a West Virginia woodland. Relatively small changes in grade, which in turn affect available moisture, can dramatically influence the composition of the herbaceous layer. The occurrence of many species coincides with readily identifiable slope and hydrologic conditions.

FAR RIGHT Extensive colonies of running ferns including New York fern (*Thelypteris noveboracensis*), shown here in a Pennsylvania woods, are increasingly common in the herbaceous layer in areas where white-tailed deer predation is high, since deer find the ferns unpalatable. Such colonies play an important role in preventing soil erosion; however, seedlings of many herbaceous and woody species find it difficult to establish within the tight-knit root systems of running ferns. This can be beneficial if ferns suppress exotic weeds, but can have a negative impact on the shrub, understory tree, and canopy regeneration if fern colonies are too dense and too extensive.

The beauty of living process: recycling organic material on the ground layer of a Delaware woodland in winter.

THE GROUND LAYER

Except where it is clothed with plants, the ground layer and its intricate living processes are often overlooked in gardening circles, yet the events that occur here are among the most important to life in the entire ecosystem. The forest floor is where accumulated organic material is decomposed and made available once again for plant nutrition by a myriad of fungi and bacteria, earthworms, insects and other arthropods, and mammals.

It's unfortunate that the term most often used for the accumulation of organic matter on the ground is *litter,* because this material is anything but trash. Dictionaries typically define litter as "trash or garbage lying scattered about" or as an "untidy accumulation of objects." The general connotations of worthlessness and messiness obscure the essential nature of this material, and the beauty inherent in the process of organic recycling. Ground layer litter, in the form of leaves, twigs, bits of bark and dead wood, seeds and seed pods and capsules, plays critical roles in conserving moisture, replenishing nutrients, and creating niches—microhabitats—needed by various species of animals and plants especially in their earliest stages of regeneration. *Duff* is an alternative term referring to dead plant material that that has accumulated on the ground.

The profile of typical upland woodland soils consists of vertically arranged horizons grading into one another but distinguished by individual letter names assigned by soil scientists. The uppermost horizon, called O for organic, has an upper zone containing still-recognizable dead plant and animal matter and a lower zone of unrecognizable decomposed matter (humus). Below this, the A horizon, or topsoil, has high mineral content but also incorporates significant organic matter including humus which gives it a typically dark color. The subsoil, or B horizon below, has relatively little organic

TOP Seedlings of dwarf ginseng (*Panax trifolius*) benefit from nutrients recycled from decomposing organic matter in a Pennsylvania woods in mid-April. Fallen branches and other bits of wood act as reservoirs for rainfall and provide moist shady niches ideal for germinating seedlings.

ABOVE Freshly fallen leaves of blackgum (*Nyssa sylvatica*) add color to the ground layer of a West Virginia woods in October. Bacteria, fungi, and minute decomposers including springtails break down the leaves' organic matter, creating nutrient-rich humus.

matter and a generally lighter color. Below it, the C horizon consists primarily of partially broken down rock, and below that is the bedrock, known as the R horizon.

Specialized soils may contain additional horizons, and disturbed soils may have missing horizons or the horizons present may be partly inverted. If mosses, fungi, algae, insects, arthropods, and related macroinvertebrates are counted, the ground layer including the O and A horizons support more species diversity than any other woodland layer.

Many long-evolved relationships are evident between plant and animal life in the ground layer and associated layers. One of the more interesting examples is the interaction between many early spring wildflowers and

ABOVE Unlike bacteria, fungi are capable of breaking down the high lignin content in wood.

RIGHT A mossy patch on the ground layer of a woodland in Pennsylvania's Pocono mountain region in October. Because they have no vascular system for transporting water internally, mosses typically inhabit shady moist niches that minimize the risk of desiccation. They often establish themselves where the humus-rich ground layer is exposed to filtered sunlight, in turn providing ideal conditions for germinating seedlings of vascular plants such as the wintergreen (*Gaultheria procumbens*) in this photo.

ants. Bloodroot, trillium, Dutchman's-breeches, squirrel-corn, and trout lily are among the species that depend upon ants to help with seed dispersal. Their seeds have a nutritious appendage (elaiosome), which is not necessary to the development of the seedling but is valued by ants. Ants carry the seeds back to their nest, snip off the elaiosomes with their mandibles, and feed them to their larvae. The seed itself is of no value to the ants so they dispose of it in a waste area within the nest, which happens to be an ideal place for the seed to germinate and grow into a new plant. This mutually beneficial interaction (mutualism) helps sustain ant larvae while providing low-growing spring wildflowers with a means of widely dispersing their seeds.

LEFT AND BELOW Bloodroot (*Sanguinaria canadensis*) is one of many spring ephemerals that depend upon a mutually beneficial relationship with ants for seed dispersal. The smooth green capsules of bloodroot contain multiple seeds, each with an elaiosome. The second image shows an ant carrying a bloodroot seed back to its nest. The elaiosome is the transparent appendage attached to the red-brown seed.

FAR LEFT Land snails are terrestrial mollusks that eat low-growing leaves, stems, fruit, algae, and fungi. They are most common in areas where soil calcium is abundant because they require a great deal of calcium to make their shells. Land snail shells, in turn, are an important source of calcium for many breeding birds when they are making their calcium-rich eggshells.

RIGHT So tiny that they usually go unnoticed, springtails are essential to the decomposition of organic matter in the ground layer. Typically only 2 millimeters long, springtails are macroinvertebrates that were once grouped with insects but are now classified separately. Among the most abundant of modern macroscopic animals, springtails are part of a lineage that can be traced back to the Devonian period approximately 400 million years ago.

ABOVE RIGHT A flat millipede (*Apheloria virginiensis*) makes its way through the ground layer of a Virginia woodland in May. Millipedes are important decomposers of organic matter and, along with earthworms, they play roles in working soils and creating favorable conditions for essential soil bacteria.

LEFT Salamanders, like many other inhabitants of the forest floor, require environments with consistently high humidity. Most salamander species exchange gases through their skin and this form of "breathing" requires moisture to be effective. Salamanders are active primarily at night when humidity is high and there is no exposure to the drying effects of sunlight. They thrive in habitats where abundant leaf litter and woody debris enable them to hide from predators while remaining within an envelope of moisture near the ground.

ABOVE Chipmunks and other small mammals unwittingly aid in the dispersal of acorns and other seeds since they often fail to eat all the acorns they stash in hiding places, especially in years when acorns are abundant.

BELOW While they are decomposing, fallen logs contribute to life just above the ground layer by serving as moisture reservoirs and as shelter and storage sites. What may have once been a woodpecker hole in this chestnut oak log has been filled with acorns by a chipmunk, a squirrel, or some other small mammal.

RIGHT In January in a Delaware woodland, a fallen tree provides a perch for a Carolina wren, which is dividing its time between scouting its territory and foraging in the leafy ground layer. The wren's colors closely match the ground layer, making it difficult for predators to spot as long as it stays still.

Pileated woodpeckers, one of North America's most charismatic birds, use all layers of wooded landscapes in their daily routine. Like most woodpeckers, pileateds use their beak to drill into soft wood for larvae of wood-boring beetles. This type of food is rich in protein and lipids but is hard to find, so pileateds must forage long hours each day in woody substrates from the top of the canopy to fallen logs on the ground.

Carpenter ants are even more desirable than beetle larvae. When a woodpecker senses a carpenter ant nest within a tree, it excavates as much of the nest as possible by pounding out large rectangular holes deep enough to reach the heartwood where the carpenter ants live. A large ant nest may require several excavations, usually stacked one on top of the other, to reach all of its occupants. Such rectangular tree cavities are the hallmark of pileated woodpeckers, as no other woodpeckers create holes of this size or shape.

Pileateds nest and roost in natural tree cavities such as the beech holes in the images below, but more often they create their own cavities high in the canopy. Nesting high reduces the chances that raccoons, opossums, or black, gray, and yellow rat snakes will find and eat the nestlings. Pileated woodpeckers are so-called indicator species: their presence in a forest is an excellent indication that it is a mature and functioning ecosystem.

THE DYNAMIC EDGE

If we leave the woodland's vertical layers and begin an exploration of lateral layers, the first zone that becomes apparent is the edge. In ecological terms, *edge* is a local transitional zone where two different habitats or ecosystems meet. The edge can also be recognized as a habitat in itself comprised of a dynamic mix of biotic (living) and abiotic (non-living) elements from two adjacent habitats.

Depending upon how different the habitats are, the edge may be readily apparent or quite subtle. In temperate North America, the transition from woodland interior to wetland, meadow, or grassland is among the most dramatic and most ecologically dynamic of all. The visual drama is due to the startling difference in illumination and structure: from shade to sun and from stately enclosure to expansive openness. The ecological dynamism is the result of enhanced opportunities provided by the concentration and juxtaposition of diverse environmental resources.

Similar in meaning to edge is the term *ecotone*, which ecologists use to refer to a transitional zone between adjacent ecological systems. Ecotone may be used to define a local transition but is often used to refer to transitions on a grand scale, such as the transition from the deciduous forest biome of eastern North America to the freshwater aquatic biome of the coast, or to the grassland biome of the central and western regions.

Edges and ecotones typically exhibit a high degree of flux: a constantly shifting flow of resources and organisms. They are often characterized by relatively high biological diversity; however, an excessive edge component created by disturbance can result in dramatically reduced diversity, especially in specialist species. Edges are frequently encountered features of most landscapes, but they are a defining element of suburban residential landscapes.

Increased flowering, seed production, and intensified autumn coloration are among the most obvious effects of increased available sunlight in edge habitats as the following photos illustrate. Even the form of trees may be affected as they stretch toward the sunlight.

Yet another benefit of increased available sunlight in edge habitats is better health for the plants growing there. More sunlight means increased air circulation, which minimizes the amount of time leaves and flowers remain moist from rain or dew, and thus inhibits growth of fungus on plants.

LEFT A sourwood (*Oxydendrum arboreum*) thrives in conditions at the edge of a West Virginia mountain woodland in mid-October. As is the case with so many edges in the modern landscape, this landscape is the result of clearing and re-grading for a transportation corridor.

RIGHT Backed by the bright yellow of a sassafras, a flowering dogwood growing along a sunny edge produces a heavy berry crop. Though *Cornus florida* can tolerate the low light in the understory of woodland interiors, it is less affected by the dogwood anthracnose disease (*Discula destructiva*) when growing at edges and in other more exposed habitats.

LEFT Flame azaleas (*Rhododendron calendulaceum*) are common throughout this Virginia deciduous forest, but the only ones blooming are at the woods' outer edges or at interior edges below canopy openings caused by storms or fallen trees.

BELOW A Baltimore oriole feeds its young in the distinctive pouched nest that is typical of the species, built here in a sycamore (*Platanus occidentalis*) at the edge of woods. The Baltimore oriole is an example of an avian species that is adapted to edge habitats but also relies on adjacent forests or woodlots for foraging.

TOP LEFT Shadbush (*Amelanchier arborea*), sassafras (*Sassafras albidum*), and various oaks bloom profusely while maples (*Acer* species) are already developing their bright red samaras along a woodland edge in northern Delaware in mid-May.

LEFT The tiered branching structure of blackgums (*Nyssa sylvatica*) becomes even more pronounced in trees growing toward sunlight along this edge in western Pennsylvania. The blackgums share the edge with chestnut oaks (*Quercus montana*) and sweet birches (*Betula lenta*), and, in the shrub layer, witch hazel (*Hamamelis virginiana*) and great laurel (*Rhododendron maximum*).

ABOVE Spring iris (*Iris verna*) easily pushes up through leaf cover on the ground layer of a Virginia forest, taking advantage of increased sunlight near the edge.

This population of redbuds stretches half a mile across a 50-degree slope created when a highway was cut through northwestern Maryland. The trees are the result of redbuds above the slope dispersing their seeds. Each tree began as a seedling that happened to germinate in a crevice or similar spot capable of providing the minimal shade, moisture, and nutrients it required. The top growth of each seedling increased in relation to the growing root system's capacity to support it, even in the driest summer months. These redbuds are an example of how autonomous individuals can accomplish tasks that would challenge the most capable gardener.

The ability of redbuds (*Cercis canadensis*) to thrive in very dry conditions often makes redbuds among the first trees to establish when new edges are formed. Imagine being given the task of establishing hundreds of redbud trees on a rocky slope that's so steep you can't walk or climb up it. And on top of that, you must accomplish the task without watering the trees when you plant them or at anytime afterward, not even in the worst droughts. If the task must be accomplished immediately, it is simply impossible. If it must be accomplished using standard horticultural techniques, it is probably still impossible. However, if you have time and a means of dispersing an adequate quantity of redbud seeds, the task can be done.

Self-sown redbuds along a Maryland highway edge are living proof of freedom—and wildness—in action. At its best, it is uniquely efficient and highly conserving of resources. Wildness is essential to the capacity of autonomous systems to perpetuate themselves. The resiliency of many ecosystems depends upon the role of chance in allowing adaptive mechanisms to function.

As human cultural activities re-shape the landscape, some habitats are destroyed and others are created. Many of the newly created habitats are unrecognizable in traditional terms, yet close observation proves they do have uncharted capacities to sustain life. However unnatural some may seem, their ability to afford cover, shelter, and sustenance to the indigenous flora and fauna is valuable—naturally. Is a rocky highway cut part of today's natural habitat for redbuds? As this image proves, it certainly is wildly functional. **—RD**

ABOVE Redbuds and New Jersey tea (*Ceanothus americanus*) are among the pioneer species along a new sunny edge in West Virginia. New Jersey tea can withstand considerable drought but is not tolerant of the low light in woodland interiors.

LEFT Named for its curly seed structures, curly-heads (*Clematis albicoma*) is a clump-forming member of a genus characterized by vining species. This early May photo in Virginia illustrates its ability to self-sow and thrive in very dry conditions on a shale-covered slope at the edge of an oak-maple woodland. The extensive root systems of plants established from seed on site are the key to survival.

Edge habitat in interiors may result from canopy openings due to storms but is also common along streams and creeks running through woodlands, as illustrated by this early May photo of a rocky watercourse in Virginia.

WET EDGES

Some of the most productive, biologically diverse habitats are edges where woodlands meet consistently moist ground or wetlands. This most commonly occurs when a stream or creek runs through the woods, suppressing tree growth and creating a linear opening in the canopy, or at an interface where tree growth is rather abruptly stopped by constantly wet conditions or deep water. The latter type of edge is typically created by rivers, lakes, or ponds.

Vegetated edges reduce erosion and help reduce water temperatures in summer, contributing to the health of the habitat.

Plants arrange themselves in response to a moisture gradient combined with changes in available sunlight.

ABOVE Tiger swallowtails "puddle" at the wet woodland edge. The purpose of this puddling behavior is to obtain essential salts and amino acids. Droppings of wading birds and other animals foraging along the edges of streams and creeks provide concentrations of salts, which often attract butterflies.

LEFT Wet edge habitats along ponds, creeks, streams, and other watercourses are essential for many wading birds including great blue herons, which make use of elevated perches including rocks, tree stumps, and fallen branches during scouting and foraging activities.

OPPOSITE TOP Sweet pepperbush (*Clethra alnifolia*) turns bright yellow at the end of October in a wooded edge along a slow-moving stream in southern New Jersey. The mix in this edge includes highbush blueberry (*Vaccinium corymbosum*), turning bright crimson, and Atlantic white cedar (*Chamaecyparis thyoides*).

FAR LEFT In late October, Virginia sweetspire (*Itea virginica*) stretches out from a wet edge along a pond in southern New Jersey. Like many other species that only occur in wet edge habitats, *Itea* is capable of growing in drier conditions.

LEFT An adult praying mantis waits for prey on a stalk of *Itea virginica*.

ABOVE In this edge in the New Jersey Pine Barrens, the open water in the foreground supports fragrant waterlilies (*Nymphaea odorata*). As the water becomes more shallow, smooth rush (*Juncus effusus*) becomes dominant. Further back on slightly higher ground where the soil is wet or moist but there is no standing water, highbush blueberry (*Vaccinium corymbosum*) creates a virtual hedge of crimson. At the rear, on high dry ground, pitch pines (*Pinus rigida*) and scrub oaks including *Quercus marilandica* dominate.

LEFT A male ebony jewelwing (*Calopteryx maculata*) rests on a branch leaning out from a wet edge on Ferncliff Peninsula in western Pennsylvania. One of eastern North America's most distinctive damselflies, it lives only near wooded streams and rivers. Many other plants and animals thrive along this same stretch of wet woodland edge.

ABOVE The composition of plants and rock in this section of the Ferncliff edge appears gardenlike but it is completely uncontrived. The two foreground shrubs, sweet azalea (*Rhododendron arborescens*) and smooth alder (*Alnus serrulata*), are backed by a mass of great laurel (*Rhododendron maximum*).

TOP Perhaps easily overlooked in summer, royal fern (*Osmunda regalis*) is a dramatic presence in mid-October along the Ferncliff edge, here mixed with smooth alder (*Alnus serrulata*).

ABOVE The sweetly scented flowers of *Rhododendron arborescens* appear in June.

Other shrubs adapted to this wet edge include May-blooming ninebark (*Physocarpus opulifolius*) and July-blooming buttonbush (*Cephalanthus occidentalis*), which is providing nectar to a silver spotted skipper (*Epargyreus clarus*).

Black swallowtails take nectar from a variety of herbaceous species growing along the Ferncliff edge including Turk's cap lily (*Lilium superbum*).

WETLANDS

Extensive wetlands and truly aquatic environments are uncommon in residential landscapes, and for this reason they are not covered in this book. However, since many residential landscapes do include patches of constantly wet ground, and these are most appropriately populated with wetland species, it is worth looking at a few of the plant associations representative of such habitats.

Although wetlands, swamps (a wetland populated by both herbaceous and woody vegetation), and marshes have long been judged worthless and the typical approach has been to drain them, their importance to the health of regional waters and wildlife is now understood and they are being conserved. The majority of plants that occur in wetland habitats have root systems that are tolerant of saturated soils and low aeration. This gives them a competitive advantage in wet and moist habitats; however, many are adaptable to moisture levels and soil conditions common in suburban residential landscapes.

Swamp rose-mallow (*Hibiscus moscheutos*) often grows with other species adapted to sunny wet conditions including buttonbush (*Cephalanthus occidentalis*), cardinal flower (*Lobelia cardinalis*), and blue vervain (*Verbena hastata*). This adaptable species is easily grown in garden soils of average moisture. Redstem or red osier dogwood (*Cornus sericea*) is another shrub that is tolerant of periodic standing water. It is stoloniferous and can grow to form large colonies. Winterberry (*Ilex verticillata*) often tolerates standing water for considerable periods.

OPPOSITE Swamp rose-mallow (*Hibiscus moscheutos*) blooms in mid-August in a sunny wetland in northern Delaware.

BELOW This early spring image shows redstem dogwood (*Cornus sericea*) dominating the shrub layer in a wet, open deciduous woodlands in Michigan.

RIGHT A painted turtle peers through a haze of jewelweed (*Impatiens capensis*) at the edge of a tiny Maryland pond, trying to spot the photographer. The log is an important part of the turtle's habitat.

FAR RIGHT Winterberry (*Ilex verticillata*) is adaptable to a wide range of moisture conditions but occurs naturally only in wet habitats.

BELOW Winterberry forms the shrub layer of an open wet woods in western Pennsylvania.

ABOVE This open community of red maples topping an herbaceous layer of skunk cabbage (*Symplocarpus foetidus*), tussock sedge (*Carex stricta*), and cinnamon fern (*Osmunda cinnamomea*) qualifies as a swamp. The structure, form, pattern and luminous qualities of this landscape are especially appealing late on a spring day when illuminated by slanting sunlight.

ABOVE New fronds of cinnamon ferns emerge among skunk cabbage foliage in early May. These two species are well balanced and can live side by side for decades.

ABOVE RIGHT Spring peepers (*Pseudacris crucifer*) are amphibians that need the aquatic conditions found in swamps, marshes, ponds, or ephemeral wetlands to support their early egg and tadpole stages. The adults are carnivores that are most active at night, when they emerge from hiding places in the vegetation to feed on insects and other small invertebrates. Only male frogs have the expandable vocal sac required to make the species' distinctively loud, high-pitched peep. Spring peepers typically begin breeding at dusk and often continue into morning. Their mating chorus can carry for a mile or more through the night landscape.

MEADOWS AND GRASSLANDS

In North America east of the Mississippi River, meadows and grasslands have two things in common: they are frequently encountered and yet they rarely occur except as the result of human activity, past or present. The soils and climate in this region are generally ideal for woody plants, and as a result, forests are the dominant vegetation.

Excluding places where forests have been removed by humans, meadows occur here only in places where consistently high moisture discourages woody growth. Similarly, though grasslands dominate the Prairie region to the west, they occur here only in places frequented by wildfires, along coastal areas with high salt concentrations, or in places where extremes of moisture or soil chemistry are unsupportive of woody growth. Examples are serpentine barrens, with their high-magnesium and low-nutrient levels, pine barrens, which are classic fire ecologies, and coastal sand dunes.

The vast majority of meadows and grasslands encountered within the expanse of rural, urban, and suburban landscapes where most of us live are the direct result of deliberate clearing for agriculture or other industry. Since the activities that motivated these clearings have often ceased or are waning, most meadows and grassy places in this region are transitional: they are highly dynamic habitats that are essentially ephemeral. Without intervention, woody vegetation eventually regenerates and becomes dominant. In the meantime, these often beautiful, unstable systems typically support high floral and faunal diversity.

Spontaneous meadows like this upstate New York example often provide opportunities for the local native flora. In this early September view, the meadow is enlivened by *Eupatorium maculatum*, a Joe-Pye-weed species more frequently encountered in northern states.

LEFT Sweeps of ironweed (*Vernonia noveboracensis*) and boneset (*Eupatorium perfoliatum*) mix with goldenrods (*Solidago* species) and grasses in a moist western Pennsylvania meadow in late August. Such meadows are naturally occurring only if the definition of natural includes human activity. Once forested, this land was cleared long ago for pasturing. The ironweed's heavy presence today is in part because long-gone cows found it unpalatable and avoided it.

ABOVE Ironweed is a popular nectar source for many lepidopterans including tiger and black swallowtails.

ABOVE Cutleaf coneflowers (*Rudbeckia laciniata*) and ironweed (*Vernonia noveboracensis*) are responsible for the late August show in this eastern Pennsylvania floodplain meadow. In background, sycamores (*Platanus occidentalis*) and black willows (*Salix nigra*) follow the course of the adjacent White Clay Creek. Continual regeneration of this community depends upon periodic flooding plus maturation and dispersal of the yearly seed crop of these colorful forbs.

LEFT In transition from its former role as a small pasture, this self-seeded meadow in northern Maryland owes its early September color to goldenrods (*Solidago species*), roundleaf thoroughwort (*Eupatorium rotundifolium*), and slender false foxglove (*Agalinis tenuifolia*), a locally native annual species.

ABOVE LEFT Maximilian sunflowers (*Helianthus maximiliani*) mix with bushy beardgrass (*Andropogon glomeratus*) in an east Texas farm pasture turned to spontaneous meadow, with a large burr oak (*Quercus macrocarpa*) in background. Though moist, the moisture is insufficient to discourage woody growth, and in a few years, this meadow will again become woodland unless woody plants are selectively removed.

ABOVE A black swallowtail takes nectar from Maximilian sunflower.

Though this meadow was once forested, something has changed and the area is now frequently inundated. The newly wet conditions have caused the death of most of the trees while creating ideal conditions for golden ragwort (*Senecio aureus*), which is thriving in the increased sun and moisture.

ABOVE The capacity of switchgrass (*Panicum virgatum*) to tolerate low-nutrient soils and moisture conditions that annually run from extremely dry to water-logged allow it to out-compete most other species on this sandy slope edging a slow-moving stream in the New Jersey Pine Barrens, creating a localized grassland within the forest.

LEFT The dry, low-nutrient conditions of this sloped ground on a former farmstead in upstate New York have resulted in a self-sown near-monoculture of locally native little bluestem (*Schizachyrium scoparium*).

BIRDS IN EVERY LAYER

The degree of diversity in the physical structure of a landscape determines the amount of living diversity that can exist there. Restoration ecologists have known this forever, and they call variation in vegetation structure "habitat heterogeneity." Many scientists, including Paula Shrewsbury and Michael Raupp in 2000, have shown that, as the vertical and horizontal heterogeneity of a landscape increases, so does the number of species that can make a living within that landscape.

Increasing habitat heterogeneity increases the number of niches in a landscape, thus enabling plants and animals to divide the finite resources of a particular place (for example, food, shelter, water, nesting sites, and hunting sites) in ways that minimize competition with each other. This was demonstrated as far back as 1917 by Joseph Grinnell and again by G. Hutchinson in 1957. Competition is fierce in the natural world, and when a new niche appears in a landscape, it does not stay empty very long. This reality long ago inspired the idiom "Nature abhors a vacuum."

Birds illustrate these ecological principles perfectly, as research by Martin Cody in 1974 and by R. MacArthur and colleagues in 1966 shows. Birds can be found using every layer of the landscape, including the subterranean layer if you consider a robin's (or any thrush species) yanking a worm from its tunnel in the soil such a use. Some birds are niche specialists that do nearly everything they need to do within one vegetation layer. Others use several layers over the course of their lives, but are very specific about which layer is used for a particular purpose.

A good example of a layer specialist is the ovenbird, a neotropical migrant so named because it makes its nests on the ground out of leaf litter in shapes that resemble little ovens. Not only do ovenbirds nest on the ground, but they also forage for arthropods in ground litter and low-growing groundcovers such as mayapples, foamflower, and ginger. In fact, ovenbirds spend so much time

ABOVE A fledgling great horned owl peers from the safety of its perch high in the canopy. It takes a young owl up to three weeks to learn to fly well; during that time fledglings do not stray far from the nest. Parents help feed their young for five months after they leave the nest.

LEFT Ovenbirds spend most of their life in the ground layer of forests. They hunt for food, build their nests, and raise their young among the litter on the forest floor. The only time you can see them in the understory is when males perch on a branch and belt out a crescendo of notes to advertise ownership of their territory.

within the ground layer that they have taken on the appearance of chestnut-brown leaf litter to hide from their enemies. The only time ovenbirds leave the ground layer is when males are seeking a mate and delineating their territories. Then they will move to the understory, where they a sing a crescendo of loud notes that seems far too powerful for such a little bird. Other layer specialists include Carolina wrens and yellow-breasted chats (shrub layer); white-breasted nuthatches and all woodpeckers (canopy); rufous-sided towhees and worm-eating warblers (ground layer); and great crested flycatchers and cedar waxwings (understory).

Bluebirds (eastern, western, and mountain) are one of many common bird species that hunt for food exclusively in one layer but nest in another. The eastern bluebird, for example, is a tree-hole nester that prefers snags on the edge of, or isolated within, grazed meadows. When it comes time to eat, and particularly to feed their nestlings, bluebirds hunt for insects and spiders on the ground. Bluebirds evolved when ungulate grazers were abundant in North America, even in the well-forested East. They developed a preference for caterpillars, particularly fat cutworm and armyworm larvae that develop on the forbs of well-grazed pastureland, as well as for scarab beetle larvae that feed on grass roots. Free-hunting spiders that frequent the ground layer are also favorites and comprise about 10 percent of their diet. Diet preferences that evolved over many millennia have become hardwired into birds like the bluebird and now dictate where birds forage—or whether they will be in your landscape at all.

Many other birds nest in elevated layers of the canopy, understory, or shrubs but forage for food on or near the ground. Catbirds, mockingbirds, and brown thrashers nest in low shrubs or understory trees, but spend a good deal of their time foraging for insects that eat detritus (dead plant parts) on the ground. Perhaps the most beautiful fruit-lover, the cedar waxwing nests on horizontal branches

TOP Bluebirds, like the great majority of North American birds, rear their young on insects, but they hunt almost exclusively on the ground. This male has just captured a June beetle. Before taking it to his nest, he will search the area for predators to be sure he does not lead any to his young.

ABOVE Catbirds build their nests in dense shrubbery and lay 3–5 brilliant blue eggs. Egg color intensity reflects the quality of the mother's diet: the bluer the eggs, the better the diet.

as high as 50 feet but will seek out fruits from shadbush, elderberry, black cherry, and red cedar in lower landscape layers as soon as those fruits ripen in the summer and fall. Pileated woodpeckers the largest remaining woodpecker species in North America, nest in tree cavities high in the canopy, but because they love to eat carpenter ants, they will forage wherever carpenter ants may be, including within fallen trees on the ground. Even birds we do see commonly, particularly species at our feeders like the Carolina chickadee and tufted titmouse, prefer to nest in canopy tree holes, but forage for fall and winter seeds in meadows.

ABOVE **Although chickadees nest in canopy tree holes, they move to meadows in the fall and winter months to feast on the bounty of seeds this layer offers. In fact, chickadees would not make it through the winter without patches of meadow plants to sustain them. Here a chickadee plucks black-eyed Susan seeds one by one from a flower head.**

RIGHT **Many common birds including chickadees, titmice, and all woodpeckers nest in canopy tree holes, and they are very specific about the size of the tree hole they will use. If a chickadee chooses a hole too large, it will likely be evicted by a downy woodpecker, red-bellied woodpecker, or even a screech owl. A consistent problem for all tree hole nesters is the shortage of tree holes.**

ABOVE **Eastern red cedars (***Juniperus virginiana***) can be common in late-successional habitats where they provide excellent cover for birds as well as copious amounts of nutritious wax-covered cones, often called juniper berries. Juniper berries are favorite winter foods of many bird species, especially cedar waxwings. A single berry will pass through a cedar waxwing's gut in only 12 minutes, but that short internal treatment improves the germination of red cedar seeds threefold.**

Layer specialization by birds is not always static and can change with the seasons. This is usually driven by seasonal changes in diet. The hermit thrush for example, behaves like other thrushes while breeding: it nests in the forest understory but forages for arthropods and worms almost exclusively within the ground layer. Unlike its thrush relatives, however, the hermit thrush does not migrate to the neotropics where insects are abundant all winter. Instead, it remains in the temperate zone, albeit in mid rather than high latitudes, and subsists largely on berries such as those produced by winterberry (*Ilex verticillata*), American holly (*Ilex opaca*), and flowering dogwood (*Cornus florida*). These berries can be an abundant and convenient source of food for hermit thrushes, but they are typically claimed and aggressively guarded by another, larger winter berry-eater, the northern

mockingbird. Rather than frequenting the ground layer as they do in the spring and summer, hermit thrushes spend the winter months sitting quietly near such berry sources, darting into a berry shrub for a quick snack whenever the mockingbird on duty turns its back.

Although many birds commonly use lower layers in landscapes, the canopy is required at some point in their lives by more birds than any other layer. Moreover, many species like the scarlet tanager, woodthrush, red-eyed vireo, and most warblers are considered interior forest species because they are only comfortable where trees are numerous enough to create a closed canopy.

Habitat heterogeneity is not only created by the addition of vertical niches to the landscape; horizontal layers also add much to the structural diversity of habitats. The eastern meadow is a distinct

OPPOSITE TOP Poison ivy produces very few caterpillars for birds to eat during the summer, but come fall its white berries provide valuable nutrition for migrating warblers. Here a yellow-rumped warbler prepares to feast.

OPPOSITE FAR LEFT Hermit thrushes breed in northern states and Canada but often spend the winter months at mid and southern latitudes in the United States. They forage for arthropods in leaf litter as long as weather permits, but when the ground layer freezes, they rely on berries to sustain them. Here a hermit thrush eyes one of the few remaining on a winterberry (*Ilex verticillata*). He has to grab it quickly before the resident mockingbird who has claimed the holly for himself chases him off.

OPPOSITE NEAR LEFT In the spring and early summer, male yellowthroat warblers sing from bushy scrub for many hours each day to attract females and to warn off competing males.

LEFT Scarlet tanagers are residents of mature forests with tall canopies. The difference between males and females is extreme in this bird: males are a striking contrast of red and black while females are uniformly tan.

ABOVE Although they breed in the boreal forests of Canada, white-throated sparrows are common winter residents in fields and scrub habitat throughout eastern North America. Like so many other birds, white throats depend on the large seed stocks of unmown meadows to see them through the winter.

horizontal layer in many landscapes because both the plants and the animals that depend on it for their existence differ from those using the ground, edge, or shrub layers.

Birds are no exception; many grassland birds nest and forage exclusively within the sunny habitats provided by meadow and grassland vegetation. Despite specializing within the most open habitats of the landscape, grassland birds are more secretive than other birds, particularly when they are nesting, because their love of the grasses and forbs that comprise early successional sites in the east makes them easy targets for predators that canopy birds need not worry about.

Rather than flying to escape predators, grassland birds like the bobwhite, meadowlark, and grasshopper sparrow typically run among the clumps of warm season bunch grasses. In fact, the clumped growth habit of warm season grasses is essential to the survival strategy of North American grassland birds, and these layer specialists will not nest in dense grasses that fail to provide escape runways.

Another unique horizontal layer in many landscapes is the edge habitat. Both terrestrial and wet edges are ecotones, or places where two communities meet and integrate. The mixing of two plant and animal communities makes edges the most diverse habitats. Birders know that scrub habitats—the transitional habitats between forest and meadow—are often rich in both forest and grassland birds. Some species, like the golden-winged and chestnut-sided warblers, brown thrasher, indigo bunting, and orchard oriole, will only breed in scrub transitional zones. Others, like forest-loving scarlet tanagers and meadow-loving bobwhite quail, forage frequently in edge habitats because they are so rich in insect prey.

Aquatic-terrestrial interfaces, those stream, marsh, and lake edges referred to as "wet edges" here, also host a variety of specialized birds. Wading birds, such as the great blue, little blue, and green herons, as well as the great egret, spend

ABOVE **A little blue heron waits out a rain shower at a river's edge. The transitional zone between water and land is favored by the small fish, frogs, and insects that little blues hunt throughout the day.**

RIGHT **A female ruby-throated hummingbird nectars at a jewelweed flower growing along the wet edge. Jewelweed species, both the orange-flowered** *Impatiens capensis*

and the yellow *I. pallida*, **are important sources of nectar for hummingbirds, particularly during their September migration from North America to Central America.**

much of their lives in wet edges. Only there is the water shallow enough to provide access to the frogs and fish that are the main food sources of these birds and the vegetation thick enough to provide the cover these birds need when danger approaches. And the willows, birches, and alders that comprise much of the woody vegetation in wet edges are preferred breeding and foraging sites for many smaller birds, such as the beautiful and quite vocal yellow warbler. In fact, the ruby-throated hummingbird will build its nest on a sloping branch over water whenever the opportunity arises.

Landscapes with many vegetation layers are landscapes with many birds, because they are landscapes with many plants making many things to eat. Layered landscapes provide a complex of interacting organisms that are both beautiful and fascinating to those who learn to see. More important than their beauty and interest, though, is the fact that layered landscapes are functional landscapes. **—DT**

RIGHT **Great egrets are stunning birds that were hunted nearly to extinction at the turn of the twentieth century to support the fashion** **industry. They are now common in marshes and pond edges where they use their formidable bill to stab small fish and frogs.**

THE CULTURAL LAYERS

The word *landscape* was formed by combing the word *land* with old German and English words meaning *to shape*. Literally meaning "land that has been shaped," the word came into use only a few hundred years ago by painters wishing to distinguish between a literal, physical view of the land and a scenic view that recognizes the narrative content—the story—of the land. Though many forces contribute to these stories, in recent centuries no force has been more powerful than human culture.

Through agriculture, industry, home building, and a myriad of other activities, human culture continually adds to the physical and narrative layers of the landscape. The word *palimpsest*, originally referring to a page from an ancient scroll or book that was continually reused after the text had been washed or scratched off, has been expanded

LEFT A rusty tiller rests at the edge of an old farm field, now a meadow, in New York's Catskill Mountain region in October. The neat line of birches edging the meadow look as if they were planted, but this is merely the result of spontaneous regeneration in response to current conditions created by past cultural activities.

RIGHT The eventual impact of cultural activities on local ecologies is heavily influenced by time, place, and subsequent management. These three images show a road being cut through a Pennsylvania forest for a residential development. The abrupt new edge allows the sun to penetrate deeply into formerly shaded areas, radically changing both light and moisture conditions for plants and animals. The steeply graded slope adds to the drying effect. Species tolerant of the new conditions, including a range of introduced weeds, will thrive along the new edge. Moisture-dependent species will decline unless the site is re-vegetated.

to define any surface that has been written on repeatedly, each time the previous writing having been imperfectly erased and therefore remaining partly legible. Cultural layers are very much like this. They are often easily read when first written, but inevitably become partly masked by successive writings and by environmental processes. The stories inherent in cultural layers can be incorporated in the garden narratives, and insights gleaned from the interactions of culture and ecology can inform the sustainable design and management of gardens. —RD

LEFT A railroad once traveled this path. In the near-century since its demise, the forest regrew except in the old bed of cinder ballast. Now part of a preserve, the trail is kept clear partly by crews with saws but largely by human foot traffic. The dark circular vanishing point is the result of shadows in the otherwise sunny early spring landscape, hinting at a turn to the right. In mornings, this trail is full of birdsong.

TOP RIGHT Local residents wondering about this grand allée of trees might assume it was planted or follows a watercourse, but it follows the rail bed and is the result of mostly native trees taking advantage of opportunity. The pastures on both sides have been kept clear of trees since the trains stopped running, but once the tracks were removed, the railway was neglected, creating a new linear niche for seedling trees. The community of trees that established along the railbed 80 years ago is different from what would establish today due to changes in local climate, hydrology, and the presence of naturalized exotic species.

RIGHT In October, the allée follows the old railway across a local road. The line of trees in the distance follows the course of a creek.

Walking south along the former railroad right of way in early summer.

TOP This population of wild ginger (*Asarum canadense*) has been increasing for decades, apparently adapted to current conditions along the shoulder of the cinder bed, just before it slopes down toward the creek.

ABOVE LEFT Nodding trillium (*Trillium cernuum*) is the only trillium species native to this section of the local watershed. Never common, it is diminishing in its traditional niches due to the spread of multiple exotic weeds. For reasons unknown, it is finding new habitat along the shoulder of the railbed. Ants certainly play a role in this.

ABOVE RIGHT The pendent flower of nodding trillium in early May. —RD

ABOVE Relict cultural landscapes can be as beautiful as the best of gardens. The visual order in this scene is the result of vegetation responding to former human activity. This scene at Whitesbog in the New Jersey Pine Barrens was graded more than a century ago by engineers creating conditions suitable for commercial cranberry production. Long abandoned agriculturally, the resulting accidental landscape still reflects this early shaping of the land.

OPPOSITE TOP Also created decades ago when the land was engineered for cranberry production, a nearby drainage swale now provides ideal habitat for possumhaw (*Viburnum nudum*) in the foreground. Highbush blueberries (*V. corymbosum*) form a self-sown hedge of scarlet along the bank of the swale.

RIGHT Again quite gardenlike, this scene is the result of frequent human foot traffic through a self-seeding population of Virginia bluebells (*Mertensia virginica*) on a floodplain along the Susquehanna River in Maryland. No steel or plastic edges, no mulch, no deliberate maintenance by humans is necessary. —RD

THE TEMPORAL LAYERS: TIME AND COMMUNITY

Temperatures outside Ithaca, New York, had been near freezing for days before I arrived one week into November. I was in the area to present a program on woodland gardens for Cornell Plantations and as usual I'd brought my camera in hope of capturing events in the local landscape that might add to the presentation that evening.

Though the ground was nearly frozen, the air temperature was unseasonably high, and this was creating dense fogs that were moving in the brisk wind. A decade earlier, I might have thought there was nothing worth photographing, but on this day, I stopped along the road to watch the fogs rolling through tall woods on a facing slope. The landscape was exceedingly gray—nearly devoid of color—and yet the forest structure reduced by the fog to black and white seemed unusually beautiful. I stood mesmerized as the fog alternately obscured and revealed elements in the vast woodland canopy.

Inspired by the visual appeal of the scene I began imagining what would be required to create such a composition deliberately. The fog would have to be left to happenstance and good fortune, but certainly I could begin with an inventory of the trees needed, couldn't I?

I then noticed that except for the younger growth in the foreground, at the bottom of the slope where the road cut through, there were very few symmetrical trees evident. Hardly any resembled the evenly formed specimens produced by a well-run tree nursery. Though the same oak and maple species were repeated almost endlessly, the woods was comprised of profound individuality. Some trees were clearly younger and thriving; others were older and perhaps declining. A few were so reduced by wind, weather, age or unknown events that I could no longer guess their species from my stance. Yet this intriguing cast of characters together seemed a graceful fit—because that's exactly what they were.

I was observing a community of trees that had grown up with each other, had fitted themselves to one another. They competed; they made use of every opportunity. Their irregularities and imperfections, if properly called that, were proof of years or decades of adaptation to ever-changing conditions on the slope. Each tree had begun as a seedling, sown by no one, fitting itself to chance. I realized then that to reprise such a finely crafted scene in a designed landscape my two most essential elements would be seeds—and time. **—RD**

31 July 1994

24 October 1995

12 April 2000

20 April 2012

THE TEMPORAL LAYERS: TIME AND OPPORTUNITY

Climate change and the increased presence of naturalizing exotic species have profoundly altered the way many modern landscapes regrow after disturbance. This series of photographs charts the regrowth of a section of woods in Pennsylvania's White Clay Creek Preserve following a tornado in July 1994.

I'd hiked and botanized in this area for decades and was familiar with the richness of its layering. A variety of oaks, tulip trees, beeches, maples, and hickories formed the canopy. Dogwoods and ironwoods were frequent in the understory. The shrub layer included spicebush, arrowwood viburnum, and mapleleaf viburnum. The herbaceous layer was especially diverse, including white wood asters, wild ginger, multiple ferns and a number of species that are uncommon locally including puttyroot orchid (*Aplectrum hyemale*), cranefly orchid (*Tipularia discolor*), and devils'-bit (*Chamaelirium luteum*).

The tornado twisted the tops off more than half of the canopy trees in a wide swath, and many others were broken or toppled. The ground layer was cleared of decades of accumulated organic matter and much of the soil was laid bare. I knew the preserve had no budget to do much more than clear debris blocking the road and I was curious to see what would evolve in the absence of human intervention.

Choosing one distinctive broken tulip tree as a reference point, I began photographing from the same approximate position in July 1994. By late October one year later, regrowth was well underway, but it consisted mostly of annual weeds and exotic shrubs and vines including multiflora rose, Japanese honeysuckle, and Oriental bittersweet along with tulip tree seedlings and stump sprouts from beeches.

A photo taken approximately five years later in April 2000 shows the exotic growth dominating the lower layers and climbing over the broken tulip tree. I couldn't find any oak or hickory seedlings and only white wood asters and Christmas ferns were still common in the herbaceous layer. Twelve years later in April 2012 the vines and roses had grown to such proportions that I could barely get near the spot I'd originally photographed from in 1994.

At one time the most common advice following disturbance was "Let nature take its course," with the implication that in time everything would return to the way it was. This may once have been appropriate, but it no longer is in many instances. The forest section I've watched is re-vegetating, but with profoundly different structure and composition. The trees felled by the tornado remain on the ground, and as they decompose and release their stored minerals and nutrients, they provide habitat and sustenance for woodland fauna. This is desirable. However, if the desire is also for the woods to regenerate some semblance of its former diversity, human intervention is essential—but at what cost?

If one were to start with the landscape in 2012, huge effort would be required just to clear the exotic woody growth. Since many of the native species that would once have dispersed seeds are no longer present, deliberate planting would be necessary.

Imagine beginning the same task in 2000 and it would require less effort. Beginning in 1995 would have been even easier.

The best opportunity presented itself in 1994. Embarking on a program to watch the ground and remove weed seedlings so that indigenous species could re-establish was then a relatively low-cost option. Continuing this over the years would have provided a more desirable outcome at a fraction of the total resource cost.

Parks and preserves may not have the staffing to do this, but it is a realistic option for residential landscapes. The amount of discretionary time two stereotypically busy people can devote on a per-acre basis to taking care of their home garden greatly exceeds the staffing of most parks. The key is to be watchful and intervene efficiently in response to opportunity. —**RD**

WHAT DO WE MEAN BY *NATIVE*?

Life would be simpler if we could discuss the complex relationships between plants, animals, place, and time without relying on the word *native*, but this isn't likely to be the case anytime soon. Typically poorly defined or undefined, *native* often confuses more than it clarifies. Definitions, when provided, sometimes rely on geographic or political boundaries such as "naturally occurring within 200 miles" or "naturally occurring in Pennsylvania." These definitions fail to connect organisms to ecosystems, which rarely coincide with arbitrary boundaries.

Another prevailing approach relies on human influence as a deciding criterion such as "occurring in a given geographic area without human involvement" or "occurring within the state boundaries prior to European contact." These definitions perpetuate the ideological separation of humans from all other organisms, a concept soundly rejected by modern ecological science.

If the term is to have clear relevance now and in the future, it requires a definition recognizing that native status accrues from origin, evolution, and functionality. What is native in any given place today wasn't native if we look back far enough in time, and it is certain that what will be native in that same place in the future will be different from what is native now. Functional ecological relationships take a long time to evolve—often thousands of years—but they do evolve. Humanity's challenge is to reduce its introduction of rapid environmental changes that are currently causing extinctions to occur faster than the evolution of new species.

With all the above in mind, for the purpose of this book and future discussion we've created the following definition:

The tiny blue dot (circled) is a great blue heron with a 5-foot wingspan flying 50 feet above the surface of the White Clay Creek, photographed from a helicopter flying 300 feet above this intricately layered Pennsylvania landscape.

native: a plant or animal that has evolved in a given place over a period of time sufficient to develop complex and essential relationships with the physical environment and other organisms in a given ecological community.

The Community of Living Organisms: Why Interrelationships Matter More Than Numbers *by Doug Tallamy*

THE PROMINENCE OF SPECIALIZED RELATIONSHIPS

In the mountain cloud forests of Central America a brilliant green-and-red bird with tail feathers twice the length of its body sits motionless among the epiphytes growing on a branch some 120 feet off the ground. After several minutes, it darts through the air to a nearby tree limb, plucks an inch-long fruit off the branch, and returns to its perch. Once settled, the bird swallows the fruit whole . . . and sits. Perhaps 20 minutes later, the bird regurgitates the large pit of the fruit and the process starts again.

Birders worldwide recognize this as a description of the resplendent quetzal pursuing its favorite food, fruits of the wild avocado tree (*Persea americana*), the progenitor of our cultivated avocados. To characterize avocados as a favorite food of quetzals is an understatement, because at this point in its evolutionary history, avocados are essential to the quetzal's existence. Although they also eat insects, frogs, and lizards, as well as fruits from other plants in the Lauraceae, quetzals have grown so dependent on the rich fats and proteins provided by avocado fruits that they can no longer live where there are no avocado trees. When the forests of Central America were intact, this degree of diet specialization was not a problem for quetzals.

Today, however, with wild avocados themselves threatened, dependence on avocado fruits has placed quetzals firmly on the road to extinction.

For those interested in quetzal conservation, the solution to their dwindling numbers is obvious; plant avocado trees! The same can be said of other tropical creatures with specialized diets. To save the great green macaw, plant the mountain almond (*Dipteryx panamensis*) as fast as possible. To sustain populations of jaguars, save the palm trees that make the palm nuts that support large peccary populations, the wild pigs that are required components of jaguar diets.

To be sure, highly specific relationships between food and consumer are more common in tropical ecosystems, but some level of diet specialization is easily found in temperate zones as well. In fact, one or more species of the bolas spider, one of the most specialized predators in the world, can be found in residential landscapes throughout much of the United States. Rather than spin an intricate web, adult female bolas spiders use a single strand of silk tipped with a bolas of sticky goo. They then hang off the end of a leaf, patiently holding their line as if they were fishing. The chances that an insect will fly into the sticky bolas by accident seem infinitely small, yet often within minutes a moth flies directly to the bolas and becomes entangled.

How can this happen? It can happen through extraordinary chemical mimicry. Over the eons, bolas spiders developed the ability to manufacture the female sex pheromone of a particular species of moth. A hunting bolas spider appears to be waiting passively for a moth to fly to its bolas, but, in reality, it is releasing copious amounts of the moth's sex pheromone, a chemical that can attract male moths of the appropriate species from hundreds of yards away. Each species of bolas spider has mimicked the pheromone of a single moth species, forming a unique relationship between predator and prey.

LEFT **A pipevine swallowtail lays eggs on** *Aristolochia macrophylla* **in mid-June.**

ABOVE **Resplendent quetzals depend on the fats and protein in wild avocado fruits during much of the year.**

Most people are unaware of the bolas spiders hunting in their yard, even though this is a common occurrence. A specialized relationship that many *have* observed involves the Carolina chickadee. If asked what chickadees eat, most people would confidently answer "seeds." Their confidence would be borne out of personal experience. Chickadees are one of the most common customers at our backyard birdfeeders and they do indeed spend the winter months eating a variety of seeds. When it comes time to reproduce, however, chickadees become diet specialists.

Like 96 percent of the terrestrial birds in North America, Carolina chickadees rear their young on insects. And not just any old insect; they feed nestlings caterpillars, the larvae of moths, butterflies, and sawflies. Chickadee parents could feed their young crickets, millipedes, sow bugs, crane flies, katydids, treehoppers, click beetles, spiders, cockroaches, horse flies, or bumblebees, but 95–100 percent of the insects they hunt for their offspring are caterpillars.

The bolas spider (*Mastophora phynosoma*) mimics the sex pheromone of a single species of moth to attract them to its sticky bolas.

Because chickadees rear their young exclusively on caterpillars, there will be no chickadees where there are no caterpillars. We really should say that there will be no chickadees where there are not *enough* caterpillars to bring a clutch of eggs to independence from parental care. An environment that produces *almost* enough caterpillars just won't do.

How many caterpillars *are* enough to produce a clutch of chickadees? 75? 150? Not quite. Carolina chickadees bring somewhere between 390 and 570 caterpillars to their nest *each day*, depending on how many chicks are in the nest. Parents feed nestlings in the nest for 16 to 18 days before the young fledge, and then for several more days after fledging. If we focus only on the caterpillars required to reach fledging, it takes 6,240 to 10,260 caterpillars to fledge a single clutch of chickadees, an astounding number, even to those who study bird behavior.

What's more, chickadees are tiny birds; a Carolina chickadee weighs a third of an ounce, the equivalent of four pennies. In comparison, a red-bellied woodpecker, which also rears its young on insect larvae, weighs eight times more than a chickadee. How much insect biomass is required to create a red-bellied woodpecker? How many insects are required to sustain an entire population of chickadees and woodpeckers . . . and titmice, and orioles, bluebirds, woodthrushes, robins, and all of the other birds that signal healthy temperate zone ecosystems? The numbers are mind-boggling.

Before we consider what types of landscapes are capable of producing such large numbers of insects, we have to consider another type of relationship: the relationship between the insects that eat plants and the plants they eat. Most insect herbivores, some 90 percent in fact, are diet specialists. Just like breeding Carolina chickadees, they are restricted to eating very specific types of plant food.

First, herbivorous insects select a particular part of their host plant to consume. All plant parts support some species of insects. There are insects that only eat flower petals while others eat only flower anthers, stamens, or ovaries. Many species specialize on roots; others eat cambium or dead xylem. A great many species are seed specialists. By far, though, most insect herbivores eat only leaves, and even then they specialize. Some only eat young leaves; others only eat older leaves. Many species only eat leaves that are exposed to direct sunlight because those leaves are higher in nitrogen than leaves that are shaded. Some insects eat the entire leaf while others only eat the soft tissues between leaf veins, causing a skeletonized appearance of the leaf. Finally, there are many insects that are so thin they can tunnel, or mine, if you will, between the upper and lower surfaces of a leaf, eating only soft parenchymal cells.

Not only do insects rely on a particular part of the plant for their nutrition, they also restrict their feeding to particular plant lineages. Let's consider the caterpillars that support my chickadee friends. The great majority of caterpillar species are leaf specialists. Like katydids, grasshoppers, and beetles, caterpillars have chewing (as opposed to sucking) mouthparts and cannot eat a leaf without bursting the tiny vacuoles within the leaf's cells that store defensive chemicals.

Plants, of course, do not want to be eaten. They want to capture the energy from the sun and use it for their own growth and reproduction, so they manufacture nasty tasting chemicals specifically to deter plant-eaters. These chemicals are secondary metabolic compounds that do not contribute to the primary metabolism of the plant. Their job is to make the leaf taste bad or be downright toxic to any insect that may try to eat the leaf. Some well-known plant defenses include toxic compounds

TOP Carolina chickadees feed their young almost exclusively on caterpillars. If there are not enough caterpillars in the landscape, chickadees cannot reproduce.

ABOVE The red-lined panapoda is a caterpillar that develops only on native *Quercus* such as black oak.

like cyanide, nicotine, cucurbitacins, and pyrethrins; heart-stoppers like cardiac glycosides; and digestibility inhibitors like tannins.

If plants are so well defended, how can insects eat them without dying? This question dominated plant-insect interaction studies for three decades, but at this point, the answer has been thoroughly delineated. Caterpillars and other immature insects are eating machines; some species increase their mass 72,000-fold by the time they reach their full size. If humans grew to such proportions, an infant that is 7 pounds at birth would weigh 504,000 pounds by the time it reached its twentieth birthday. Because caterpillars necessarily ingest chemical deterrents with every bite, there is enormous selection pressure to restrict feeding to plant species they can eat without serious ill effects. Thus, a gravid female moth will lay eggs only on plants with chemical defenses their hatchling caterpillars are able to disarm.

There are many physiological mechanisms by which caterpillars can temper plant defenses, but they all involve some combination of sequestering, excreting, or detoxifying the nasty phytochemicals contained in leaves before they interfere with the caterpillar's health. Caterpillars typically come by these adaptations through many generations of exposure to the plant lineage in question, although occasionally they coincidentally possess enzymes that are able to disarm a plant the caterpillar has never encountered in its evolutionary history. In short, by becoming host plant specialists, insect herbivores can circumvent plant defenses well enough to make a living.

Does this mean specialists have won the evolutionary arms race with plants? Yes, but only in relation to the plant lineage on which they have specialized. When viewed across all lineages, plant defenses are very effective at deterring most insects. The rose hooktip moth (*Oreta rosea*) provides an excellent example. This caterpillar is a specialist on New World members of the genus *Viburnum* that use various forms of toxic irridoid glycosides to protect their tissues. Because of its specialized adaptations, the rose hooktip moth can eat viburnums that are not viable host plants for most other insect herbivores. The advantage of this relationship is obvious for the moth, but there are real disadvantages to specializing as well. Unfortunately for the hooktip moth, the ability to detoxify iridoid glycosides in viburnums does not confer the ability to disarm the chemical defenses found in other plant lineages. This means that of the 1385 plant genera in the Mid-Atlantic states, the rose hooktip moth can develop on only one, the genus *Viburnum*. The evolutionarily history

The rose hooktip moth (*Oreta rosea*) is a good example of thousands of species that have evolved to use only one plant lineage for growth and reproduction. Rose hooktip moths are specialists on North American *Viburnum* species, with a special affinity for *V. dentatum*.

of this moth has locked it into a dependent relationship with viburnums and if viburnums should disappear from a landscape, so would the hooktip moth.

What type of landscape is capable of producing insects in the numbers required to support viable food webs? A landscape built from a diversity of plants that have each developed specialized relationships with a diversity of insect species. A landscape occupied by organisms that have interacted with each other over evolutionary rather than ecological time spans.

As we have explained, diet specialization is the rule among insect herbivores, not the exception. Without the plant lineages that support insect herbivores, there would be no insect herbivores. If there were no insect herbivores, all of the creatures that depend on insect herbivores for their nutrition, that is, the insectivores of the world, would also disappear. A world without insectivores would be a world without spiders; insect predators and parasitoids; frogs, toads, and other amphibians; lizards; bats, rodents, skunks, opossums, as well as mammals we don't think of as insect eaters, such as foxes and black bears, both of which get a quarter of their nutrition from insects.

Studies have shown that even some freshwater fish get more than 50 percent of their protein from terrestrial insects that fall into the water. And let's not forget that a world without insect herbivores would also be a world without 96 percent of the terrestrial bird species; with the exception of doves, finches, crossbills, and our largest birds of prey, terrestrial birds rear their young on insects and the spiders that ate insects to become spiders. Most important, a world without all of these creatures would not only be a world without biological diversity, it would be a world in ecological collapse.

BIODIVERSITY AND ECOSYSTEM PRODUCTIVITY

Research over the decades has tied the number of interacting species in an ecosystem to both ecosystem function and ecosystem stability. Let's first consider ecosystem function.

We can define ecosystem function in several ways: the ability to hold energy captured from the sun within biological systems before it escapes back into space; the ability to produce products or perform services useful to humans and other species; the ability to create living and dead biomass; and so on. In 1955, famed ecologist Robert MacArthur predicted that ecosystem function would increase linearly as the number of species within an ecosystem increased. Diverse ecosystems with many equally abundant species would be more productive than species-poor ecosystems

The great gray dart in the beak of this bluebird feeds on birch trees and blueberry bushes. Insects that eat plants are essential components of nearly all terrestrial food webs.

dominated by one or a few species. Although no one had tested this prediction, it was logically appealing and soon came to be known as the Law of Nature.

It was not until 1981 that MacArthur's Law was challenged by an analogy between species populating an ecosystem and the rivets that once held airplanes together. In their rivet hypothesis, Paul and Anne Erhlich suggested that ecosystem productivity was indeed tied to the number of species in an ecosystem, but only to a point. Their hypothesis introduced the concept of species redundancy; the Erhlichs reasoned that there was redundancy in the species performing particular roles within ecosystems just as there was redundancy in aircraft rivets. An airplane could lose some rivets before a wing fell off the plane, and an ecosystem could lose some species before it suffered a measurable loss in productivity.

Pollinators provide a nice example of species

redundancy. A black-eyed Susan needs to be pollinated before it can produce seeds, but many species of bees, moths, butterflies, beetles, and even ants are capable of doing the job (although not all do it equally well). The redundancy in black-eyed Susan pollinators implies that one or even several of these pollinator species could disappear from the system without a reduction in seed set in black-eyed Susans.

The rivet hypothesis was somewhat comforting to ecologists because it predicted that the local or global extinction of some species would not send ecosystems spiraling into collapse, at least not right away. The question then became, how many species could an ecosystem lose before it reached that threshold number predicted by the Erhlichs that *would* trigger ecosystem collapse.

Replicated studies of entire ecosystems in which distracting variables are controlled are extremely difficult to conduct, and so the compelling logic of the rivet hypothesis remained untested for many years after it was proposed. Slowly, however, reliable studies were performed that allowed scientists to measure the relationship between ecosystem function and the number of species within. Although evidence is still accumulating, it now appears that MacArthur's predictions were closer to reality than was the rivet hypothesis.

We still do not know the exact shape of the relationship, but consensus is growing that ecosystem function increases directly with the number of species in an ecosystem. Redundancy in the roles species play within ecosystems surely exists, yet studies now show that it does not buffer ecosystems from a loss of productivity every time a species disappears from the system. Not good news. If this relationship is borne out by additional research, we can no longer be complacent about the loss of species from local ecosystems.

It is worth emphasizing that we do not need

Rather than being redundant, a diversity of pollinators creates stability in vital pollinator communities.

to wait for the global extinction of a species to become concerned. Ecosystems function locally, not globally. Local extinction, the disappearance of a species within, say, the woodlot down the street, or even your front yard, is now predicted to compromise the productivity of that woodlot and your yard.

Unfortunately, local extinction is rampant in human-dominated landscapes. A simple experiment conducted by one of my students illustrates this problem well. Melissa Richards measured what happens to caterpillar diversity and abundance when Asian plants like autumn olive, porcelain berry, Chinese privet, and Japanese honeysuckle displace indigenous plants in hedgerows. Controlling for the amount of vegetation searched, Melissa found that hedgerows dominated by plants indigenous to the study sites in Delaware, Maryland, and Pennsylvania, that is, hedgerows with few invasive plants, produced five times more species of caterpillars and twenty-two times more caterpillars than hedgerows in which invasive Asian plants had replaced much of the native vegetation.

Does the twenty-two-fold reduction in caterpillars matter? For those who consider caterpillars to be yucky worms that must be squished at every opportunity, perhaps not. But the loss of caterpillars from breeding sites certainly matters to birds and other insectivores that rely on caterpillars to feed their young. Caterpillars function for birds in exactly the same way money does for us; caterpillars are the currency on which birds live. If you reduced your bank account twenty-two-fold, you would notice. And so do birds.

Bird reproduction is limited by food availability. Whenever food is increased for breeding birds, fledgling number or weight or both also increase. A good general rule then is that breeding birds are never satiated but instead take every suitable caterpillar they can find. What do you imagine happens to breeding bird success in habitats where food availability is *decreased* twenty-two-fold?

In 2009 Karin Burghardt documented the relationship between caterpillars and the birds that eat them within suburban landscapes and, like Melissa, found that landscapes dominated by Asian ornamentals were correlated with a significant loss in breeding bird species and abundance. Not only does a reduction in the number and diversity of organisms with dependent relationships reduce ecosystem productivity, as we shall now see, it also threatens the long-term stability of the ecosystem.

BIODIVERSITY AND ECOSYSTEM STABILITY

There are several definitions of ecosystem stability and several ways that biodiversity contributes to various forms of stability. Some consider stability to be the amount of time required for an ecosystem to recover from an ecological perturbation, while others define stability as being ecosystem resistance to change from outside forces. Regardless of the definition applied, stable ecosystems are more productive over the long term than unstable ones that fluctuate wildly in both species numbers and diversity.

Both the physical and the biotic environments contribute to ecosystem stability. Warm, wet regions of the world tend to support more-stable ecosystems because moisture and warmth encourage the evolution of biodiversity, and, as we shall see, diverse ecosystems are more stable. Drier ecosystems are more sensitive to perturbations, are more easily knocked out of kilter, and can take far longer to return to a stable productive state after a perturbation. Few people realize that the dry Mediterranean region, including the original breadbasket of civilization in what is now Iraq, was once a forested ecosystem. When humans cut those forests thousands of years ago, rainfall became even more scarce than it already was and the entire region became and has remained an extremely fragile and far-less-productive desert-scrub ecosystem.

The relationship between biodiversity and ecosystem stability may best be illustrated by the relationship between biodiversity and food web stability. Food webs are most stable when comprised of many interacting species, that is, when they are complex. Let's return to the Carolina chickadees nesting in my yard for an example. Recall that chickadees are caterpillar specialists while rearing young and they need thousands of caterpillars to complete the job successfully. Now, imagine two landscapes, each with a breeding population of chickadees.

The first landscape is dominated by one tree species, the tulip tree, while the second has a more diverse plant community that contains four species of trees: black cherry, tulip poplar, red oak, and eastern red cedar. In the first landscape tulip trees produce large inch worms called tulip tree beauties, while in the second landscape black cherries produce the speckled green fruitworm, oaks produce the ilia underwing, red cedars produce the curve-lined angle and the juniper geometer, and the tulip trees, as in the first landscape, produce the tulip tree beauty. Chickadees in the tulip tree–only landscape must rely on a single species of caterpillar to meet the nutritional needs of their young, while chickadees in the more diverse landscape can rear their young on five species of caterpillars.

Now let's add a dose of reality to our two landscapes. Populations fluctuate; in good

Autumn olive (*Elaeagnus umbellata*) and Oriental bittersweet (*Celastrus orbiculatus*) dominate a Delaware hedgerow in early May.

times they increase in size and in bad times they shrink. Sometimes the weather causes populations to grow or shrink, but other times the cause is biological in nature: too many parasitic wasps, not enough assassin bug predators, or the outbreak of a species-specific disease can cause the numbers of a given species to rise or fall. Because the causes of population fluctuations are both density dependent and density independent, there is no synchrony in the behavior of different populations; thus, in our example, the population of one species of caterpillar can grow at the same time that the population of another species is falling.

This illustrates why a complex food web with many interacting species is more stable than a simple food web with few interacting players. Chickadees in the tulip tree-only landscape are entirely dependent on the population success of a single species of caterpillar, the tulip tree beauty. If the population of this caterpillar is not sufficiently large to supply the breeding chickadees with enough food to rear their young, the chickadees will experience reproductive failure and their own population numbers will fall. If, in contrast, the tulip tree beauty suffers a population crash in the landscape that produces prey alternatives, the chickadees in that landscape will simply hunt the more numerous speckled green fruitworms, ilia underwings, curve-lined angles, and juniper geometers. Chickadee reproduction will succeed, their population numbers will not plummet, and the food web will remain stable, all because it was comprised of multiple species of productive trees instead of just one tree species.

There is a second reason that diversity lends stability to food webs. Because predators must capture more energy than they exert while hunting, they typically focus their attention on prey species that are easiest to find, that is, prey that are the most common. This ensures that the predator will not waste energy searching for

uncommon prey and risk falling into an energy deficit, a state no predator can survive for long. When several prey species are available in a food web, a predator will hunt the most numerous prey item until it is no longer the most numerous. At that point, the predator will switch to the next most numerous species, and so on. This is a fortunate circumstance for the heavily hunted prey species, because once the predator no longer targets it, the beleaguered species can rebuild its numbers before it is hunted to local extinction. When a food web consists of only one or two prey species, the predator has no choice but to hunt them to dangerously low numbers.

Again, we see that diversity in caterpillars, derived from diversity in caterpillar food plants, enables all species to persist in a food web over long periods through an intricate dance of density dependency led by reproducing chickadees. When we expand our example from unrealistically simple landscapes with only chickadees and caterpillars to the complexity that is the hallmark of highly productive ecosystems—thousands of species of plants making tens of thousands of species of insects that support dozens of species of insectivores and several species of top predators—we can begin to visualize the role of interacting species in maintaining ecosystem function.

TIME AND RELATIONSHIPS

If you were to visit ecosystems all over the world and count the number of species in each, an unmistakable pattern would soon emerge from your efforts: ecosystems built from indigenous organisms would contain more species than ecosystems infused by non-native organisms. Quite simply, indigenous organisms are enmeshed within a greater network of relationships than non-indigenous organisms, and so wherever species are native, more species accumulate. Plants and the caterpillars that eat them offer a powerful example, as the accompanying graph shows.

There are, on average, nearly thirteen times more species of caterpillars that develop on woody plants indigenous to the Mid-Atlantic states than on plants not historically found in that area. Why should this be so? It may be simply a matter of time. Most plants indigenous to the Mid-Atlantic states have been exposed to most native caterpillars for hundreds of thousands, if not millions, of generations: plenty of time for those caterpillars to evolve the specialized adaptations necessary to circumvent the defenses of one or more plant lineages. Plants that originated outside of local food webs have, in evolutionary time frames, just met local caterpillars.

Non-native plants will eventually develop the complex relationships that characterize indigenous communities, but the speed with which new relationships form is proving to be surprisingly slow. For example, L. Tewksbury and others found that the European genotype of the common reed (*Phragmites australis*) supports

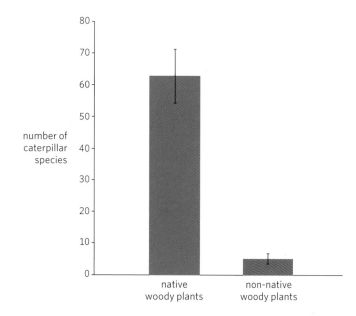

On average, native plants support thirteen times more caterpillar species than non-native plants.

170 species of insect herbivores in Europe where it evolved, but only five insects have adapted to its defenses in the three centuries since its introduction to the United States. A slow process, indeed. In that same time the aggressive European genotype has displaced countless North American plant species. And *Phragmites* is not an exception.

A century after its introduction, *Eucalyptus stelloleta*, a tree planted worldwide for lumber and ornamental purposes, supports only one species in California but 48 species of insects in its Australian homeland according to D. Strong and colleagues. In 1995, research by S. Costello and team showed that *Melaleuca quinquenervia*, the infamous invader of the Everglades, supports 409 species of insect herbivores in its native Australia, but after 120 years in Florida, only 8 species have figured out how to develop on this plant.

We can say with confidence that introduced plants have not had the time required to develop the relationships with local organisms that lend stability to ecosystems. And because of studies by K. Burghardt and myself published in 2010 and 2013, we can say with certainty that, on average, ecosystems built from indigenous plants are more species-rich than ecosystems infused with non-natives. But can we say that all native plants are equal contributors to local animal diversity? No we cannot, and a quick look at the tables at the back of the book tells us why.

There is extraordinary variation in the degree to which different genera of indigenous plants support local food webs and thus local biodiversity. If we use caterpillars as surrogates for all insect herbivores, we see that, in the Mid-Atlantic states, native oaks are the most productive plants because they act as host plants for 557 species of caterpillars. The loss of oaks (*Quercus*) from an eastern deciduous forest would trigger an immediate and destructive drain of species from that ecosystem. In contrast, the loss of American yellowwood (*Cladrastis kentukea*) would hardly be missed, at least in terms of the other species it supports, as there are no records of caterpillars using this tree. Yet yellowwood is a native tree.

Many such comparisons illustrate the wide variation in productivity among indigenous plants. Native cherries (*Prunus*) support 456 species of caterpillars while leatherwood (*Dirca palustris*) supports one; willows (*Salix*) support 455 species while tulip tree (*Liriodendron tulipifera*) supports 21. Ferns are exceptionally well defended by nasty phytochemicals and consequently support very few insects. Their contributions to local food webs are therefore less than those made by many other indigenous plants.

It's worth noting that ferns are one of the most ancient native plant lineages. Insects have had hundreds of millions of years to adapt to fern defenses, but few have succeeded. Although time is generally a necessary part of the process of becoming a productive contributor to local ecosystems, it is obviously not the only factor involved. It seems that the defenses of some plant lineages can never be breached by most insect herbivores, no matter how much time they have to adapt. In fact, it would be easy to construct a landscape entirely from native plants with long geographic histories in local ecosystems that contributes very little to the diversity, productivity, and stability of the local ecosystem. The point here is that "being native" does not always translate into "being productive."

There is another reason we should be cautious about the ecological ramifications of the label "native." Most people talk about native plants within the context of their geographic origin rather than their ecological function. This has lead to long debates that have distracted from rather than enhanced the restoration of ecosystem function in our landscapes. For example, *Ginkgo biloba*, the oldest living tree species on earth, used to have a global distribution. Over

The European genotype of *Phragmites australis* now dominates countless acres in the Hackensack Meadowlands of northern New Jersey.

millions of years, its range contracted until now wild populations are only found on Xitianmu mountain in Zhejiang, China. Ginkgo disappeared from North America seven million years ago, yet because it once lived in what is now Virginia, some claim that it is a tree native to Virginia. From a geographic perspective, I understand this reasoning, but does this make sense from the perspective of ecosystem function? It is likely that North American ginkgoes once supported a large and complex food web, including many insect herbivores that specialized on

its leaves. Once ginkgo disappeared, however, what do you think happened to those insect specialists? It is most parsimonious to assume that they too disappeared from North America.

Today there are records of five species of caterpillars using the many ginkgoes that have been planted widely as ornamentals in the Mid-Atlantic states, but they must use it sparingly; I have never encountered any caterpillars on ginkgo, nor have I seen any evidence of ginkgo caterpillars or any other insect in the form of feeding scars. Today ginkgoes are contributing little if anything to local food webs compared to most contemporary indigenous plants. Regardless of whether it was once a native in North America, the complex food webs ginkgo may have supported in the past did not survive its seven-million-year hiatus.

An ecosystem is the combination of an interacting community of living organisms and their physical environment, functioning as an ecological unit in a given place. The operative word in this definition is "interacting." Organisms in co-evolved ecosystems have relationships with each other that have developed over time to benefit at least one member of the relationship.

There are so many specialized relationships in ecosystems that we can easily say ecological specialization is the rule rather than the exception. Most organisms depend on relationships with particular species or particular kinds of species for their existence; any old species will not do. The species that evolved within an ecosystem are what created that ecosystem over time and they cannot be interchanged willy-nilly without destroying the relationships that drive function in that particular ecosystem.

We have also learned that, in the absence of human tinkering, the more interacting species there are in an ecosystem, the more stable and productive is that ecosystem. Evidence to date shows that scrambling age-old relationships causes a precipitous loss of species from

A mature white oak (*Quercus alba*) in a southeastern Pennsylvania forest.

ecosystems. The bolas spider would not persist in our yard if there were not also a viable population of the moth species it chemically mimics. The chickadees that nest in our yard could not rear their young if there were not thousands of caterpillars in enough diversity in the landscape to persist through normal population fluctuations. And there would not be a diversity of caterpillars in our yard without a diversity of their co-evolved host plants. On it goes, with one species inextricably linked to many others.

What happens, then, when humans create new groups of organisms by assembling species from around the world that have never before had the opportunity to interact with each other? This experiment is underway nearly everywhere. Richard Hobbs has estimated that more than 85 percent of the earth's ecosystems is now what he calls "novel" ecosystems—ecosystems containing many species with *no* prior history of interacting together and *no* relationships honed over evolutionary time. Such ecosystems are built, at least in part, from *non-relational* biodiversity. A linguist could successfully argue that, without functional interactions, such collections of organisms do not constitute an ecosystem at all.

It is worth emphasizing that novel ecosystems are not just phenomena developing in Australia, Brazil, and Italy. They are being created all around us and we are responsible for their proliferation. Traditional residential landscapes built from turf grass and Asian ornamentals are novel ecosystems, as are our county, state, and national parks that are overrun with Bradford pear, kudzu, Oriental bittersweet, privet, multiflora rose, bush honeysuckle, buckthorn, Japanese honeysuckle, ailanthus, Japanese knotweed, Norway maple, and burning bush. These ecosystems have lost many of the relationships sustained by indigenous plants.

Although alarms have been raised about the exchange of novel organisms all over the world, and the rising ecological costs that result from such exchanges, many people are still ambivalent about whether this is really a problem. Scientists have done a poor job of articulating how ecosystems work, why we can no longer rely on the Adirondacks and the Great Smoky Mountains to produce all of the ecosystem services needed in the eastern United States, and even why we need functioning ecosystems at all. It is quite possible, however, to recreate ecological function where we live and work and even where we farm if we do not lose sight of the relationships that create that function.

Adapted to modern conditions, the large ginkgo tree in the center of this photo was planted by the Peirce family approximately two hundred years ago on land that is now part of Longwood Gardens.

In a novel ecosystem along a Delaware highway in November, blazing red self-sown Callery pears (*Pyrus calleriana*) introduced from Asia mix with the European genotype of common reed (*Phragmites australis*), with autumn olive (*Elaeagnus umbellata*) introduced from Asia, and with locally indigenous red cedars (*Juniperus virginiana*), winterberry (*Ilex verticillata*), little bluestem (*Schizachyrium scoparium*), and goldenrods (*Solidago* species).

In this chapter, I have focused on the ecological aspects of functional landscapes. I have emphasized the specialized relationships that characterize food webs because no ecosystem can exist without them, but interactions among organisms in different trophic levels are hardly the only specialized relationships in nature. Many birds and rodents have specialized relationships with tree holes; thousands of species of soil organisms have specialized relationships with the damp leaf litter above them. Many birds have specialized relationships with dense vegetation for nesting cover, and so on.

We must not forget that humans also have relationships with the landscapes around them. Fully functional residential landscapes must meet the physical, cultural, and aesthetic needs of humans while generating ecosystem services required by diverse other species. We may use ferns even though they contribute little to local food webs because they provide cover for wildlife, are beautiful, are durable ground covers, help replenish atmospheric oxygen, aid in hydrologic recharge, and can be the vegetational backbone of soil ecosystems. We may use splashes of colorful plants even if they are not indigenous to our region because they are beautiful and they will draw us into our gardens to experience the life around us. And we will not skimp on the core group of plants that support most of the biodiversity vital to ecosystem function.

To paraphrase Abe Lincoln, you can create multifunctional residential landscapes using all-natives some of the time, and some natives all of the time, but you cannot meet all landscaping goals using all natives all of time. We will see why in future chapters.

LEFT Polypody ferns (*Polypodium vulgare*) cover the top of a Pennsylvania streamside rock outcrop while evergreen wood ferns (*Dryopteris intermedia*) occupy the more consistently moist niches just below.

BELOW Another example of a novel ecosystem: a great blue heron wades along the edge of a Delaware stream in search of the small fish and aquatic insects that make up much of its diet while Asian multiflora roses (*Rosa multiflora*) dominate the shrub layer and lesser celandine (*Ranunculus ficaria*) from Eurasia makes up the majority of the herbaceous layer.

CHAPTER THREE
The Ecological Functions of Gardens: What Landscapes Do *by Doug Tallamy*

Gardens and the greater landscapes that surround them occupy such enormous areas of the country that they have great potential to address many of the environmental challenges facing us today if given half a chance. Gardens are made of plants and plants deliver, either directly or indirectly, many of the ecosystem services that support human populations. Landscape designers, landscape architects, gardeners, and even homeowners who have no interest in gardening have within their power the ability to protect our watersheds, cool and clean the air we breath, build and stabilize top-soil, moderate extreme weather, sequester carbon, and protect the biodiversity that drives ecosystem function. Before I expand on these new opportunities for our gardens, I want to share an inspiring example from South Florida of the ecological power of residential landscapes.

SPECIES CONSERVATION

On a recent trip to Florida, I learned about an accident that has occurred there; Florida gardeners have *accidentally* brought the atala butterfly back from the brink of extinction. Here's how this happened: South Florida was once home to a thriving population of coontie (*Zamia pumila*), a slow-growing cycad that the Seminole Indians used as a starchy food. When Florida was occupied, first by the Spanish and then by newly minted Americans, the Seminoles showed

ABOVE **An essential Florida relationship: Atala butterfly (*Eumaeus atala*) on coontie (*Zamia pumila*).**

RIGHT **An atala larva on coontie.**

the newcomers how to pound coontie roots into a powder that could be used to enhance a number of dishes. The colonists loved coontie root so much that soon all the coontie, except for a few plants in private gardens, was gone.

What the colonists didn't know was that coontie was the sole host plant for the atala (*Eumaeus atala*), a gorgeous lycaenid butterfly whose only foothold in North America was southern Florida. Not surprisingly, when coontie disappeared, so did the atala butterfly. Last-minute efforts in 1974 to put the atala on the endangered species list failed because there was no evidence that the butterfly still existed.

About that time, landscape designers recognized the ornamental value of coontie in residential plantings. Here was a low-growing, long-lived evergreen shrub with interesting habit that was adapted to the dry conditions of South Florida's sandy soils. Homeowners agreed and in short order coontie was restored to Florida landscapes—not in the wild, but in formal landscape plantings. Soon after coontie became widespread once again, the atala butterfly reappeared. Apparently, some remnant atala population had survived, perhaps on undetected coontie deep in the Everglades, and is now colonizing residential coontie plantings throughout South Florida.

I want to stress the *accidental* nature of this extraordinary conservation success. Even though saving the atala butterfly could so easily have been a goal of homeowners when coontie was restored to Florida landscapes, it was not. It simply had not occurred to them. In fact, in step with a culture that only values plants for their aesthetic qualities, many Floridians still ask for instructions from extension agents on how to

The low, evergreen presence of coontie (*Zamia pumila*) is a beautiful and ecologically functional component in the visitor center landscape at Bok Tower Gardens in Florida, photographed on a misty January morning.

kill atala caterpillars before they mar the perfect fronds of their coontie.

The return of the atala in Florida illustrates the untapped, indeed, unrecognized, conservation power of residential landscapes. If our landscaping choices can rebuild populations of a butterfly thought to be extinct without listing it under the Endangered Species Act and without investing one dime of limited conservation funds—that is, without even trying—imagine what we can do if we include conservation as one of the goals of our gardens.

ECOLOGICAL BENEFITS FOR HUMANS

Think of *all* of the ecosystem services we could produce in our managed landscapes: the carbon that could be sequestered, the watersheds that could be protected, the air that could be cleaned and cooled, the pollinators that could be produced and nourished, the isolated natural areas that could be linked, the food webs that could be stabilized and expanded, and, yes, the biodiversity that could be saved if we designed landscapes with function, as well as beauty, in mind. Considering that the earth's ability to produce ecosystem services has already been degraded 60 percent, according to a report by the Millennium Ecosystem Assessment in 2005, building landscapes that produce such services everywhere we live and work could go a long way toward mitigating such losses.

Carbon Sequestration

To expand on just one example, let's consider the carbon sequestration potential of our residential landscapes. Billions of tons of carbon that have been buried out of harms way miles beneath our feet for millions of years are being released in an geological instant into the earth's atmosphere by the burning of fossil fuels. Because plants are made of carbon, and dense plants like hickories, black locust, and oaks can

lock up 10 to 40 tons of carbon per individual for centuries, well-vegetated landscapes can help buffer the atmospheric effects of carbon dioxide while they deliver many other ecosystem services.

Trees do not sequester carbon overnight, but the sheer scale of their effectiveness is worth thinking about. Let's say you decide to plant five oak trees on your property. In 55 years, those trees will have removed 216,053 pounds of carbon from the atmosphere. In 75 years, this figure would grow to 425,492 pounds of carbon. If one thousand homeowners in your city also planted five oaks each, over 425 million pounds of carbon would be sequestered. And if 1000 cities across the United States did the same, 425 billion pounds of carbon could be locked away for many decades. Of course, this would require the participation of 1 million homeowners in this tree-planting effort, but considering that there are approximately 82 million detached homes in the United States as reported by the U.S. Census Bureau in 2010, and the average suburban lot contains only 10 percent of the tree biomass that it could contain, as soon-to-be-published research by myself and colleagues shows, this seems doable.

Shading and Evaporative Cooling

The positive effect of increasing the amount of plants in residential landscape can also be estimated in terms of other critical ecosystem services. For example, shading and evaporative cooling from tree canopies can reduce summer temperatures from uncomfortable to pleasant ranges. What's more, the effect is additive: the more your neighbors add trees to their properties, the cooler the air mass within your neighborhood will be and the longer it will stay cool during extended heat waves.

You can easily experience the power of forest cooling by visiting your nearest forested park. As soon as you step from the deforested park perimeter into the forest itself, the air temperature will drop 10 degrees. This effect is magnified within built structures. Research published by the U.S. Environmental Protection Agency in 2009 showed that when solar radiation is blocked from striking the walls, roof, and windows of your home by trees, the temperature inside your house drops 10 to 45 degrees *without* air conditioning. Trees can reduce heating bills during the winter just as well as they can reduce air conditioning bills during the summer. By blocking cold winter winds, trees reduce the rate of air exchange between the warm interior of your home and the cold exterior. Thus, the air you have heated with your furnace stays in your house longer when trees are strategically placed on your property, a benefit more thoroughly explored in *Energy-Wise Landscape Design: A New Approach for Your Home and Garden* by Sue Reed.

Watershed Protection

Another underappreciated ecological function of plants in our landscapes is their role in watershed management and protection. We all live within a discreet watershed: a matrix of streams

that flow to a single large river, which, in turn, carries water to the sea. The quality and amount of water that reaches our streams and the speed with which it does so is a function of both the topography of the watershed and the plants within the watershed.

Imagine a watershed with no plants: perhaps a watershed shortly after a volcanic eruption. When it rains on such a landscape, gravity immediately pulls water down hill toward sea level. With no plants to absorb the rainfall through their roots, or build a thick layer of humus and litter to soak up the rain as it falls, there is little to impede the progress of the water and it flows with increasing speed and volume toward the sea where it becomes nearly useless to creatures that need fresh water. With no leaf canopy over the land or leaf litter on the ground, there is nothing to lessen the force of driving rain as it hits vulnerable top soil, and with no thick matrix of roots and rootlets to hold that soil in place, soil erosion is rapid and rampant. By slowing water movement across land surfaces and by excavating deep channels in soil with roots, plants encourage the infiltration of rain water which replenishes subterranean aquifers that can then be tapped as freshwater sources long after the rain has ended.

Perhaps the most immediate watershed benefit that well-vegetated landscapes deliver to humans is protection from floods. Studies have shown that 100 mature trees intercept on average 100,000 gallons of rainfall each year in the eastern United States, reducing storm water runoff and the frequency and severity of floods. Intercepted water enters the water table gently where it moves slowly through the dense root horizon toward the nearest stream. On its way, plant roots and rich organic humus filter nitrogen, potassium, and phosphorus as well as deadly heavy metals from the water before these elements reach aboveground aquatic systems where they can be serious sources of water pollution. All of these services are easy to see and appreciate if you compare the water clarity and volume of a stream that originates within a forested landscape after a rain event with a stream that travels through landscapes with few trees.

Moderation of Extreme Weather

An increasingly valuable service provided by both managed and natural ecosystems that are built from large volumes of plants is the moderation of extreme weather events, particularly droughts. When they are not dormant, most plants are thirsty: in mesic environments they pull water out of the ground in daily cycles and transport it up through their vascular system to their leaves where the water evaporates through millions of tiny stomata into the air. The combined effect of such transpiration in a landscape

Trees help reduce storm water runoff by intercepting falling rain and holding a portion of it on the leaves and bark. A mature tree can hold 100 gallons of water on its many surfaces during a rainstorm. Part of this water soon evaporates and the rest is gradually released into the soil below.

adds large amounts of water vapor to the atmosphere, which frequently condenses as rainfall, particularly during the hot summer months when rainfall is most needed.

So important are large tracts of vegetation to the water cycle that, according to D. Sheil and D. Murdiyarso, more than 50 percent of the precipitation that falls on an ecosystem can be generated by that ecosystem. Remove those plants and rainfall amounts plummet. Can we reduce the frequency and severity of droughts in this age of climate change by increasing the amount of vegetation in our yards? Climate models predict that we can. With all of the other ecological benefits derived from the plants in our gardens, why not capitalize on drought buffers as well?

Air Filtration

Before we consider the benefits our gardens provide for the birds and the bees, we need briefly to mention the ability of plants to filter pollutants from the air that moves through our landscapes. Although research into the interaction between air pollutants and plants continues, particularly in urban centers, the statistics from early studies are impressive. Trees in small urban parks have been shown to remove 48 pounds of particulates, 9 pounds of nitrogen dioxide, 6 pounds of sulfur dioxide, and half a pound of carbon monoxide daily during the growing season. Toxic heavy metals are also sequestered by plants; K. D. Coder found that in a single season a roadside sugar maple removed 60 mg of cadmium, 140 mg of chromium, 820 mg of nickel, and 5200 mg of lead from the air. We should not focus on the specific amounts of these pollutants that are removed from our air by urban trees because they will vary with season, location, temperature and a host of other factors. What is important is that plants *do* remove such pollutants—just another benefit of the plants in our lives.

ECOLOGICAL BENEFITS FOR WILDLIFE

As we have seen, there are measurable ecological benefits for humans that accrue from investing in well-vegetated landscapes, even if we only consider interactions with the physical environment. What, however, can gardens do for us if they are designed to support animal life as well as beautiful plant designs: the birds that turn silent landscapes into vibrant displays of color and sound; the caterpillars that feed those birds; the box turtles that disperse the seeds of our mayapples, and the butterflies, beetles, bees, flies, and moths that pollinate the plants in our landscapes?

Support Pollinator Communities

Let's consider those pollinators as one example. We typically think of pollinators as being important to us because of their role in agriculture. And, of course, they are, but 80 percent of all vascular plants, not just agricultural crops, are pollinated by animals, while only 20 percent are pollinated by the wind. This makes maintaining large and diverse populations of pollinators everywhere there are plants essential if we would like most plant reproduction to continue.

For centuries, we have relied on managed colonies of European honeybees to carry out the bulk of our pollination needs in agricultural systems. Plants indigenous to North America, however, evolved in concert with over 4000 species of bees that met all of their pollination needs through co-evolved mutualistic interactions. Native bumblebees, carpenter bees, colletid bees, halictid bees, mellitid bees, and andrenid bees all require two things to persist in human-dominated environments: nesting sites, and a continuous sequential source of pollen and nectar from April through September. These conditions are rarely met in today's industrial and agricultural landscapes and native

A bumblebee takes nectar while pollinating a redbud.

bees consequently are in decline or are absent altogether from these areas. Fortunately, our gardens are a wonderful opportunity to make up this habitat shortfall; with a little planning our landscape designs can provide both a variety of pesticide-free nesting sites as well as a continuous bloom capable of sustaining dozens of local bee species that, in turn, will service the woody, perennial and annual plants in our landscapes—an important ecological function, indeed.

Connect Viable Habitats

Sprawling development of the past several decades has positioned residential and corporate landscapes perfectly to perform a new-yet-essential ecological role even though it is a role these landscapes were not designed to perform. Human-dominated landscapes must now serve as viable connections between the isolated habitat remnants of natural ecosystems. Such connections are often called biological corridors, but this implies that their primary role is to provide an avenue for safe travel between habitat fragments. Today, however, our landscapes must be more than areas through which animals and plants can move; they must also be places in which animals and plants can successfully reproduce. That is, our yards and corporate landscapes must be ecologically enriched to the point where they can support entire life cycles of local biodiversity.

Why do residential landscapes suddenly have to shoulder this new ecological responsibility? Quite simply, the natural world is now so fragmented that any given piece is no longer large enough to sustain most of the species within it for very long. Long-term studies from all over the world, some approaching 100 years in duration, are showing with shocking clarity that even our largest national parks and preserves are not large enough to serve as permanent safe sites for the biodiversity within them.

It is easy to understand why habitat fragments

bleed species at a steady rate if we consider the dynamic nature of all populations. Populations of plants and animals naturally fluctuate over time; in good times (when the weather is favorable, when food and nest sites are plentiful, when there are few predators and diseases, and so forth), survival is good, reproduction is successful, and populations increase in size. When times are difficult, in contrast (poor weather, little food, many predators), reproduction is often poor, mortality levels are high, and populations become smaller.

If populations are large, as they can be in large habitats, even after losing members during unfavorable periods there are still enough individuals remaining to breed successfully and increase population numbers when conditions improve. In small habitat fragments, however, populations of plants and animals are correspondingly small and often disappear altogether when conditions cause their numbers to fall. A hurricane, disease outbreak, drought, or cold snap is all it takes to eliminate the remaining few individuals and the species disappears from its habitat fragment, a condition known as local extinction. The return of good conditions is no longer enough to foster population growth because there are no individuals left to reproduce.

Residential, corporate, and public landscapes can help mitigate the effects of habitat fragmentation by linking fragments to each other with viable habitat. If we provide food, shelter, and places to reproduce right in our yards, our neighborhoods will no longer be the "no man's land" that isolates one fragment from another. Instead, they will become corridors of life that link fragments to each other. And this is the key: if fragments become linked by our managed landscapes, they will no longer be isolated. If they are no longer isolated, the populations within them will no longer be tiny, and if they are no longer tiny, they will no longer be vulnerable to natural population fluctuations. Building viable habitat at home and work promises to be such a powerful approach to conservation that it may very well make the difference for many species in trouble. The monarch butterfly provides a timely example.

Monarch Butterflies: An Example

The monarch has long been the most charismatic insect in the United States, not only because it is a beautiful butterfly, but also because it undertakes the longest and most spectacular migration of any insect species on earth. Like so many moths and butterflies, it is a host plant specialist; monarchs can only reproduce on milkweeds in the genus *Asclepias*. Late each summer, monarchs stop laying eggs on various species of milkweeds and start converting flower nectar into fat stores capable of fueling flight from southern Canada, through Texas, to a tiny region deep in a fir forest in the mountains just west of Mexico City. With the exception of a few populations in Florida and along the gulf coast, all of the monarchs east of the Rocky Mountains aggregate by the millions within a few acres of the Mexican mountains where they hang all winter clustered together from tree trunks and limbs. The monarchs have selected a spot in the mountains that is just warm enough to keep them from freezing but also cold enough to prevent them from burning up the energy they need to make it through the winter. In early spring, the aging monarchs mate and the females fly north once again, laying the eggs that will become the next generations on their milkweed host plants as they go.

Habitat islands in a virtual sea of ecologically impoverished suburban residential lots.

Millions of monarchs sound like a lot, but in fact, monarch populations have plummeted 90 percent since their winter refuge was first discovered by Canadian entomologists in 1976. As so often happens, several events have converged to threaten the eastern monarch population. First, the forests in which the monarchs find perfect overwintering temperatures are being thinned by logging, exposing monarchs to weather they cannot handle physiologically. Equally threatening is the loss of milkweed breeding sources throughout the U.S. Midwest because of the wide-scale adoption of Round-up ready corn and soybean technology that eliminates milkweeds from millions of acres of cropland as well as the conversion of fallow land that once supported milkweed populations to corn for the productions of ethanol. Finally, the repeated droughts in recent years in the Midwest and Texas have killed the wildflowers that support monarchs as they fly south in the fall, as well as the milkweeds that spring migrants use to produce the next generation of monarchs as they fly north in March and April.

Although conditions in natural and agricultural areas along fall and spring migration routes have become deadly for monarchs, conditions within private gardens have been ideal. Thousands of gardens that include irrigated flowering plants during the dry weeks of the monarch's fall migration have provided the only nectar sources available for thousands of migrating monarchs and should be credited with the survival of a large portion of the monarch population that reached the Mexican mountains in recent years.

Similarly, butterfly gardens that feature milkweed plants are enabling returning monarchs to breed successfully within greater landscapes from which milkweeds have been largely eliminated by development, agriculture, and drought. One small 15 by 15 foot garden in a courtyard in the center of Dover, Delaware,

produced 150 monarch adults in a single season by including several *Asclepias syriaca* plants as one of its species. Such successes are truly exciting and demonstrate the importance and potential of private gardens in providing the resources needed by declining wildlife.

ECOSYSTEM COMPLEXITY

For years now, I have embraced the standard anthropocentric view of ecosystem services: I have adopted the view that we humans have to maintain functioning ecosystems, both in our natural areas *and* our residential landscapes, so that we will have the ecosystem services we need to live as we do in the future. Indeed, the term *ecosystem services* was defined by the Millennium Ecosystem Assessment in 2005 as resources and services produced by ecosystems that benefit humans.

In 1997, R. Costanza and team suggested that to justify ecosystem conservation we have to assign monetary values to services such as water purification and pollination. But this is where I have come to question the anthropocentric focus of this definition. If an ecosystem product does not directly benefit humans, does this mean that it has no value for humans? When red cedars produce a bumper crop of waxy cones, should we dismiss the importance of red cedars because humans do not eat their cones or should we recognize that the cones are essential food for many overwintering birds that, in turn, become important sources of pest control in the summer months when they become insect-eaters? And what about the lichens and Jack-in-the-pulpits and boxelder bugs that do not seem to intersect with human needs at all?

Perhaps we should not ask how every individual component of an ecosystem benefits humans but instead appreciate that it is ecosystem complexity itself that humans require because it is complexity that drives function: complexity in ecosystem design, complexity in ecosystem food webs, complexity in ecosystem interactions. All living things require ecosystem services to make it in this world, not just humans, and there will be no ecosystem function without the myriad of life forms that create it. Perhaps one of the most important ecological functions of our gardens will be to sustain the diversity of life that sustains us.

The relationship between landscaping practices and the production of vital ecosystem services has created ethical issues never before faced by gardeners. Because the resources and services that support all humans come from functional landscapes, and function starts with plants, the planting and management choices we make at home impact our neighbors and indeed, our greater society as a whole.

In essence, the relationship between plants and ecosystem function makes the ecological functionality in our landscapes a public resource, just like a reservoir, a river, and a national park. Unfortunately, this new reality is in direct conflict with Western culture's tradition of private land ownership. The plants

Cindy and I select for our landscape determine the type and amount of ecosystem services our garden will provide. If our landscape does not provide all of the services we need, we will have to borrow ecosystem services produced by someone else's landscape. If everyone designs landscapes in ways that force them to borrow services from someone else . . . well, you see the problem.

In the past, our natural areas were large enough to produce what humans and most other species needed to lead productive lives regardless of how we designed private gardens, but no longer. Natural areas are now far too small and fragmented to meet the needs of the expanding human population. Fortunately, we can help mitigate the destruction of the natural capital that sustains us by valuing the ecological potential of residential gardens. By planting our landscapes with productive plants, we can create diverse, stable, and balanced food webs that meet our own ecological and cultural needs while enabling life around us.

All living things require ecosystem services, not just humans: (above) a small-eyed sphinx moth and a baby cardinal (right).

CHAPTER FOUR
The Art of Observation

This chapter is devoted to the art of observation and its relevance to gardeners seeking to enhance their ability to understand and appreciate the beauty of living processes. It presents a variety of short essays and visual tools useful as observational models.

Restoring functional biological layers to residential landscapes affects the way they look. Opting for increased functionality doesn't mean sacrificing beauty—functional landscapes can be extraordinarily beautiful—but it does introduce beauty of a somewhat different nature. Some of the change results from the look of different materials, such as site-produced leaf mulch instead of store-bought mulch. The main shift in aesthetics results from adopting management strategies that support a greater diversity of living relationships and processes. There is beauty in these processes; however, it is not always apparent to the untrained eye.

Learning to see deeply and clearly is one of life's most rewarding, artful enterprises, with benefits that accrue throughout our lives. The opportunity to pursue this incrementally—each day, in all seasons—is among the most enduring gifts of the garden and the larger landscapes that inspire it. **—RD**

Neither of these images is a photograph in the traditional sense: they were both created by laying objects on the bed of an inexpensive scanner. The left image shows beech leaves collected one early April day. I sought the darkest and lightest leaves and a sampling of those in-between to make a record of how objects that were once nearly identical had been changed by varied exposures and processes in the ground layer over winter. The image at right from an August walk during a drought records a pocket's worth of blackgum, tulip tree, and dogwood leaves, tulip tree seeds, hickory nuts, an acorn, and a jay feather.

CHARTING LANDSCAPE COLORS

Landscape colors change at different rates each year in response to varying conditions. In our area, we can count on blackgums (*Nyssa sylvatica*) beginning to drop a few red or gold leaves sometime between mid-July and late August, even though most of our garden and the surrounding woods appear quite green at this time.

The images on this page first show turning leaves on a blackgum growing at water's edge, then a group of fallen leaves laid out on a rock for grading, and finally a color-graded series. The intensity of this concentrated color trains our eyes to see turning leaves yet to drop from branches.

At right is another exercise employing a flatbed scanner to learn about landscape colors. First, a group of mapleleaf viburnum (*Viburnum acerifolium*) leaves representing the range of colors on just a few shrubs in October was scanned. Next, an even-sized series of blocks was created using photo editing software. The software was then used to sample actual colors one at a time from the scan and to fill the blocks individually. The resulting chart makes it easy to see the color range in the leaves, from light yellow and green through reds and improbable purples. The process of creating the chart makes it easier to appreciate the colors in the landscape without it. —RD

LIFE AT A DIFFERENT SCALE

Before you continue reading, please take ten seconds to commit the image at left to memory.

Water striders are frequently found in ponds and along the margins of slow-moving creeks and streams, displaying their capacity literally to walk on water. This is something many humans have wanted to do for a long time. Water striders can do this because their legs are covered with thousands of microhairs. The hairs distribute the insects' weight so efficiently that at no point is it sufficient to break the surface tension of the water.

While observing these gracefully gliding insects on a hot summer day it occurred to me that perhaps I'd like to trade places with one of them. Then I noticed the many tiny bits of organic debris floating on the surface that seemed to be sticking to the water striders' legs. I imagined this must feel like gardening in Wellington boots in mud season.

I was about to change my mind about becoming a water strider and then I looked more closely. The weight on each leg wasn't breaking the surface but it was depressing it enough to create a concave mirror. The darkness around the legs wasn't debris—it was a mirror image of the canopy trees and sky above. **—RD**

BANKING ON OLD LOGS

Most birds rear their young on insects, but those that spend the long winter months where insects are few must turn to other sources of food. Protein-rich seeds are an obvious source, but they are produced in abundance only once in the early fall. Birds have two choices: spend each day searching for seeds that become increasingly scarce as the winter progresses, or gather as many seeds as they can in the fall and cache them for later use.

The Carolina chickadee is a cacher. In the fall, watch one at your feeder. It will not sit and eat the seeds one after another like a house finch or goldfinch, but instead will take one seed at a time and, more often than not, fly off and hide it. Trees with exfoliating bark are great hiding places, but so are tree holes. Then, when the flush of seeds dwindles later in the winter, the chickadee returns to its many caches to live off its fall labors. Chickadee behavior in the fall is so predictable that blue jays have learned to follow them—and steal their precious seed caches one after another.

In 2003, Colin Saldanha at Lehigh University wondered how a chickadee could remember where it had hidden thousands of seeds months later. This simple question led to an amazing discovery about chickadee brains. In the fall, when chickadees face extraordinary memory challenges, their hippocampus increases its size by 30 percent. The hippocampus is the part of the brain responsible for memory, and by adding new cells to its mass, it can increase the storage capacity of cache locations. Brains, however, are energy hogs, so in the spring, when insects once again become abundant and chickadees no longer need to think about where they hid their seeds, their hippocampus shrinks back to its normal size. **—DT**

GOING WITH THE FLOW OF OPPORTUNITY

On a late-November day, I was bicycling back from a meeting at the university along the old road that follows the White Clay Creek. The vibrancy of colors and patterns reflected on the surface compelled me to stop for a photograph, and though the unmanipulated image looks like a painting it is merely a record of woods and water a few weeks before winter.

I then turned my lens to the old Pomeroy railroad bridge piers while contemplating the ways in which local plant life had adapted to these ruins. I later used this photo in a course titled *Plants and Human Culture* to ask students a simple question: Which way is the creek flowing? I qualified the question by saying that the answer could not rely on gravity for its reasoning, but must be derived from the observation of biological process. So, reasoning that the creek must be flowing away from my stance (it is) because it appears lower in the distance and water always flows downhill doesn't qualify.

Surprisingly I got the answer I was looking for not from a botany or ecology major, but from a young woman studying marketing. She used common sense and powers of observation to say, "I see tall trees growing on the far side of each of the piers but none on the near sides. I think this is because any seedlings that germinated on the near sides were eventually washed away by floodwaters. The far sides of the piers offer protection from floods and a chance for seedlings to grow into trees. The water must be flowing from near to far."

The lesson here for gardeners and anyone seeking to take advantage of opportunity is that conditions can be radically different in niches just yards from one another depending upon their exposure to periodic but inevitable processes. Thoughtful observation can reveal which sites will make all attempts at establishment futile, and which will produce dramatic results from modest resources. No matter how small in scale a planting project is, the key to long-term success is to begin with a visual inventory of the larger landscape and the forces influencing its life processes. —**RD**

LEFT **An unmanipulated photograph of the late autumn Pennsylvania woods reflected on the White Clay Creek.**

RIGHT **Remnant railroad piers create unlikely but viable habitat in the middle of the creek.**

SAFETY IN RECYCLING

Red-spotted purple butterflies and their close relatives have discovered an unusual and effective way to defend themselves during their early larval stages. It all starts with the adult female, who takes care to lay her eggs singly at the very tip of a black cherry leaf, the favorite host plant of this species. A gravid female will land on a leaf and inch her way down toward the narrow end until the tip of her abdomen is perfectly aligned with the apex of the leaf. She then taps the leaf with her abdomen, leaving an ornate egg that turns from creamy white to tan as it nears hatching. As soon as the tiny larva emerges from the egg, it makes the protein-rich egg shell its first meal.

This is the young larva's most vulnerable period, for it is the perfect prey size for foraging ants. To defend itself, it eats, and eats, and eats. Its goal, oddly enough, is to create as much frass (caterpillar poop) as quickly as it can. As soon as it has a reasonable collection of frass to work with, the caterpillar cements each piece together with silk to form a sturdy frass stick that it fastens to the leaf edge. Once the stick is in place, the caterpillar crawls out onto the frass and rests. It will have to leave its frass stick every time it returns to the leaf to eat, but if the larva senses the slightest vibration on the leaf, it rushes back to the safety of its frass stick.

Apparently, ants would rather go hungry than walk out onto the stick made of frass! When the larva grows too large for protection from its own frass, it is also too large for ants to attack. The larva is never too large for birds to eat, however, so it mimics a bird dropping in its later instars. Since actual bird droppings are common sights on plant leaves, looking like one is an excellent way to avoid being eaten.

The red-spotted purple is a common butterfly wherever black cherry remains in the landscape. Like many butterflies, it prefers to develop on low-growing, young trees, so this fascinating sequence of events is easy to watch from start to finish if you include small cherries in your garden. —DT

AVOIDING DETECTION: CRYPSIS

Chances are your garden is full of life that you have never seen. Don't feel bad; there is an excellent reason these animals are difficult to see. Any animal that is easy to find quickly becomes a predator's next meal.

A mother bird that must find thousands of caterpillars in just a few days to feed her young becomes very good at finding caterpillars. Over the eons, this has made caterpillars equally good at looking like their background, a condition known as crypsis. Insects that come to resemble a decayed section of leaf, a conifer needle, the bark they are resting on, and so forth are more difficult to locate than insects that contrast with their background. Often that's all it takes to discourage a bird from searching for cryptic insects.

Birds must hunt quickly and efficiently; they must find lots of food to feed their hungry chicks *and* they must do it as quickly as possible to minimize their own exposure to predators. If a caterpillar looks just like a twig, a bird would have to look closely at every twig to find it. Looking like a twig, then, elevates the cost of searching beyond what the bird can afford both energetically and ecologically.

Fortunately, gardeners can learn to find even the most cryptic species themselves by learning where to look, when to look, and what to look for. The rewards are great from this investment, for cryptic insects are true marvels of evolutionary design.

A camouflaged looper hides from its enemies by fastening petals of the blazing star (*Liatris spicata*) to its back with silk. This strategy has earned this caterpillar its common name and ensures that it will always perfectly resemble its background, no matter what flower it feeds on.

The varied textures and shades of tree bark provide excellent opportunities to "disappear" from sight. Here a nocturnal waved sphinx moth goes undetected by foraging birds by remaining motionless by day amid the lichens on this tree trunk.

Few caterpillars blend in with their food plant as well as the curve-lined angle. This specialist on juniper (*Juniperus virginiana*) resembles the needles it eats so well that even sharp-eyed birds have difficulty seeing it.

Yellow-flowered legumes such as partridge pea (*Chamaecrista fasciculata*) and various *Senna* species provide the perfect backdrop (and food) for larvae of the cloudless sulfur butterfly. As long as they stay within a flower, these caterpillars are very difficult to see.

The richly layered Riska-Dunson garden in Delaware is brimming with life yet is highly functional and profoundly livable.

CHAPTER FIVE
Applying Layers to the Home Garden

What brings life to a landscape? Gardening is unique among the arts because its primary materials are literally alive, but are gardens merely beautiful arrangements of living objects?

A growing awareness of a broad range of environmental relationships suggests the traditional object-oriented approach to garden-making is unable to guide us in the design and care of landscapes that are genuinely sustainable. Informed by ecological science and cultural studies, we have an opportunity to adopt new ethics outlining a modern recipe for inclusive habitat: ethics that embrace the changing dynamics of our world while recognizing the need to protect and conserve what is vital and irreplaceable.

We can promote intensely local approaches to design that are simultaneously cognizant of global realities, with the understanding that even our most humble, necessary journeys can be guided by a universal language of landscape stewardship. Plants will always be at the heart of gardening, but instead of beginning with a set of objects, we can start with a set of goals to ensure the landscapes we live in are beautifully layered, biologically diverse, and broadly functional.

Don't be afraid to ask a lot of your garden. With a bit of thought and a modest amount of care a garden can be many things—even things that might seem incompatible or contradictory. For example, a good garden must be practical. The care it requires should be balanced with our

capacities, yet it must provide for essential needs that vary as gardeners do: safe surfaces on which to walk, run, sit, or play; shelter from storms; a cool place in summer and perhaps a warm place in winter. But that same garden can also be a sensual place that brings varied pleasures into life's routines: color, texture, fragrance, an outdoor dining room, birdsong in the morning, and perhaps a chorus of peepers at night.

As David Abram suggested in 1996, "the sensual world is always local." Much of the sensuality, breadth, and beauty of local landscapes derives from long-evolved associations between flora and fauna, yet it is also profoundly influenced by local and global culture. Fortunately, the divide separating biological and cultural landscapes is diminishing. A garden devoted to the conservation of a unique ecosystem need not banish a bit of human history that survives in its midst, just as a landscape devoted to human artifice need not neglect a vital remnant of ecological richness within its bounds.

No matter what size it is, a well-designed garden can be both intimate and expansive. It can include intimate spaces that encourage appreciation of infinite detail as well as outwardly focused spaces that direct us to contemplate

A resident phoebe takes advantage of a leafless branch of the venerable dogwood that stretches gracefully from the side of the historic farmhouse in the Riska-Dunson garden.

Applying Layers to the Home Garden

BELOW Steps and low retaining walls handcrafted of local stone contribute to planting niches while furnishing an intimate but functional route up and down the gently terraced site in the Riska-Dunson garden. Essential no-more-than-necessary patches of sturdy turf invite strolling and provide for gatherings of friends.

BELOW RIGHT Fresh lettuce with your native plants—why not? Though the Riska-Dunson garden's principle plant palette is made up of indigenous species, its broad range of functions includes providing locally grown sustenance for humans.

infinite expanse. The intimate space might be as modest as a nook defined by richly layered vegetation. The expansive space could simply be a deftly placed bench with a clear view of the sky through a window in the canopy.

Reliability and spontaneity may seem like opposites, but they need not be. An inspired design can offer both. We should be able to count on a garden to do many specific things on time and reliably, but each time we return to it, there should be some element of chance, some delightful presence or event that we could never have anticipated.

The local landscape is the most influential because we spend the most time in it. Because it is so close at hand, a residential garden is the ultimate local landscape. For these reasons, two of the most essential qualities of a garden are that it be both walkable and watchable. It should offer practical paths, sensual paths, and a

variety of other routes to get us to where we need to be. All the while, these paths should provoke us to watch more closely, ask more questions, and contemplate the dynamic beauty of interdependent processes.

Gardens are often intended to provide us with refuge: a personal place away from the crowds, offering myriad opportunities for individual expression. A personal garden or landscape is a place we can tell our story in our way. It can provide reassurance and offer new insights, even when we're the only listener. On a different day or during a different mood, that same garden can be most alive when we invite others to share it with us: reacting to it, enjoying it, and finding new meanings in it. When sharing extends beyond human presence, a garden contributes to the sustenance of many forms of life, and they in turn help sustain all of us.

This small spring-fed pool and other moist
niches in the Riska-Dunson garden support
wood frogs, pickerel frogs, green frogs,
bullfrogs, spring peepers, and toads.

SPACE-MAKING WITH ORGANIC ARCHITECTURE

No aspects affect the way we experience a garden more than the quality and arrangement of its spaces. Among limitless possibilities, garden spaces can function as outdoor living rooms, dining rooms, playgrounds, bathing or swimming rooms, stages, shelters, museums, wildlife habitats, workshops, nurseries, or food-producing areas. Well-built garden spaces offer living experiences unlike anything that can be attained with indoor architecture. As with all architecture, the characteristics of the materials used profoundly influence the nature of the results, and the relationships between the spaces and the paths connecting them are also integral to their success.

Like building architecture, landscape architecture typically relies mostly on hard materials to create paths and spaces—mortared brick and stone, tile, wood, metal, and glass—and extensive re-grading is usually employed to fit these to the landscape. This approach is both expensive and durable, but there are additional costs to the durability of hardscapes. Hard designs are durably static: they do what they do reliably but with little intrinsic capacity for spontaneity.

Perhaps more important is the relative immutability of hard designs. They are difficult and expensive to modify or to adapt to changing circumstances in the landscape or in the vital routines of the inhabitants. Hard designs are sometimes the only practical architectural solution to required landscape functions; however, in many situations there is a softer, more imaginative option and that is to rely principally on literally organic architecture—plants—for space-making.

The word *organic* may refer to materials made principally of carbon, as plants are. It is also used (first and perhaps most famously in 1954 by Frank Lloyd Wright in *The Natural House*) to refer to non-living things such as architecture that have been constructed or have evolved in ways that emulate the growth forms, patterns, and processes of living organisms.

There are many benefits to space-making with truly organic architecture. Spaces made of plants are infinitely mutable. They, and the passages between them, can be shaped and reformed in small increments or with dramatic gestures at a fraction of the cost of hard materials. Spaces made of plants are inherently evolutionary and responsive, since the living materials that define them are constantly reacting to changing conditions, events, and seasons. Perhaps most importantly, a reliance on organic architecture means that more of a garden will be made of plants. If residential landscapes are to play increasing roles in sustaining floral and faunal diversity, this last point is essential.

This outdoor living room at Mt. Cuba in Delaware is a superb example of space-making with organic architecture. The space is defined by a curving multilayered wall planting that includes herbaceous plants, shrubs, understory trees, and canopy trees. This living wall separates the seating from the sunny meadow above and beyond to the right. In late April (top), the wall allows a bit of spring sunshine through to illuminate a blooming sweep of golden ragwort (*Senecio aureus*). By the end of July of the same year (bottom), plum azalea (*Rhododendron prunifolium*) is at peak and fragrant sweet pepperbush (*Clethra alnifolia*) has just finished.

The intensely layered
design of the Darke-
Zoehrer garden includes
a high degree of diversity
in composition, structure,
and scale, resulting in
spatial experiences that
make the landscape seem
larger than it is and that
change dramatically
with the seasons.

For more than two decades, a 1.5-acre garden in Pennsylvania has been the home habitat my wife and gardening partner, Melinda Zoehrer, and I share with countless friends, family, and other creatures. It is a highly architectural landscape, yet other than a portion of the asphalt driveway that pre-dates us, there is no mortar used beyond the house itself. Dry-laid stone is employed for areas that must withstand very heavy use and a few low wooden screens have been built for privacy, but all other paths, surfaces, and spaces have been constructed entirely with living materials: grass, moss, herbs, shrubs, and trees.

There are no single-layer borders in this garden: all plantings have at least two or three layers. Few edgings are used. The connecting turf directly meets edge plantings, with the ethic being "green to green." The garden's connected spaces offer a wide range of experiences, with "rooms" for many human purposes and highly varied functional habitat for local wildlife. **—RD**

This May aerial photo illustrates the central part of the garden's spatial organization. Low-maintenance turf is the principal walking surface material. In two decades, it has never been watered and no herbicides, pesticides, or fertilizers have been used to maintain it. It is mowed at casual height with a mulching mower, so organic matter and nutrients are continually recycled.

Creating spaces in the garden is often no more complicated than establishing a deftly placed sweep or row of separating vegetation. As the fothergilla (*Fothergilla ×intermedia*) in this November image illustrates, the beauty of vegetative material is that it doesn't have to be completely opaque to be an effective spatial organizer. The opacity will vary with the choice of plants and plant combinations, with seasons, and with pruning and other maintenance techniques.

This outdoor living/dining room is both separated from other spaces in the garden and connected to them by pathways comprised entirely of vegetation. Some paths are obvious, others are partly obscured deliberately, adding to the element of surprise while strolling the garden.

OPPOSITE TOP An allée in the garden pales in comparison to the formality of Versailles, yet it demonstrates that highly ordered space can be achieved entirely with layered vegetation.

LEFT In contrast to the relatively expansive mood and experience of the view down the allée, this transitional space in the front of the garden offers shelter and intimacy. The chairs are at the north edge of a small wooded section that has been re-forested almost entirely with trees and shrubs that began as seedlings in the garden. This May view looks northward to a south-facing edge comprised of a proven site-adapted mix of native and non-native vegetation. —RD

Normally unseen by humans and other surface dwellers, the extensive root system of this beech has been unearthed by floodwaters scouring the bank of a creek. The foundations for much of life above ground extend well below. In addition to roots and rhizomes, life below ground includes diverse fungi, bacteria, and micro-invertebrates essential to the recycling of organic matter and nutrients. It also includes more familiar animals such as ground-nesting bees, cicadas, salamanders, small mammals, reptiles, and turtles.

LIFE BELOW GROUND

Modern science still offers relatively few certainties about life below ground level, except that there is a huge, diverse amount of it. The larger, more obvious organisms are well known, especially those that live parts of their lives above ground, but even for these, the subterranean events in their life cycles are least understood.

A majority of terrestrial insects spend at least some time in the soil, as do many amphibians and turtles. Below-ground organisms including micro-invertebrates and bacteria are essential to the decomposition of organic matter and the recycling of nutrients required for plant growth. Mycorrhizal fungi in the soil form mutualistic relationships with many, perhaps a majority, of vascular plants. The fungi benefit by access to carbohydrates produced by the plants, and the plants benefit from the fungi's aid in absorbing water and mineral nutrients.

Plant roots represent a significant portion of the life below ground in many habitats and in most gardens. Because roots require oxygen for respiration, and oxygen levels decrease with soil depth, the majority of root systems are found in the top 24 inches of soil. Along with microbes and mycorrhizal fungi, roots release organic compounds into the soil including proteins, enzymes, sugars, and amino acids. These compounds play complex but little-understood roles in sustaining soil heterotrophs (organisms including animals, fungi, and bacteria that cannot fix carbon but must rely on organic carbon compounds produced by photosynthesizing plants). Roots help stabilize soils, especially in areas prone to erosion or flooding. Dead or alive, the extensive root systems of woody plants contribute to the value of soils as important carbon sinks.

The simple lesson is to anticipate that there is a great diversity of life and essential processes below ground, and that respecting and conserving the health of these contributes to the health of life above ground. Unnecessary mechanical disturbance should always be avoided. When preparing areas for planting, dig only as much as needed. Use less destructive hand tools such as trowels, shovels, and spades instead of power tools such as rototillers whenever practical. Instead of pulling weeds, clip, mow, or use a hoe to scrape the surface. These weeding methods minimize the disturbance of life below ground level. A conservation-based approach to garden management also greatly reduces or eliminates the use of pesticides, herbicides, and other toxic substances that may leach into or be absorbed by soils.

Ground-Nesting Bees

When we think of important pollinators, we most often think of the imported European honeybee (*Apis mellifera*). However, there are over 4000 species of indigenous bees that pollinated North American plants for millions of years before the arrival of the honeybee and most reproduce in solitary nests below ground. These bees can be common residents of our gardens if we provide pesticide-free patches of ground and a diversity of plants that bloom sequentially in April, May, and June.

Bees in the families *Colletidae* and *Andrenidae* are the most commonly encountered bees in early spring and play important roles in pollinating early bloomers like redbud and phlox. Because they are solitary nesters, these ground-nesting bees are not aggressive and rarely sting, even if provoked. Spring ground nesters prefer to excavate their nests in sunny spots of soil on a gentle south-facing slope to help them warm up on cool spring mornings.

Ground-nesting bees, one of the most important members of the soil community, are active above ground during the spring and summer,

BELOW **A colletid bee on redbud (*Cercis canadensis*).**

RIGHT **A colletid bee emerging from its solitary underground nest in early April.**

FAR RIGHT **An andrenid bee on woodland phlox (*Phlox divaricata*).**

Cicadas

Adult cicadas provide yet another example of life below ground. These insects devote their short surface lives to reproduction, with males "singing" in loud chorus to attract females. After mating, adult females lay their eggs in slits they make in the bark of small branches. The eggs hatch in summer and the nymphs drop to the ground and burrow up to 1 foot down, where they spend the next 17 years. Branches used for egg-laying typically die back to the point of incision and although this can make a large tree look messy for while, there is no more harm done than by a very gentle pruning. Small woody seedlings with few branches to spare are more vulnerable.

Some periodical cicadas have 13-year cycles, and others have much shorter cycles of 2 to 5 years. Because the life cycles of these latter groups overlap, some appear each year and are commonly called annual cicadas. Unlike 17- and 13-year cicadas which appear in May or June, annual cicadas appear in the sultry dog days of summer and are often called dog-day cicadas.

Cicadas are often called locusts, but this is incorrect, since cicadas are insects belonging to the order Hemiptera and locusts belong to Orthoptera (which includes crickets and grasshoppers). All cicadas are incapable of biting or stinging. —**RD**

There's more than one generation X. After spending 17 years underground feeding (harmlessly) on fluids in the roots of a large oak in the Darke-Zoehrer garden, this periodical cicada has emerged from the shell of its nymph stage to spend its last few weeks of life above ground. It is a member of brood X, the Great Eastern Brood, which emerged in the spring of 2004 and will next emerge in 2021.

but their subterranean nest sites need protection all year long. Ground-nesting bees spend much of the year as pupae in tunnels 3–15 inches below the surface. They require well-drained sites with small patches of bare soil in sun or partial shade. Frequent mowing or watering in such areas prevents nesting or kills bees already nesting. Constant walking on nest sites compacts the soil and renders it useless to bees. Needless to say, tilling of any kind destroys nests, as do typical pesticides applied to lawns and gardens. The best approach to protecting ground-nesting bees is to identify areas of your property that have proved to be suitable nest sites and then leave them alone as much as possible. The bees will thank you with valuable pollination services throughout the growing season.

Eastern Box Turtles

Lost in the suburbs? Why are eastern box turtles in a section on life below ground? Because these turtles spend time below ground in infancy and each winter of their adult lives, which can last a century.

Like most other reptiles, eastern box turtles lay eggs that need to be incubated to complete their development. Box turtle females do this by digging a hole in a sunny spot that receives enough heat to promote egg development.

Box turtles differ from most other reptiles, and indeed most other turtles, in that after hatching, the young turtles remain underground for more than a year. Little is known about the life of hatchling box turtles because they are only encountered by accident.

This particular turtle spent much of a late-June day foraging in our front garden. Because we regularly see eastern box turtles in our home landscape, it seems reasonable to assume they are finding what they need. —RD

Cindy and I dug up the turtle here when we were planting a fringe tree in our front yard. Fortunately we did not injure the turtle in the process, but the event was a reminder that the life under our feet is nearly as abundant and varied as the life we see above ground every day. —DT

THE GROUND LAYER

Though mowed turf has become the default ground layer choice for the majority of residential gardens, its functionality is very narrow. For high use areas in full sun, turf is sometimes the sturdiest, simplest option in terms of installation and maintenance. The stereotypically perfect lawn kept free of forbs (broad-leaved herbaceous plants) and critters by use of toxic herbicides and pesticides is injurious to the health of humans and wildlife; however, it is possible to maintain functional but much less uniform turf without these materials.

However maintained, mowed turf contributes little or nothing to the cover, shelter, and sustenance necessary to sustain wildlife. Grass turf, especially on ground compacted by heavy riding mowers, is relatively impermeable. Very little rainfall is absorbed and therefore most runs off much like it does over a paved surface. No-mow lawn areas planted with low-growing hard fescue grasses are an alternative, offering better absorption and therefore better groundwater recharge, but they will not tolerate heavy foot traffic or play.

If the goal is to design and manage for a wide range of ecosystem services, the sensible approach is to restrict mowed turf to areas that truly require its utility. A more imaginative, creative approach to the ground layer will add immeasurably to the beauty, diversity, and functionality of all layers in the garden.

Mid-October light plays on a moss lawn at the Cecchi residence in northern New Jersey. This no-mow alternative to turf is a beautifully functional choice for this gently sloping ground under a high canopy of native oaks. Unlike the monotony of grass turf, the colors of this mossy ground layer resemble the abrash of a fine vegetal-dyed rug in which the hues and tints vary in with the nature of the dyes used in different parts.

Fallen Leaves and Other Organic Material

Leaves and other organic matter cover significant portions of the ground layer in many habitats; however, in gardens, leaves are often perceived as messy or even unsightly. Recent horticultural trends toward discarding fallen leaves and purchasing neatly uniform commercially produced mulches are counterproductive and unsustainable. Bought mulch is often the only option in new gardens lacking sufficient woody growth to produce enough leaves for mulching purposes, but when fallen leaves are available, they are best included in on-site management practices.

If autumn leaves are run over with a mower (most efficiently in the course of mowing the lawn), the resulting material is finer and less likely to smother more fragile plants when used as mulch. Composting leaves, even for one year, is another way of making them more suitable for mulching between mixed vegetation.

In many places, the most conserving, functional, low-maintenance approach to autumn leaves is to let them lie where they fall. This is exactly what happens in unmanaged forest ecosystems. Though a too-heavy leaf layer can have a negative effect on delicate herbaceous plants, most trees and shrubs and a wide range of sturdy perennial herbs grow well under natural leaf fall.

The characteristics of leaf mulch vary significantly with different plant species. The relatively thin leaves of trees such as birches (*Betula* species), ironwood (*Carpinus caroliniana*), and American hop hornbeam (*Ostrya virginiana*) make the least-smothering mulch. Leaves of oaks (*Quercus* species), blackgum (*Nyssa sylvatica*), and sweetbay magnolia (*Magnolia virginiana*), all of which have waxy surfaces, make better mulch after they've been composted for at least a year or more.

Though neatness may be a virtue, too much neatness in a garden is a vice. A more relaxed approach that allows for a scattering of leaves, acorns, or other essential foodstuffs around the garden can make a huge difference in the life of a landscape. **—RD**

OPPOSITE TOP This pile of raked leaves can be used directly to cover the ground, conserve moisture, and suppress weeds in areas without vegetation or in areas where the vegetation is tolerant of a degree of leaf cover.

OPPOSITE BOTTOM This "mitten mulch" was produced without human effort by a small grove of sassafras (*Sassafras albidum*).

TOP LEFT A leaf-covered ground layer in between a planting of Christmas ferns (*Polystichum acrostichoides*), asters, and shrubs contributes to the moist conditions necessary to sustain an American toad (*Bufo americanus*).

TOP RIGHT A cardinal forages for seeds and insects in February in-between ferns in a garden. The bird wouldn't be here if the ground was covered in uniform turf or if the natural organic accumulation on the surface had been removed in favor of sterilized commercial mulch.

ABOVE These bluejays aren't waiting for a meal at the table in this December photo. They're foraging for acorns that have fallen from the large oak tree overhead.

RIGHT Newly germinated seedlings of American beech (*Fagus grandifolia*) appear under beeches in our garden. Seedlings at this stage are easily transplanted.

CENTER These Oriental bittersweet (*Celastrus orbiculatus*) and Japanese honeysuckle (*Lonicera japonica*) seedlings established quickly on disturbed open ground. Removing any unwanted plants is easiest while they are still young.

BELOW Mosses established themselves in the interstices of this dry-laid stone patio on the north side of our house, which is never irrigated. Knowing that mosses are an ideal substrate for germinating bluets (*Houstonia caerulea*), we scattered seeds and now enjoy blooming bluets each year from late March to early May.

Weeds and Seedlings

A ground layer covered in leaves provides ideal conditions for the germination and growth of many plants, some desirable, some not. When gardeners grew a majority of their plants from seed, most were familiar with what a wide range of plants look like as young seedlings. Now more than ever, the skill to identify seedlings is important to environmentally sound garden management.

The ability to spot spontaneous seedlings of desirable plants at early stages is an important tool for making the most efficient use of existing resources. For example, when tree seedlings appear, if there is room in the garden for them, the most conserving approach is to edit the excess and allow a desired quantity to mature in place. This editing process can be thought of as addition by reduction.

Similarly, the ability to identify and remove seedlings of pernicious weeds, especially woody vining species such as Oriental bittersweet (*Celastrus orbiculatus*) and Japanese honeysuckle (*Lonicera japonica*), is essential. Early detection and removal can be done with a small fraction of the resources required to eliminate mature plants.

Moss

With no sacrifice in function, a varied approach to the ground layer is certain to increase the beauty and biological diversity of any residential garden. One option is to replace mowed turf with no-mow moss. Although moss can't withstand the heavy foot traffic that turfgrass tolerates, it is lightly walkable. Mosses often establish themselves in lightly shaded areas that receive occasional moisture, where they nurture germinating seeds of other plants, which in turn are visited by insects when in bloom. —RD

LEFT What child isn't captivated by a hover fly, here resting momentarily on a bluet? Also called flower flies or syrphids, these non-stinging, non-biting insects belong to the insect family *Syrphidae*. They ward off predators by mimicking the colors and patterns of bees and wasps. Adults subsist principally on nectar and pollen. As adults, syrphids pollinate many types of flowers, but as larvae, they are efficient predators of aphids.

The mossy ground layer of art gallery owner John Cram's North Carolina garden is an ideal foil for sculpture and the sculptural forms of old trees and stone benches.

THE HERBACEOUS LAYER

The potential botanical diversity of a garden's herbaceous layer is much greater than that of any other aboveground layers—there simply are more species of herbaceous plants than of woody plants. Designing for high biodiversity in the herbaceous layer can benefit both humans and wildlife. Greater diversity results in more color, texture, form, fragrance, and seasonal interest pleasing to gardeners. It also increases the likelihood of determining which species really are best adapted to site conditions.

From the perspective of wildlife, a more diverse herbaceous layer provides more varied shelter and cover. An overlapping sequence of bloom throughout the season translates to a continual source of nectar and pollen along with a steady supply of ripening seeds and fruits. If diversity is sufficient to ensure that multiple plants are capable of fulfilling each of these vital functions at any one time, this "system redundancy" becomes a hedge against gaps or complete failures.

One potential down side of plant diversity in gardens is that it is often concentrated at too small a scale. For the love of plants, gardeners sometimes group too many species with distinctly different growing needs into areas that are too small or not diverse enough to sustain them. The usual results are plantings that are difficult or impossible to maintain in the long run. Looking to healthy natural habitats as models is a reminder that while the overall plant diversity of a landscape may be high, in any given space or localized ecosystem there is considerable repetition of a few key species.

When designing for diversity, it's important to aim for the highest supportable biodiversity overall but to avoid unsustainable variety in any one spot. Developing a working knowledge of the dynamics of mixed plantings—the relative

LEFT An herbaceous layer consisting primarily of ostrich fern (*Matteuccia struthiopteris* var. *pensylvanica*), wild ginger (*Asarum canadense*), and fernleaf phacelia (*Phacelia bipinnatifida*) covers a large area at Mt. Cuba Center in Delaware in late April, with occasional wood poppies (*Stylophorum diphyllum*) adding to the mix. All of these plants are adapted to the site conditions, and their rates of growth and spread are well enough balanced that this planting can be maintained indefinitely with minimal intervention by gardeners.

RIGHT Also at Mt. Cuba Center, the herbaceous layer in this area is more diverse on a per-square-yard basis, with complex intermingling of interrupted fern (*Osmunda claytoniana*), trillium (*Trillium flexipes*), Virginia bluebells (*Mertensia virginica*), and wood poppy (*Stylophorum diphyllum*). Managing this composition requires more effort than the previous image, but because the group dynamic is fairly balanced, the maintenance isn't excessive.

This juxtaposition of creeping phlox (*Phlox stolonifera*), eastern foamflower (*Tiarella cordifolia*), and mayapple (*Podophyllum peltatum*) makes an attractive photograph, but maintaining this composition in the landscape is a high-maintenance proposition. The phlox spreads strongly enough that it will overrun the foamflower from one direction and the mayapples will overrun it from the other. While plantings like this may be maintainable on a small scale, they are not practical for creating a durable, low-maintenance herbaceous layer over larger areas.

growth rates and abilities of plants to spread or resist spreading neighbors—is also necessary to efficiently managing diversity.

Maintenance strategies greatly influence the effective functioning of any amount of plant diversity. For example, cutting a plant back prematurely in the interest of neatness may shorten its lifespan or reduce its capacity to suppress weeds sprouting around it. It may eliminate seed production or dispersal and, with this, the plant's ability to perpetuate itself. It is also likely to reduce the food, cover, and shelter value to wildlife.

Biennials comprise a highly functional group of herbaceous plants that are often overlooked because their life cycles are less familiar than those of annuals or perennials. After germinating, a biennial produces only vegetative growth in the first growing season. It flowers the second year, then dies after producing seed. Within a population of biennials there will always be first-year plants and second-year plants, meaning that there will almost always be foliage present (except in winter) and there will be flowering plants each year.

Though annuals and biennials should not be discounted, perennial species comprise the majority of herbaceous plants suitable for residential landscapes. The word *perennial* suggests a capacity to live indefinitely; however, the likelihood of this is entirely dependent upon how well a plant is matched to site conditions. Though much can be done to improve the soil and growing conditions on a residential property such as adding organic material, changing the grade, improving drainage, or in extreme cases replacing the soil, the most conserving approach is to begin with a realistic assessment of existing conditions and to look for plants capable of thriving with a minimal amount of intervention.

Balance and Durability in Diversity

The herbaceous layer provides a wealth of habitat niches that vary in structure and composition and provide cover, shelter, and sustenance for a hugely diverse population of invertebrates. Among the many that live amid the herbaceous and ground layers, click beetles are important detritivores—they eat organic detritus. There are nearly 1000 click beetle species in North America, and most play important roles in breaking down coarse woody debris. They are best known to humans by their escape mechanism. A spine on the ventral surface of their first thoracic segment hooks into a notch on the second segment. Applied muscular pressure causes the spine to snap loose with a loud click, flinging the beetle several times its body length out of harm's way. Many other fascinating creatures are supported by the herbaceous layer.

When pairing or mixing herbaceous plants in a planting, it is important to consider their individual growth rates and, ideally, to select species with similar rates. Asters and heucheras, for example, are commonly used together in gardens. If white wood aster (*Aster divaricatus*) is paired with American heuchera (*Heuchera*

LEFT Aromatic aster (*Aster oblongifolius*) and large-rooted heuchera (*Heuchera macrorhiza*) are both relatively large, strong-growing, long-lived plants that are well matched against each other. This fall-blooming heuchera species is a southeastern North American native that is sun and heat tolerant. It is semi-evergreen except in far northern locations. Botanists sometimes include it in *H. villosa*, but that species lacks the large woody rhizomes of *H. macrorhiza*. The commercial name Autumn Bride refers to *H. macrorhiza*.

ABOVE A click beetle about to fly uses a foamflower stalk as a take-off point.

ABOVE RIGHT American heuchera (*Heuchera americana*) is a relatively long-lived clump-former, but it is not as strong as white wood aster (*Aster divaricatus*). Maintaining a mix of the two will require occasionally pulling the aster away from the heuchera.

Both woodland
phlox (*Phlox divar-
icata*) (above) and
creeping phlox (*Phlox
stolonifera*) (right) are
durable spreaders.

americana), however, the aster will overrun the heuchera. For a balanced pairing, try aromatic aster (*A. oblongifolius*) and large-rooted heuchera (*H. macrorhiza*). They make a reliable combination for covering large areas in sun, and the heuchera can also be planted in shade.

The key to a durable herbaceous layer is to rely primarily on a mix of clump-forming plants that are inherently long-lived, plants that regularly perpetuate themselves by self-sowing, and spreading plants that have a capacity for self-repair. Phloxes meet these criteria.

Maintenance Strategies

Though herbaceous plants are commonly selected for their ornamental flowers, they often contribute other necessary qualities in the landscape. A disproportionate focus on species with showy flowers has long obscured the functionality of plants such as barren strawberry (*Waldsteinia lobata*). Despite its small flowers, this southeastern native produces a dense mat of shiny green leaves in even tough sites and requires little maintenance in the process. It has high functional value in the biodiverse garden.

Herbaceous plants with low maintenance requirements are especially attractive to today's busy gardeners. Plants don't have to look tough to be durable, as delicate-looking maidenhair fern (*Adiantum pedatum*) and Virginia bluebells (*Mertensia virginica*) demonstrate. When grown

TOP Low-growing cold-hardy barren strawberry (*Waldsteinia lobata*) has insignificant yellow flowers, but the evergreen foliage makes it an ideal ground cover in shade or part sun.

LEFT A delicate new frond of maidenhair fern (*Adiantum pedatum*) unfurls in early May.

The fern's refined appearance belies its long-lived nature.

ABOVE A shade-tolerant mix of maidenhair fern, woodland stonecrop (*Sedum ternatum*), and zigzag goldenrod (*Solidago flexicaulis*) has a good dynamic balance and can be maintained with little effort.

within a ground-covering layers of other plants, the fern can persist indefinitely, and the bluebells, for decades.

The natural cycle of Virginia bluebells and most native spring ephemerals makes them well suited to provide early bloom in areas of the garden that are very dry later in the season. Summer drought is no threat to these plants because they are dormant by that time. However, because they can leave a "hole" in the herbaceous layer when they go dormant, spring ephemerals are often ignored by gardeners. The answer is a mixed planting in which ephemerals are interspersed with plants that have a presence through the growing season.

In early April the foliage and flower buds of Virginia bluebells (*Mertensia virginica*) push up through evergreen layers of woodland stonecrop (*Sedum ternatum*) (above) and Christmas fern (*Polys-* *tichum acrostichoides*) (above left). Among the earliest blooming spring ephemerals, Virginia bluebells provide essential pollen and nectar services at the very beginning of the growing season (top).

Roots of river birches (*Betula nigra*) planted a quarter century ago make competition for moisture in summer a serious issue in this area off a walkway in our Pennsylvania garden. Despite this, an herbaceous layer consisting of woodland stonecrop, Christmas ferns, white wood aster (*Aster divaricatus*), Virginia bluebells, and three non-native species—snowdrops (*Galanthus nivalis*), epimedium (*Epimedium pinnatum* subsp. *colchicum*), and wood tulip (*Tulipa sylvestris*)—thrives without irrigation and with minimal refereeing on our part. —RD

Mayapples (*Podophyllum peltatum*) cover a large partly shaded area in our garden in mid-April (above). There's little in the herbaceous plant palette anywhere in the world that can provide this much textural drama with so little effort. We've integrated woodland stonecrop, white wood aster, woodland geranium (*Geranium maculatum*), and various evergreen ferns including Christmas fern into the mix, so the ground remains vegetated after the mayapples subside (right). —RD

Weed Suppression

Fernleaf phacelia (*Phacelia bipinnatifida*) is a biennial that produces showy lavender-blue blossoms in April and May, which in turn provide copious quantities of nectar and pollen for native bees and other hymenopterans. It self-sows readily, but can easily be kept in bounds by grubbing out any excess plants when young. It has the capacity to establish itself in highly shaded conditions below and between shrubs and trees, and the low foliage of first-year plants makes an effective drought-tolerant weed-suppressing ground cover.

Like fernleaf phacelia, Virginia waterleaf (*Hydrophyllum virginianum*) is also in the waterleaf family (*Hydrophyllaceae*). The family name refers to the light gray-green markings on mature leaves that resemble water marks. Virginia waterleaf is a deciduous perennial with attractive but relatively small white spring flowers. It creates a 4- to 6-inch tall mat of foliage that beautifully covers the ground for the remainder of the growing season. It is easily grown in part sun or dense shade. Though it is dense enough to have real weed-suppressing value, the foliage and root system are delicate enough that other perennials can persist within it.

Virginia waterleaf creates a no-maintenance groundcover under native azaleas, as new leaves of pinkroot (*Spigelia marilandica*) and maidenhair fern (*Adiantum pedatum*) begin to emerge and a non-native bluebell (*Hyacinthoides hispanica*).

ABOVE In April, fernleaf phacelia fills the shady spaces behind a bench at Mt. Cuba Center with a carpet of lavender-blue flowers.

RIGHT Foliage of first-year plants of fernleaf phacelia makes an attractive shade- and drought-tolerant ground cover.

Wildlife Support

Strongly running species such as mountain mint (*Pycnanthemum muticum*) are often avoided when selecting plants for the herbaceous layer; however, in the right place and for the right purpose these plants can be the ideal choice. Mountain mint, for example, is a food source for butterflies, bees, and wasps in midsummer and can provide a durable presence through changing light conditions in a garden. —RD

We planted mountain mint around the interior margin of a circular space in our garden that will in the long term be defined primarily by trees and shrubs. The mint proved adaptable enough to tolerate the initial full sun conditions (above), yet has persisted even as conditions have become increasingly shady (left). Herbaceous species that can survive such transi-tions are an important part of the functional palette.

TOP Mountain mint attracts large numbers of tiger swallowtails in late July (left). The nectar also attracts the blue winged wasp (*Scolia dubia*) (right). Like most ground-nesting solitary wasps, this species is docile and does not attack humans. It is a useful predator of the grubs of Japanese beetles.

RIGHT **Common blue violet makes an attractive flowering groundcover.**

BELOW **A self-sowing, self-perpetuating population of naturalized violets serves as a deciduous ground cover under large trees while providing plenty of material for fritillary larvae to eat. The violets are easily kept in check by mowing along the edge were they meet the turf.**

Plants such as the common blue violet (*Viola sororia*), long dismissed by gardeners as a weed, can be reconstituted as desirable components of the herbaceous layer when their ecosystem functionality is re-evaluated. Violets are the sole larval food source for fritillary butterflies. Eliminating violets eliminates fritillaries, but finding ways to incorporate violets in garden design supports fritillaries.

With proper plant selection and management, a diverse herbaceous layer can provide beauty and ecosystem services for all late into the season. Plants in the aster family (*Asteraceae*) are among the latest blooming, and most provide edible seeds throughout winter if allowed to stand.

The striped cream violet (*Viola striata*) has proved an easily managed choice for the edge of this layered planting that includes white wood asters, wood geraniums, shrubs, and trees.

ABOVE A New England aster (*Aster novae-angliae*) provides nectar to a female tawny-edged skipper in mid-September.

RIGHT A bee and monarch butterfly share a heart-leafed aster (*Aster cordifolius*) in early October.

Providing Water for Birds

Though we take great pleasure in observing birds in our home landscape, our goal has been for the landscape to provide enough bird food that we don't need feeders. However, since our property is relatively high and dry with no natural water running through it, we decided we would provide an avian facility for drinking and bathing.

Rather than buying something generic, I began with a large stone from a local quarry. With protective goggles on, I used a hardened bit to drill a circle about 2 inches deep. A cold chisel and hammer were then used to excavate the circle while creating a pleasingly textured surface.

We set the freshly filled bathing and drinking stone amid the herbaceous layer, where a mix of cinnamon fern (*Osmunda cinnamomea*), white wood aster (*Aster divaricatus*), woodland wild oat (*Chasmanthium latifolium*) had previously been established. We counted on these and nearby shrubs and trees to provide sufficient cover to make birds feel safe using the stone bath.

The stone is strategically placed at the corner of a path away from the house but within view from two favorite sitting areas. As long as it is kept full of water, the stone sees continuous use. In early December (opposite top right) a black-capped chickadee avails itself of the bathing facility. —**RD**

The Ecological Functionality of Hybrids

A frequent question prompted by hybrids and cultivated varieties of natives produced by selection is "Do they still function as natives?" In most cases, if hybridization has not changed the chemical makeup in ways that make it unpalatable to native insects, the plant will still function as a native in this regard. If hybridization or selection hasn't changed the physical form or structure of reproductive parts in ways that make them inoperative, then the hybrid is likely to function much like an unmodified plant.

In some cases, hybridization or selection of native species produces garden plants that bloom at times that are out of sync with typical forms of the species. This may result in plants that are no longer contributors to the development of local gene pools and/or plants that are not providing ecosystem services such as pollen, nectar, or seeds at times when they are needed by local fauna. Hybridity and selection can also positively or negatively affect adaptability and longevity, both of which are important qualities to consider when designing sustainable layers.

Sanguinaria canadensis 'Multiplex' is a cultivated variety of a common native species. Instead of functioning reproductive parts, it has additional petals. Because of this, 'Multiplex' is sterile—it is incapable of producing seed. If you're an ant looking for eliasome-appendaged seeds, you're out of luck. But does this mean the double bloodroot has no function? Of course not. It functions as a beautiful element in the garden and that has value. It also still has all

TOP LEFT **A variegated fritillary takes nectar from a patented hybrid coneflower, *Echinacea* 'Tomato Soup'.**

CENTER **Double bloodroot (*Sanguinaria canadensis* 'Multiplex') is surely one of the most elegant** cultivated varieties derived from a common native species.

LEFT **Functioning reproductive organs are at the center of a typical bloodroot flower and enable the species to perpetuate itself.**

the adaptability of the typical form of the species except that it is unable to perpetuate itself. As long as the garden as a whole is comprised of functional layers, there is no reason not to include a measure of single-function elements.

To ensure that even long-lived species such as Jack-in-the-pulpit (*Arisaema triphyllum*) remain part of the herbaceous layer, it is best to allow seeds to mature, be dispersed, and germinate.

Variation within a species can add to the beauty and resilience of plant populations in the garden. The flower color of woodland geranium (*Geranium maculatum*) varies in different parts of its native range. Though plants in most Pennsylvania populations tend to produce light lavender to pink flowers, elsewhere plants may be typically deep blue-purple. —**RD**

We acquired woodland geranium plants from a Virginia friend's property years ago and established them in our Pennsylvania garden. Though individual plants live for years, this darker flowered form continues in our garden through self-seeding.

Natives in Formal and Informal Designs

Though native plants are sometimes considered appropriate only for informal design styles, there's no reason for this. Style, and formality or informality, have more to do with management than with plant selection.

Ferns are among the most adaptable and durable possibilities for the herbaceous layer. Though many are deciduous, a few including marginal shield fern (*Dryopteris marginalis*) and Christmas fern (*Polystichum acrostichoides*) are fully evergreen. Two running species, hay-scented fern (*Dennstaedtia punctilobula*) and New York fern (*Thelypteris noveboracensis*), can be used to create highly durable herbaceous layers at a large or a relatively small scale. Ferns come about as close to being immune to deer damage as any group of native plants in eastern North America.

Providing fragrance is a function of plants and gardens that is important to human sensibilities, and good design will make the most of this potential.

The sweet fragrance of strategically placed summer phlox (*Phlox paniculata*), a native of eastern United States, is readily accessible in this July image.

OPPOSITE BOTTOM The vegetation edging this bluestone walk is mostly white wood aster (*Aster divaricatus*). A quick trimming with hand shears twice over the course of the growing season keeps this native aster looking neat enough for most eyes.

LEFT Native mayapples dominate the spring herbaceous layer on a wooded slope above an outdoor dining area at Patterns, the private residence of Governor and Mrs. Pierre S. du Pont in Delaware. Patterns includes an inspired mix of informal and highly formal plantings.

ABOVE In this late-November image, Christmas ferns function as an evergreen edge defining a woodland path.

In lieu of lawn, sunlit sweeps of hay-scented fern (*Dennstaedtia punctilobula*) and New York fern (*Thelypteris noveboracensis*) cover the landscape in front of Russ Jones' historic Pennsylvania cabin.

Managed Wildness

Pinkroot or spigelia (*Spigelia marilandica*) is an excellent example of a showy, highly desirable native perennial that is difficult to propagate commercially but is easily naturalized in the garden. Though spigelia can be rooted from cuttings, the success rate is typically low. It grows easily from seed, but is explosively dehiscent: as the seed capsules ripen, they propel the seeds far from the plants, making seed collection problematic in a production setting.

The species is a member of the logania family (*Loganiaceae*), which is closely related to the gentian family (*Gentianaceae*). The relationship can be observed in the opposite leaves and tubular flowers shared by spigelia and many gentians.

Spigelia's native range is concentrated in the southeastern states. Although garden literature typically says it grows only in moist woods and along stream banks, I've seen it growing wild in Tennessee at the bottom of a dry sunny slope below a shrub layer dominated by fragrant sumac (*Rhus aromatica*) and with American smoketree (*Cotinus obovatus*) growing above. Having grown it personally for over a quarter century I can say with confidence that it is easily adaptable to garden soils of average moisture and to sites exposed to a significant amount of filtered sunlight.

I wouldn't call it a weed, but we get hundreds of spigelia seedlings each year from the naturalized populations in our Pennsylvania garden. None of them were deliberately planted—they are all self-sown.

Decades earlier when I first bought the property, I obtained *Spigelia marilandica* from three different growers whose thorough records traced the origin of their plants to different wild populations in North Carolina and Tennessee. This genetic diversity may be responsible for the vigor of the populations in our garden, but in any case, we allow spigelia to tell us where it would like to grow.

It has become a reliable presence in a number of areas, blooming in June and often re-blooming later in summer. Whenever it gets too rambunctious, we dig up the seedlings and give them to gardening friends. Managed wildness and an invitational approach to chance happenings can sometimes accomplish things that would be impossible through more deliberate methods. —**RD**

BELOW LEFT Hundreds of self-sown plants of pinkroot bloom among shield ferns and cinnamon ferns in late June.

BELOW The tubular flowers of spigelia betray its affinity with gentians.

ABOVE Spigelia makes up a significant part of the herbaceous layer in this sitting area in the Darke-Zoehrer garden, where it mingles with white wood aster (*Aster divaricatus*), showy trillium (*Trillium grandiflorum*), Virginia waterleaf (*Hydrophyllum virginianum*), zigzag goldenrod (*Solidago flexicaulis*), maidenhair ferns (*Adiantum pedatum*), and many others.

RIGHT Spigelia is a reliable presence in the garden, blooming in spring and often reblooming in summer.

A Window on Diverse Functionality

This following series of images illustrates the transformation of a relatively sterile space off a north-facing bathroom window of our Pennsylvania home. Though a bathroom view may seem mundane, like the view from a kitchen window it is a small but significant element in our daily experiences—our "necessary journeys" to quote Ralph Waldo Emerson. Bringing life into these little landscapes can add immeasurably to the joy, the intrigue, and the functionality of the garden as inclusive habitat. —**RD**

Installed by the original owners 40 years earlier as "foundation plantings," these Japanese yews may have provided some cover for wildlife, but their contributions to the overall livability of our landscape were minimal. It occurred to us that there was something oddly poetic about a bath window view staring at the backside of a yew, but this was insufficient argument for leaving them in place.

LEFT These mid-May (top) and late-October (bottom) images show the same window view after replanting. It has remained like this with minimal care for 20 years. The planting takes advantage of partial shading from our single-story house and the higher-than-average moisture conditions resulting from this. Our management ethic is to irrigate plants only during the period of establishment and to rely on rainfall in subsequent years. The mix includes North American natives—Christmas fern, cinnamon fern, Jack-in-the-pulpit, white wood aster, and threadleaf bluestar (*Amsonia hubrichtii*)—in the herbaceous layer, along with exotic but perfectly adapted and compatible snowdrops. The shrub layer includes sweetshrub (*Calycanthus floridus*), witch hazel (*Hamamelis virginiana*), open-pollinated native azalea (*Rhododendron arborescens*) crosses, and possumhaw (*Viburnum nudum*) including the cultivated variety 'Winterthur'.

THIS PAGE Mid-May views from outside looking back at the north side of the house (above) and a bird's-eye view from the roof (right) explain the patterns in the planting. The cinnamon ferns are placed closest to the house (but not directly under the eaves) to take advantage of the shade and moisture there. Virtual rivers of white wood asters flow around sweeps of threadleaf bluestar and around and below the woody plants. —RD

OPPOSITE A top-down view in October shows the viburnums and bluestars at their autumn color peak. The asters have finished flowering by this time but their developing seed-heads are still standing, mostly obscured by the lax stems of the bluestars.

THIS PAGE We allow the herbaceous layer to stand through fall and winter. By late November, the bluestars have turned tawny and are more upright than they were in October (above). Their needle-like leaves begin dropping at this time and by spring they have contributed a significant amount of organic material to the ground layer. Along with leaves from the asters and shrubs, this material all but eliminates the need to spread mulch in this area. If we do need additional material, we use composted leaf mulch produced on site. We find the aster seed-heads quite beautiful (left), and take pleasure in knowing that they provide food for birds all winter long as well as new aster seedlings in spring to fill in any gaps in the herbaceous layer. —RD

OPPOSITE BOTTOM As this November image illustrates, the winter appearance isn't exactly tidy but it is reasonably attractive, especially with snow cover.

OPPOSITE TOP LEFT Because our herbaceous layer provides winter cover, this cardinal can safely forage on the ground below without fear of being spotted by a hawk.

ABOVE AND OPPOSITE Attracted by the cover and food provide by our layered planting, this hermit thrush, photographed through the window (above and above left) has made regular visits in January for a few years now, and by February we can count on robins (opposite top right) and many other birds arriving to feast on viburnum berries.

LEFT If we had wished to cut the bluestars back in fall, we would have needed clippers or shears. As the stems stand through winter their materials break down, and by March, they are fragile and brittle enough that they can easily be snapped off near the crowns with gloved hands, eliminating the need for bladed tools. The aster stems are also removed easily and quickly for composting at this time. —RD

Another fragrant native azalea, the piedmont azalea (*Rhododendron canescens*), greets visitors to this indoor-outdoor entry space at Ashland Hollow in Delaware.

THE SHRUB LAYER

Though not as diverse as the herbaceous layer, the shrub layer offers unique opportunities to add to the beauty, diversity, and year-round functionality of the garden. Along with trees, and accompanied by functional ground and herbaceous layers, shrubs are a gardener's principal space-making materials.

Sweetshrub (*Calycanthus floridus*) is one of the most distinctively scented native shrubs. For many weeks in April and May, it fills the garden with the scent most people associate with fresh strawberries. These photos are of the horticultural selection 'Michael Lindsey', which is fragrant for more hours each day and more spring days each year than most sweetshrubs. It is also more upright and taller than many sweetshrubs and the foliage is unusually glossy (top). It is fertile and seedlings are true to form, and 'Michael Lindsey' may actually represent a botanical type, not a chance selection. All sweetshrubs turn gold in autumn, and the color lasts quite a while as illustrated by this late-October image (above). The dense twigginess of sweetshrub provides functional cover for birds and it is frequently chosen as a nesting site.

Taken in mid-May, these photos give two different perspectives on spaces in our garden defined by woody plantings that are anchored by shrubs. In the arcing sweep of shrubs nearest the chairs, *Fothergilla ×intermedia* and sweet pepperbush (*Clethra alnifolia*) are repeated for visual simplicity and to simplify maintenance; however, other shrubs are interspersed to add to interest and functionality. The single white blooming shrub (to the right in photo above) is coastal azalea (*Rhododendron atlanticum*) and it alone is capable of scenting this section of the garden with its sweet clovelike fragrance. Later in the season fragrance will be provided by the sweet pepperbush.

Native azaleas are easy-to-grow, long-lived plants if provided with good drainage, slightly acid soil, and filtered sunlight. This mixed planting of pinxter azalea (*Rhododendron periclymenoides*) and piedmont azalea (*R. canescens*) has thrived in our garden for over 20 years with no pruning, fertilizing, or irrigation. —RD

ABOVE AND LEFT The colors of the highly fragrant Florida flame azalea (*Rhododendron austrinum*) vary from deep orange to orange-yellow in a mixed planting at Mt. Cuba Center in Delaware (above). Elsewhere at Mt. Cuba, a planting of pinkshell azalea (*R. vaseyi*) demonstrates that native azaleas can be used in relatively formal, refined designs (left). The ground-cover is eastern foamflower (*Tiarella cordifolia*). Though this pinkshell azalea is not fragrant, its flowers are unequalled for their clarity of color.

OPPOSITE Early May (top) and late-October (right) views of the same multilayered planting anchored by repeated fothergillas and river birches. Though the herbaceous layer has evolved and additional shrubs have been added, the fothergillas and birches have been growing together for over 20 years, depending almost entirely on rainfall. The main reason this works is that the foth-ergillas and birches were planted at modest size and at the same time. This isn't always possible, but when it is, it is ideal, allowing shrubs and trees to develop simultaneously the extensive root systems necessary to sustain them in times of drought. This is especially important when plant-ing shrubs with surface-rooted, highly moisture-competitive trees such as river birch or American beech. The herbaceous layer also benefits from the opportunity to develop root systems before the ground is dominated by tree roots. Deeper-rooted trees such as blackgum (*Nyssa sylvatica*) and most of the oak species allow later planting of the shrub and herbaceous layers without risk of failure or the need for regular irrigation in dry times.

FAR LEFT Juncos and white-throated sparrows enjoy the late-January cover afforded by fothergillas planted with river birches.

LEFT A red-banded hairstreak takes nectar from arrowwood viburnum (*Viburnum dentatum*) in mid-May. Viburnums are one of the larger and most useful groups of native shrubs. Most have white flowers in flat-topped clusters and most produce colorful berries of great value to wildlife.

ABOVE LEFT Possumhaw (*Viburnum nudum*) naturally occurs in moist or wet habitats but is easily grown on a wide range of soils except those that are highly alkaline. The ability of its root system to tolerate the relatively low oxygen levels of wet habitats translates into an adaptability to poorly drained garden soils. The berries begin porcelain-pink in color and gradually turn indigo blue, making for striking contrast with the wine-colored fall foliage. The plants shown here are of the cultivated selection 'Winterthur'. *Viburnum nudum* doesn't have separate male and female plants; however, two genetically distinct plants are required for fertilization and berry production. For this reason, if a clonal cultivar is planted, it should be accompanied by a different cultivar or a seedling. The cultivars 'Winterthur' and 'Brandywine', if planted together, will ensure plentiful berry production.

LEFT An abundant berry crop ripens on *Viburnum nudum* 'Brandywine' in late September at the University of Delaware Botanic Garden.

ABOVE This yellow-shafted northern flicker filled up on *Viburnum nudum* berries in our garden as snow began falling on a late-January day. —RD

Fothergilla and mapleleaf viburnum (*Viburnum acerifolium*) provide the necessary separation to make this seating area feel cozy and intimate in April even before most of the garden has leafed out (top left). The viburnum blooms in late May (top right) and by mid October it has become a virtual kaleidoscope of colors (above left and right) rivaling the fothergillas.

Illustrating the opposite side of the same planting from page 187, these two images reveal the composition and seasonal dynamics of the herbaceous layer. Virginia bluebells bloom with the fothergillas in April (right) accompanied by the bright green new leaves of Allegheny pachysandra (*Pachysandra procumbens*) and bicolor barrenwort (*Epimedium ×versicolor* 'Sulphureum'), a hybrid with East Asian origins. In mid-November (below) the semi-evergreen foliage of the pachysandra and barrenworts provides rich green contrast to the shrubs.

ABOVE Extensive shrub plantings at Longwood Gardens in Pennsylvania demonstrate how effective combined native shrubs can be in organizing spaces or edging walks. In this mid-July image, the low-growing selection of sweet pepperbush (*Clethra alnifolia* 'Hummingbird') transitions into a sweep of Virginia sweetspire (*Itea virginica*).

LEFT Sweet pepperbush attracts a zebra swallowtail in July.

Always multistemmed, witch hazel (*Hamamelis virginiana*) has a reliable upright vase shape which makes it useful in a wide variety of settings in residential gardens. It is extremely long lived, continually sending up new stems and can be maintained at almost any desired height from 5 to 14 feet by removing the older taller stems. One of the most adaptable of all native shrubs, it can grow in deep shade or full sun, in deep organic soil, clay or thin rocky soil. It tolerates prolonged droughts or periodic inundation. *Hamamelis virginiana* blooms for a few weeks in October and November. For maximum flowering impact, select a seedling that drops its leaves before flowering. These images show the same 8-foot tall plant in mid-November (top left) and mid-February (far left).

THIS PAGE Witch hazel creates a sense of enclosure around an outdoor shower area that doubles as a garden workspace. The clear yellow autumn color illustrated in this mid-October photograph is reliable and lasts for a couple of weeks (top). This particular plant was selected because it always drops its leaves before blooming as illustrated by this mid-November image (left). The two wine-colored shrubs flanking it are Korean spice viburnum (*Viburnum carlesii*). Chosen for its delightful spring fragrance and adaptability to the site conditions, this eastern Asian shrub does not naturalize in eastern North America. The last photo (above) shows the top-down view of the outdoor shower space in September.

RIGHT Though spicebush (*Lindera benzoin*) is a common and wide-ranging native shrub, its clear yellow always brightens the autumn garden and its presence provides sustenance for spicebush swallowtails.

Fragrant sumac (*Rhus aromatica*) is among the relatively small group of truly low-growing native shrubs whose rate of growth, adaptability, and durability make them suitable for ground cover use. A mass planting by Restaino Design beautifies and stabilizes a steep slope at The Flags in New York's Catskill region (right). When grown in sun, fragrant sumac colors vividly in autumn (above).

LEFT Black huckleberry (*Gaylussacia baccata*) is another low, colonizing shrub that makes a sturdy groundcover. This October image illustrates a planting on a dry slope in a New York garden.

Bottlebrush buckeye (*Aesculus parviflora*) is a large, highly adaptable spreading shrub that makes a dramatic addition to residential landscapes with adequate space (left). Its June-to-July flower spikes are followed by smooth red-brown chestnutlike seeds (above). Beautiful but not edible for humans, the seeds are valued by many small mammals and insects.

ABOVE Many experienced gardeners believe growing blueberries is for the birds. Highbush blueberry (*Vaccinium corymbosum*) grows best in full sun on moist soil with high organic content. It is worth growing as a well-formed shrub with vivid crimson autumn color even if birds manage to eat most of the berries. There are two ways to approach this. One is to cover the shrubs with netting as berries ripen. The alternative is to plant enough blueberry shrubs to produce sufficient berries for avian and human consumption.

ABOVE RIGHT Redstem dogwood (*Cornus sericea*) can grow over 10 feet tall but can be maintained at much lower heights by cutting back nearly to the ground periodically. This image shows the cultivated variety 'Cardinal', which is not quite as brightly colored as its namesake but can be one of the more colorful elements in the winter landscape.

Before cutting back any shrub, inspect it for signs of other life that might otherwise be overlooked. This February photo shows a praying mantis case on a dogwood stem (above). Postponing cutting back this shrub until the following year will allow the mantids to hatch in spring. Another option is to cut the stem with the case and position it near other vegetation somewhere else in the garden until hatching occurs. Assuming the mantid egg case is not eaten by woodpeckers, chickadees, or titmice during the winter, up to 200 tiny replicas of their parents will hatch and emerge sometime in May (above right). The entire clutch hatches within minutes and the young mantids move away from their siblings as fast as they can. Even when small, mantids are voracious predators and will attempt to eat anything they can grasp, including small flies, aphids, and each other. Many of the tiny hatchlings will fall victim to insect and bird predators and only a small percentage will live to become adults.

Alabama snow wreath (*Neviusia alabamensis*) happens to be rare in its native range through the southeastern states but it is an easily cultivated and beautifully useful addition to the shrub layer in gardens. It literally covers itself with starry white flowers in late April or early May (top and above), and is pretty enough that for years we've been using it as a cut flower (above right). Its greatest value to us is as a deer-proof screening shrub.

Though deciduous, this running species produces a dense profusion of red-brown stems that form nearly opaque mass that stands through winter. It is easily increased by division in late winter or early spring. —RD

Oakleaf hydrangea (*Hydrangea quercifolia*) occurs in woodland habitats in the southeastern states from Tennessee to North Carolina and south to Louisiana and Florida, typically on alkaline soils. In recent decades, interest in indigenous North American species has propelled it from a relatively obscure "native" to a popular shrub widely valued for its beauty, adaptability, and utility. Although lower-growing selections are increasingly available, the typical form can grow over 10 feet tall. This would be too large for many residential gardens; however, oakleaf hydrangea tolerates repeated pruning or even occasional cutting back to the ground. It is a superb example of a native shrub that is suited to a wide range of design styles and purposes. It can be used as a space-defining mass (above), or as these two examples at Longwood Gardens demonstrate, a backdrop for a casual space (top right) or a bold-textured presence in a highly formal design (bottom right).

197

ABOVE Though uncommon in cultivation, leatherwood (*Dirca palustris*) is an accommodating shrub with a naturally rounded form that requires no pruning or shaping. It is very shade tolerant but can also be grown in full sun. It is adaptable to wide a range of moisture conditions including continually moist soils, as seen in this October image in a New York garden.

RIGHT Known as rosebay rhododendron or great laurel, *Rhododendron maximum* is a cold-hardy, long lived, relatively easy-to-grow evergreen shrub that blooms white in summer. Pruning can be used to shape it or to keep it in check, as demonstrated by this walkway planting on the grounds of Frank Lloyd Wright's Fallingwater in western Pennsylvania. Without intervention, this rhododendron easily reaches 10 feet in height with equal or greater spread, which is impractical for gardens of modest scale.

ABOVE Drooping leucothoe (*Leucothoë fontanesiana*) and great laurel (*Rhododendron maximum*) help stabilize a slope and provide evergreen interest along a driveway in this New York garden.

Coast leucothoe (*Leucothoë axillaris*) is an evergreen, under-four-foot tall presence along this walkway (above). No pruning is necessary to maintain it at this height. It mixes well with deciduous species and its spring flowers provide pollen and nectar services for local bees and butterflies, as illustrated by this April image of a question mark butterfly taking nectar (left). For screening and organizing purposes and to provide green color in winter, evergreen shrubs that don't grow too tall are essential components in most residential landscapes, yet native shrubs that fit this description are very limited in number. This reality presents one of the most sensible arguments for why broadly functional landscapes usually require a mix of natives and well-chosen exotics.

LEFT Inkberry holly (*Ilex glabra*) is one of relatively few easy-to-grow, adaptable evergreen shrubs native to primarily deciduous regions in the eastern United States. The plant shown here is 'Densa', a cultivated variety that retains leaves on its lower branches into maturity, unlike many forms of this species. *Ilex glabra* offers a native alternative to *I. crenata*, the Japanese holly that has forever been the default choice for an evergreen hedging shrub. Unfortunately, even with regular pruning it is virtually impossible to maintain *I. glabra* at heights of 4 feet and under. Rather than opting for an exotic species, an alternate approach is to cut it to the ground every five to ten years, in late winter or early spring. A healthy shrub with an established root system will sprout quickly and within a year will have formed a dense, shorter plant.

FAR LEFT Winterberry (*Ilex verticillata*) adds color to the autumn and winter landscape and then, just before spring arrives, flocks of robins and other birds descend and devour them.

LEFT A mixed planting of winterberry (*Ilex verticillata*) and wild oat (*Chasmanthium latifolium*) proved highly functional for this junco, which is using the holly as a perch from which to eat the large nutritious seeds of the oat grass. The stalks of the grass are sturdy, but not enough to support the junco's weight.

THE UNDERSTORY TREE LAYER

Trees of all sizes contribute immensely to the structural beauty, functionality, and habitat value of a garden. Though the relatively small scale of many residential landscapes often limits the number of truly tall-growing canopy species that can be included, even the smallest gardens have room for lower-growing understory trees. Because of the scale difference between home gardens and forests, trees that inhabit the understory in wild habitats often form the canopy of residential landscapes.

Whether the "roof" of a home garden is comprised of understory or canopy species, it is rarely continuous. The need for sunny spaces to suit various purposes usually dictates that there be sufficient openings in the tree layers.

Because they have the potential to live longer than plants in the shrub and herbaceous layers, and because they profoundly affect growing conditions beneath them, trees of all sizes warrant special care in their selection and placement.

OPPOSITE TOP Two understory trees, umbrella magnolia (*Magnolia tripetala*) and the large-flowered two-winged silverbell (*Halesia diptera* var. *magniflora*) bloom in May under the high canopy of a pin oak (*Quercus palustris*).

LEFT A pink dogwood blooming below a white oak (*Quercus alba*) at Mt. Cuba Center illustrates the structural beauty resulting from the juxtaposition of a delicately framed understory species and a massive canopy tree.

ABOVE In general, understory trees growing under a high canopy flower better when openings in the canopy allow more sunlight to reach them. In this late-April photo, flowering dogwoods (*Cornus florida*) bloom profusely below a canopy comprised primarily of tulip trees (*Liriodendron tulipifera*) at Mt. Cuba Center in Delaware.

Because its flowers lack showy bracts (left), alternate-leaf dogwood (*Cornus alternifolia*) has long been overshadowed by flowering dogwood (*C. florida*). It may not be able to compete based on floral beauty, but by all other counts *C. alternifolia* is a highly attractive under-story tree with year-round interest (opposite top and bottom) and high value to wildlife. It is sometimes called pagoda dogwood because its tiered horizontal branches, seen here in late April (above), are reminiscent of a pagoda; however, this name is more appropriate for the Japanese *C. controversa*, which is the larger but similarly structured eastern Asian analog to the North American *C. alternifolia*.

Well-placed understory trees can provide a graceful transition from a high canopy to human-scaled features such as this bench at the Leonard J. Buck garden in New Jersey (above). The nearly horizontal branch in the foreground belongs to ironwood (*Carpinus caroliniana*). Every autumn, ironwood reliably turns a vivid mix of gold and red-orange (opposite top).

Its fine-textured horizontal branching adds a distinctive note to the understory tree layer and provides sufficient cover for birds year-round, as illustrated by this tufted titmouse sitting inside a still-leafless ironwood in late March (right). In the Peirce's Woods garden at Longwood Garden, iron-woods create a low canopy roof over this path (far right).

LEFT Redbuds (*Cercis canadensis*) make a colorful connection from the high mixed canopy to a formal garden space at Patterns, the private residence of Governor and Mrs. Pierre S. du Pont in Delaware.

ABOVE A fringe tree (*Chionanthus virginicus*) forms a canopy over this outdoor garden room at Ashland Hollow in Delaware and also connects the space to the high woodland canopy to the left in this photo.

The relatively small scale of understory species makes them easy to work with when using trees to organize and define walkways or smaller garden rooms. Pawpaws (*Asimina triloba*) are the primary structural materials defining this path in our Pennsylvania garden (left). The filtered light below them is sufficient to sustain many species in the shrub and herbaceous layers. In good years, we have more pawpaws than we can eat (bottom right). The bold-texture foliage reliably turns gold every October (bottom left). —RD

LEFT AND BELOW The fruits of the North American native persimmon (*Diospyros virginiana*) are sweet, juicy, and quite edible but only after they are fully ripe and soft. Unripe fruits are extremely astringent. Persimmons were eaten by American Indians and since Colonial times have also been used to make persimmon pudding and pie. Persimmon trees can grow 50 feet tall but are typically much shorter. They sprout readily and persistently if cut, and for this reason persimmons often grow in groups or groves.

LEFT A bird's-eye view of the delectable (for birds, not humans) berry crop on a flowering dogwood in late October.

This persimmon grove at the back of our Pennsylvania garden is the result of discontinued mowing. For years the back corner was maintained in turf. We noticed small trees sprouting in the grass and realized they were from a population of wild persimmons on the neighboring property. Fifteen years later, we have a grove of 25-foot-tall persimmon trees that produce copiously most years. We've learned not to taste the persimmons until we're certain they're ripe—typically sometime in November or early December. —RD

Sweetbay magnolias (*Magnolia virginiana*) were selected to create a semi-transparent enclosure around an outdoor patio in the Barton garden in Pennsylvania (above). This multistemmed understory tree regularly sprouts from the base and can be maintained indefinitely at modest scale by removing older stems. In addition to its small scale and dappled shade, this magnolia is also an ideal tree for outdoor living spaces because its June blooms gently fill the air with a sweet lemon scent (left).

ABOVE Many understory trees including redbuds are grown for their flowering displays. Whenever space permits, consider planting them in groves as illustrated in this mid-April photo of the Riska-Dunson garden in Delaware. Such repetition makes a greater visual impact, simplifies maintenance, and introduces a greater amount of habitat-enriching biomass to the landscape.

RIGHT Known as eastern wahoo or burning bush (*Euonymus atropurpureus*), this North American native is an example of a useful and widely adapted native tree that is rarely seen in commerce or cultivation. As this October image in a New York garden shows, it deserves more attention.

Variously called shadbush, service-berry, or Juneberry, *Amelanchier* is an example of a genus that includes both understory and canopy tree species. In recent decades, *Amelanchier ×grandiflora* hybrids have begun to dominate commercially available shadbushes. These crosses between two native species, *A. arborea* and *A. laevis*, are typically multistemmed and form very large shrubs or small trees. They grow 15 to 25 feet tall, which is far less than the 40-foot height the often single-stemmed *A. arborea* can attain. Shadbushes are among the first native trees to bloom, usually in March or very early April. The flowers are followed in June by berries that rival blueberries for their sweetness and edibility. The autumn foliage turns a pleasing mix of peach and apricot hues.

The catkins of American hornbeam (*Ostrya virginiana*) aren't colorfully showy but they certainly are elegantly beautiful. These two photos show this long-lived, drought-tolerant tree in a formal garden at Mt. Cuba Center in Delaware.

Carolina silverbells (*Halesia tetraptera*) can grow to canopy heights in native Smoky Mountain habitats, but in residential settings, especially toward the northern limits of hardiness (Zones 5 and 6) they grow 25 to 35 feet tall. They begin flowering when only a few years old, as illustrated by these young seedlings (above), and will bloom in considerable shade. The four-winged fruits hang on the tree through most of winter, as this image of a December sunrise illustrates (right). When the fruits eventually fall to the ground, they are eaten by squirrels and others.

The large-flowered two-winged silverbell (*Halesia diptera* var. *magniflora*) is a southeastern species that has proved hardy in USDA zone 5. It is more heat and sun tolerant than the Carolina silverbell and can be sited in full sun, but it will bloom profusely under the shade of a high canopy (top). The petals of this botanical variety are split (above), unlike the fused bell-like petals of most other silverbells. All *Halesia* species provide needed pollen and nectar services in late April and early May (left).

Seen from outside or inside (below), this allée of *Halesia diptera* var. *magniflora* at Patterns is dramatic proof that native trees can be used imaginatively in formal designs.

This early November view of the Rowland garden in urban Delaware demonstrates that a multilayered planting of natives can be integrated with other plants and traditions. This section of the garden was previously planted with a monoculture of Japanese pachysandra (*Pachysandra procumbens*) which offered simplicity of maintenance but made virtually no contribution to the habitat value of the garden. The herbaceous layer of this relatively young planting now includes native sedges (*Carex laxiculmis*), barren strawberry (*Waldsteinia fragarioides*), and prairie dropseed grass (*Sporobolus heterolepis*). Natives in the shrub layer include oakleaf hydrangea, fothergilla and yellowroot (*Xanthorhiza simplicissima*). Flowering dogwoods are planted as understory trees and trumpet honeysuckle trails over the low fence. The new layers are fitted within a mature framework consisting of mountain laurel (*Kalmia latifolia*), inkberry holly (*Ilex glabra*), and non-native but well-adapted boxwoods, while retaining an overall look and feel evoking an English cottage garden.

kingbird

brown thrasher

catbird

yellow warbler

phoebe

red-eyed vireo

How Many Birds Can One Tree Nourish?

I asked myself that question some years ago when I noticed the birds in our yard eating berries produced by an alternate-leaf dogwood I had planted outside our bathroom window. So many birds visit this tree during the summer that our bathroom has become the hottest birding destination in our house. So far, I have recorded 20 bird species including those pictured here using the dogwood as a source of insects and berries. Alternate-leaf dogwood is a great reminder that our plants are our bird feeders! —DT

pewee

blue grosbeak

red-bellied woodpecker

yellowthroat warbler

orchard oriole

Few sights surpass the visual drama of strategic framing by tall-growing canopy trees, as demonstrated by this scene at Mt. Cuba Center in Delaware.

THE CANOPY LAYER

Appropriately selected and sited canopy trees can contribute to the livability, functionality, and habitat value of residential gardens of all sizes. Nothing has ever been invented that more efficiently provides cooling shade in summer and allows warming sunlight through in winter than a large deciduous tree. The architectural beauty of big trees is also unexcelled: they can organize and frame a landscape better than any other living thing.

Though the flowering of canopy trees is typically less colorful than that of smaller trees, the autumn color impact of large trees is unrivalled. The sheer mass of wood, foliage, fruit, and seed production of canopy trees far exceeds that of smaller trees, shrubs, and herbaceous plants in providing nesting cavities and sustenance for myriad mammals, birds, insects, and other invertebrates.

Whether beginning with a blank slate, building a house in the woods, or moving to a property that has seen years of prior planting, devoting careful thought to the roles of canopy trees can add immeasurably to the life of any residential landscape.

Views of the J&D Darke residence from inside (left) and from the deck offer year-round glimpses into canopy life such as this barred owl photographed in late December (above).

Our 1.5-acre residential landscape includes multiple canopy tree species including beeches, birches, blackgums, maples, and oaks, yet there is still adequate sunlight reaching the lower layers to allow for turf areas and diverse shrub and herbaceous plantings. —RD

Nestled carefully into regenerating hardwood forest in North Carolina, Copper House is a sublime example of taking a *laissez faire* approach to a landscape's processes and living diversity. Everything about the design, from the sinuous elevated entry walk (above), to tree-accommodating cutouts (above right), to window-walls framing the canopy (right), to an outdoor shower on a rear deck is dedicated to near-seamless immersion in the spontaneous wild garden surrounding the house.

ABOVE In early April, the setting sun bathes the upper portions of a river birch canopy in a warm glow. Although European white birch (*Betula pendula*) tends to be short-lived in cultivation in North America, the native river birch (*B. nigra*), sweet birch (*B. lenta*), and yellow birch (*B. alleghaniensis*) are long-lived trees useful for creating a canopy layer in residential landscapes.

ABOVE Cedar wax-wings and a couple of robins fill the upper branches of river birches in late February.

LEFT The brassy bark of yellow birch (*Betula alleghaniensis*) reflects the mid-April sun in a Connecticut garden. This species does best in areas with lower summer night temperatures.

RIGHT A single-trunked shadbush (*Amelanchier arborea*) demonstrates that canopy trees can be a dramatic flowering presence.

BELOW Though the flowering catkins of river birch usually go unnoticed, they are quite colorful when side-lit by the sun against a background of blooming redbuds.

With rare exceptions, big trees planted at small size live longer, healthier lives than trees transplanted at larger sizes. Canopy tree species can be beautiful, functional elements in the landscape as they grow to maturity. This American beech (*Fagus grandifolia*) began as a seedling in our garden and was 10 years old at the time of this photograph. —RD

TOP LEFT The lower branches of young beeches frame a view to a multilayered south-facing planting which includes an orange-berried form of winterberry holly (*Ilex verticillata*) in this late- September image.

LEFT Some of the young beeches that define this space have been limbed to allow sunlight to reach an herbaceous layer that includes goats-beard (*Aruncus dioicus*), which is at its flowering peak in this late-May photo.

ABOVE A grove of beeches that originated as seedlings forms the backdrop for mixed shrub and herbaceous layers edging the lawn in this early November photo. American beech supports more than 127 species of Lepidoptera (the order of insects that includes butterflies, moths, and skippers). Like oaks, beeches produce high-protein seeds that are essential components of the diets of numerous wild mammals and large birds such as turkey and grouse.

235

A late-October view into a canopy of white oaks (*Quercus alba*) backed by shagbark hickories (*Carya ovata*) in a Pennsylvania garden. Oaks in general are relatively deep-rooted: they don't produce a network of roots just below the surface as birches and beeches do. Consequently, it is easier to establish shrub and herbaceous layers under young or old oaks. Since the demise of the American chestnut, oaks, hickories, beeches, and walnuts now supply the protein-rich nuts that are critically necessary for maintaining populations of vertebrate wildlife. Cavities that develop in these trees, both living and dead, provide nesting sites for dozens of bird species.

Pileated woodpeckers are regular visitors to our Pennsylvania garden, as illustrated by this July photo of a male drilling for insects in a small rotted branch (hidden by the large limb) in our pin oak (*Quercus palustris*). We weren't the least bit disturbed when this particular bird woke us before 6 AM. —RD

RIGHT Swamp white oak (*Quercus bicolor*) colors nicely in early November on an urban property in Delaware. This oak species transplants with relative ease and is adaptable to soils that are poorly drained or overly moist.

BELOW A canopy of chestnut oaks (*Quercus montana*) reaches its autumn color peak in early November in this Pennsylvania garden. Chestnut oaks are especially tolerant of thin, rocky, dry soils.

ABOVE Two young scarlet oaks (*Quercus coccinea*) add their brilliant hues to the Hendricks-Curtis garden in Pennsylvania in early November. Scarlet oak is well adapted to dry conditions.

A formal allée of sweet gums (*Liquidambar styraciflua*) forms the canopy and frames the view to sculptor André Harvey's bronze *Samara Turning with the Wind* at Mt. Cuba Center in late April.

VINES IN MULTIPLE LAYERS

Vines occupy multiple layers and offer unique opportunities to add color, texture, screening, and habitat value to gardens of any size. Though some, such as Virginia creeper (*Parthenocissus quinquefolia*), sometimes spread over the surface, most vines take up very little space at ground level but can produce profuse amounts of foliage, flowers, and seeds or fruits in the upper layers.

Vines are especially well suited to providing a sense of enclosure without taking up much horizontal space.

ABOVE Known as trumpet honeysuckle or coral honeysuckle (*Lonicera sempervirens*) is one of the easiest, most adaptable native vines. Its long trumpetlike flowers are typically coral-red but yellow forms are also available. This photo at Mt. Cuba Center in Delaware shows a mature vine in full bloom in late April.

LEFT Trumpet honeysuckle creates a blooming curtain along The High Line in New York in mid-May, demonstrating how adaptable this species is to urban conditions.

RIGHT Including trumpet honeysuckle in a garden virtually guarantees that ruby-throated hummingbirds will be regular visitors. This migratory hummingbird is the only species that regularly nests east of the Mississippi River.

BELOW Yellow-flowered forms of trumpet honeysuckle also attract the ruby-throated hummingbird. This photo shows *Lonicera sem-* *pervirens* interplanted with Virginia creeper (*Parthenocissus quinquefolia*). The creeper is a stronger grower but the two can be kept in balance indefinitely with minimal intervention, usually consisting of selective pruning every two or three years. The honeysuckle has no appreciable fall foliage color; however, the creeper reliably turns crimson each autumn.

LEFT Running horizontally and creating a partial ground cover, Virginia creeper turns crimson in October and the color often lasts into November. This vine can be allowed to grow up into understory and canopy trees. Though it is a strong grower, it will not smother trees. If it becomes too rambunctious, it can easily be pulled down or cut off at the base and allowed to re-sprout.

BELOW American wisteria (*Wisteria frutescens*) adds color and coziness to this rustic porch at the Hendricks-Curtis garden in Pennsylvania in mid-May. Though this native wisteria is a strong grower, requiring a sturdy support and annual pruning, it is much more manageable than the eastern Asian wisterias.

The deciduous pipevine (*Aristolochia macrophylla*) has long been a popular choice for covering fences and porch structures. It is easily grown in sun or shade on a wide range of soils, and tolerates very dry shade once established.

Though the functionality of pipevine as a screen or drape is widely appreciated, relatively few gardeners know that it is the principle food source for pipevine swallowtail larvae. Pipevine swallowtail larvae and adult butterflies contain poisonous compounds obtained by ingesting pipevine. Birds know this and avoid them. Look-alike butterflies, including the spicebush swallowtail, eastern black swallowtail, red-spotted purple, and the black phase of the female eastern tiger swallowtail are not poisonous but benefit by their resemblance to pipevine swallowtails, which affords them similar protection from predators.

Aglow with the mid-June sun, pipevine is artfully draped over a trellis framing a woodland path at Bird Hill, the Burrell-Ellsworth garden in Virginia.

Pipevine covers a section of split rail fence in the Riska-Dunson garden in early June, creating a sense of enclosure. Though deciduous, pipevine can eventually create a dense enough mass of stems to provide semi-transparent screening even while dormant. Though the pipelike flowers are interesting, they are often obscured by the boldly textured foliage.

After pipevine swallow-tails mate in spring, adult females lay their eggs on the undersides of pipevine leaves or stems. The eggs hatch within a few weeks and the young caterpillars begin feeding on leaves and stems.

Mature caterpillars typically leave the host plant to pupate on other vegetation that may be over 25 yards away. If pupation takes place early enough in summer, a butterfly will emerge from the chrysalis that year. If it takes place in late summer or autumn, the swallowtail will remain in its chrysalis through winter, emerging the following spring.

Wild yam (*Dioscorea villosa*) is uncommonly cultivated but is an easy, extremely long-lived addition to a garden's native plant palette. The flowers are small and inconspicuous, but the foliage is quite beautiful at all stages. New leaves are deep green and glossy (far left). By summer, the gloss has been replaced by a blue-green matte finish. By October, the leaves have turned a clear bright yellow that lasts well into November. The thin leaves are highly translucent and are especially dramatic when illuminated by autumn sunlight (above). The distinctive seed pods last through winter and spring the following year (left). This deciduous vine grows from a tuber, and is tolerant of dry shade.

An edge at Ashland Hollow in Delaware makes a beautiful, low-maintenance transition from the open, sunny turfed margins of the entry drive to a tall oak-beech-tulip tree woods. Mixed sassafras and flowering dogwoods along with spicebush (*Lindera benzoin*) are branched to the ground, helping to suppress the germination of weed seeds at the juncture with the turf in this mid-Atlantic setting.

CREATING EDGES

Edges are the most common component of many residential gardens. Driveways, garages, houses, pools, and lawns all create or necessitate openings in the vegetation, and these openings are surrounded by edges. In addition, many residential properties have edges fronting roads and adjacent properties.

The sunlight and air movement associated with edges affords opportunities for healthy layered plantings that produce a lot of flower color, fruits and seeds, and autumn foliage color. The transitional richness of edges makes them favorite places for resident and visiting birds. When edges are characterized by disturbance or open ground, they are also frequent destinations for weed seeds, so while they can be dynamic and rewarding parts of the garden, edges require special attention.

A lot can be learned about how a garden is planted and maintained by looking at the edge where lawn meets plantings. Does the turf stop at thickly applied mulch creating a brown strip at the perimeter of the lawn, or does the turf transition seamlessly to layered plantings? Regular application of commercially produced mulch is expensive, resource-consumptive, and time-consuming. Except as needed to establish new planting areas, the weed-suppressing, moisture-retaining functions of mulch are better fulfilled by well-chosen vegetation.

Edges in the mid-Atlantic region are especially vulnerable to incursions by Oriental bittersweet (*Celastrus orbiculatus*), Japanese honeysuckle (*Lonicera japonica*), and by both non-native and native but opportunistically weedy grape vines. Any of these is capable of smothering and killing or damaging shrubs, understory trees, and canopy trees if unchecked. With minimized disturbance, monitoring, and removal of weed seedlings when small, such edges are sustainable.

Monitoring for weed seedlings is easiest in early spring before leafy growth of garden plantings obscures the ground layer. This April view down through a native spicebush in a woodland garden edge reveals the toothed, rounded foliage of a young bittersweet seedling that has self-sown below.

This early September image illustrates multilayered edge plantings around a lawn. No mulch is visible. An herbaceous layer comprised of long-lived perennials including large-rooted heuchera (*Heuchera macrorhiza*), aromatic aster (*Aster oblongifolius*), Christmas fern (*Polystichum acrostichoides*), woodland wild oat (*Chasmanthium latifolium*), and threadleaf bluestar (*Amsonia hubrichtii*) flows into mixed shrub, understory, and canopy tree layers.

Since weeds are often prolific self-sowers, the presence of vast numbers of seedlings is often a clue to identifying interlopers; however, care must be taken to distinguish weeds from naturalized natives. Many of the weed species that plague temperate North American gardens begin growth earlier in the season than the native vegetation and because of this it is often easy to identify exotic weeds because they are the first to produce bright new leaves in spring.

Edges that transition between woods and open sun present opportunities to create color, structure, and textural combinations that wouldn't be as viable either in a shaded woodland interior or in a full-sun space.

Vegetation surrounding the meadow garden at Mt. Cuba Center in Delaware shows striped maple (*Acer pensylvanicum*) at autumn color peak, enjoying the light levels at the edge. This species can't tolerate full sun exposure except at higher altitudes. The alternate-leaf dogwood closer to the sun is more adaptable.

The front of our property flanking the driveway was originally covered in mowed lawn up to the road edge. We wanted to take advantage of this open sunny space to create a multilayered planting which would function partly as an enclosing screen and partly as an introduction to our design aesthetic. We also are always seeking to add habitat value to any new plantings. We began by removing the turf mechanically, using a sharp spade and no herbicide. Soil from our compost area was added to bring the planting site back up to level, and then sassafras seedlings from our property and a friendly neighbor were planted at half-inch caliper size. We next planted white wood aster plugs on 9-inch centers to establish a nearly continuous herbaceous layer along with a few heart-leaved asters, thread-leaf bluestars, and rough-stem goldenrods (*Solidago rugosa*) divided from existing plantings elsewhere in the garden. Twenty years later the herbaceous layer and the sassafras trees (now 25 feet tall) are still thriving (top right), and a flowering dogwood planted by the birds has reached flowering age (right). —RD

This photo sequence tells the story of two related edge plantings, one in the interior of our garden and the other at the periphery. When I first acquired the property, it bordered on active farmland along the eastern edge, shown at the bottom of this photo (above). Years later when we learned the farm had been sold for housing development we decided to create plantings that would provide screening of the semi-circular space associated with a small cabin at the very back of our property. The cabin space had already been defined by a multi-layered planting intended to evoke a local hedgerow but comprised mostly of non-weedy local natives including asters, ferns, spicebush, witch hazel, alternate-leaf dog-wood, flowering dogwood, redbud, sassafras, silverbells, river birch, and American beech along with a grouping of katsura trees (*Cercidi-phyllum japonicum*). Our contrived hedgerow includes a path opening that allows a glimpse of the cabin from the main house and vice-versa (top right and bottom right). —RD

LEFT We began creating the screen planting along the farm edge by planting a row of switchgrasses (*Panicum virgatum*). White-tailed deer were increasingly moving back and forth from the nearby woodland preserve using the now-fallow farm field and we wanted to discourage them from entering our garden. The grasses quickly and inexpensively created a temporary hedge and as we had hoped it deflected the deer. Behind the grasses, we planted *Neviusia alabamensis* and we also nurtured redbud seedlings origi-nating from the older trees behind the cabin. Now eight years later, the grasses are being shaded out, as intended, by the woody plantings.

TOP AND ABOVE The redbuds put on a wonderful spring display in April from within and outside our garden, while providing pollen and nectar services for countless bees. The space has become a favorite place for watching birds in trees along the edge, such as this white-throated sparrow photographed from the cabin porch in January. —RD

THE LAYERING PROCESS

The first step in the layering process is to take inventory of existing layers. They're often almost entirely absent in the landscape surrounding a new home, especially one built on former agricultural land. Layers on older, traditionally planted properties are typically lacking in both diversity and without purpose other than ornamentation and screening. In either case, it is necessary to consider which functions the landscape will ideally fulfill, and to make a realistic estimate of the time and resources available for planting and maintenance both at the start and in the future.

The possibilities may seem overwhelming when beginning with a blank slate; however, it is important to establish a few basic divisions of the property and pathways between them at an early stage in the design process. Trees that will eventually form the understory and canopy of various garden spaces will be healthiest and least vulnerable to disease and drought if they are planted at small size. To minimize the time required to attain maturity in the structure of the landscape, canopy and understory trees should be planted as soon as the basic arrangement of garden spaces is determined. If time and budget permit, it is best to plant shrubs at the same time, since this ensures that they will establish their root systems along with the trees.

The herbaceous layer requires the least time to mature and can be planted later; however, if time and budget permit planting at the same time as trees and shrubs, the herbaceous layer will help with weed suppression under woody plants and will also keep the ground cooler and more moist.

When working with an older landscape, the first task is to assess the health and functionality of existing layers and the plants that comprise them. Removal of unwanted woody plants, including trees, shrubs, and vines, should be given high priority since this always requires more effort and resources if performed after new plantings have been made. When deciding what to keep and what to remove, consider how each plant contributes to the landscape. Does it provide summer shade where needed? Is it effective in screening unwanted views or creating necessary privacy? Does it contribute significantly to the garden's seasonal array of color, texture, form, or fragrance? What value does it have for sustaining wildlife by providing cover, shelter, or food? While few plants fulfill all these functions, a living landscape requires a healthy diversity of plants and purposes. In the majority of residential landscapes, the process of restoring layers involves removing lawn. Areas covered with mowed turf can be highly functional; however, most gardens have more areas in lawn than are needed or utilized.

The first step in converting turf to layered plantings is to establish the outline of the new area. This is the ideal task for a garden hose. The flexibility of a hose makes it easy to describe a proposed outline and then study it from different perspectives.

Layering is an incremental process. Removing turf in favor of new plantings should always be balanced with the resources available that season for both planting and maintaining. The great majority of cold-hardy woody and herbaceous plants are best planted or transplanted when they are fully dormant. The window of opportunity extends from late autumn through early spring, whenever the soil is not frozen or too wet to be properly worked. Plants that have been growing outdoors and are cold-hardened benefit from planting as early in the season as possible. This ensures they'll be in their new locations in time for spring rains and increases their chances of establishing new roots before summer heat and potential dry periods begin.

This March photo shows a garden hose being used to define the expanded outline of an area that will be planted with multiple layers.

Commercially purchased plants that have been grown in heated production areas are often too soft and are best planted later when likelihood of damaging frosts or freezes is past.

When describing the new border between lawn and the area being planted, use the hose to make a graceful line that pleases the eye and can easily be followed with whatever mowing equipment will be used on the turf. Inside corners and sharp angles should be avoided since they add to the maintenance time required. Once the border is established, use a sharp spade to cut the turf along the line of the hose. A small rototiller can then be used to chop up the turf, or if the area isn't very large, it can be sliced off with the spade. The turf can be immediately removed for composting. Either of these methods is faster and less toxic than using a herbicide to kill the turf. If working in an area with existing tree roots rototilling should be restricted to the top few inches—just enough to break up the turf.

After the sod is removed and before planting, cover the newly exposed area with a layer of good soil. This might be soil produced in a compost area elsewhere in the garden or soil that you purchase. Spread the soil thick enough to raise the area slightly above the level of the turf, anticipating a small amount of settling.

Once the soil is prepared, the area is ready for planting. If sufficient material is available, it is best to plant all layers together, beginning with trees, then shrubs, then the herbaceous layer. Composted leaf mulch should be applied to retain moisture and suppress weeds if available. If not, commercially available shredded root or bark mulches will stay in place at thinner application rates than wood chips.

Soil with high organic matter content is spread over a new planting area.

This May image a few years later shows the same area with herbaceous, shrub, and understory tree layers well established.

WET AND MOIST SPACES

Until recently, wet and moist places were generally thought of as useless waste places and the typical approach was to drain them, fill them, or otherwise obliterate them. Wet areas on residential properties were judged undesirable. Now, greater awareness of the biological richness and ecosystem functions of such habitats has re-defined wet and moist places as assets.

When present on residential properties wet areas afford unique opportunities to conserve and enhance the biodiversity, function, and beauty of home gardens. The single most important design goal when integrating wet areas in a garden is to keep the edges vegetated. Unless there is genuine necessity for maintaining mowed turf to water's edge, this should be avoided.

Turfed edges inevitably erode and require constant maintenance unless a hard metal or masonry barrier is installed. Vegetated edges are more stable and dramatically increase visual interest and habitat functions. When edge vegetation includes taller woody vegetation, the shade produced lowers water temperatures and generally contributes to a more livable environment for local fauna.

Visual appeal and biological diversity result from well-vegetated edges surrounding a body of water.

OPPOSITE AND BELOW Two mid-October views of the pond at Valley Farm in New York illustrate the beauty and practicality of vegetated edges. Walks maintained in mowed turf provide access to the gazebo and a delightful strolling experience around the pond.

Along with large rocks, a mix of sturdy perennials, shrubs, and trees helps stabilize the edge of a pond at Mt. Cuba Center in Delaware, while providing a wealth of color, structure, and textural interest (far left). The bright yellow drifts (left) are golden ragwort (*Senecio aureus*), a sturdy perennial adapted to moist partly shaded areas that are occasionally inundated. It spreads rhizomes and by self-sowing to create self-perpetuating masses. Shallow areas along the small run feeding the pond provide habitat for tadpoles (center), while painted turtles sunbathe on a log jutting out from the pond edge (below).

TOP A simple but gracefully curved boardwalk at Longwood Gardens provides access to a swampy area populated by skunk cabbage (*Symplocarpus foetidus*), spicebush (*Lindera benzoin*), and other species adapted to continually wet or moist conditions.

ABOVE Gary Smith's design for the south woods edge of Peirce's Woods at Longwood Gardens illustrates how gracefully vegetated edges and be integrated in highly refined landscapes. In late May (left) blue flag iris (*Iris versicolor*) leans over the water, backed by the still-new chartreuse-green foliage of sensitive fern (*Onoclea sensibilis*). In mid-July (right) a green heron fishes from a rocky perch in-between the ferns.

In early June, a small rocky stream running through the Leonard J. Buck garden in New Jersey is cooled by layered
vegetation along its edges. The beautifully textured foliage in the foreground
belongs to royal fern (*Osmunda regalis*).

ABOVE A mixed planting of woodland wild oat (*Chasmanthium latifolium*) and Virginia sweetspire (*Itea virginica*) stabilizes the edge of a pond in a New York garden, illuminated by mid-October sunlight.

The Lepidoptera Trail at the University of Delaware Botanic Garden presents a residential-scale model of walkable garden spaces planted to sustain a wide variety of local butterflies, skippers, and moths, as well as the birds that eat them. Grass paths provide a strolling experience through layered plantings and around a very small central pond.

This mid-July photo (above) shows a tiger swallowtail on hollowstem Joe-Pye weed (*Eupatorium fistulosum*) while swamp milkweed (*Asclepias incarnata*) blooms next to it. Two other Joe-Pye weeds, the white-flowered *E. fistulosum* 'Bartered Bride' and deep pink-purple *E. dubium*, have begun blooming around the pond in background, with a sweep of golden-yellow cutleaf coneflower (*Rudbeckia laciniata*) behind them. Wet and moist spots in the garden afford the chance to cultivate uncommonly grown species that really do need regular moisture, such as this monkeyflower (*Mimulus ringens*) in full bloom by mid-July around the pond edge (top), or cardinal flower (*Lobelia cardinalis*), still blooming in late July along with swamp milkweeds and Joe-Pye weeds (left).

MEADOW GARDENS

As previously discussed, in North America east of the Mississippi River meadows and open grasslands occur primarily due to human activity. Except for unusually dry places prone to wild fires, extremely wet places, and coastal areas where sand and salt limits woody growth, this part of the continent is dominated by woodlands. Consequently, unless there are similarly limiting site conditions, meadow gardens require regular effort to maintain them in primarily herbaceous vegetation. They are best thought of as large-scale perennial gardens embracing a more-casual-than-usual aesthetic.

Control of unwanted woody re-growth can be accomplished by periodic mowing, burning (where practical and where local ordinances permit), and spot removal of woody plants by mechanical or chemical means. Burning can be effective if the fuel load is sufficient to produce a fire hot enough to kill woody species. This usually requires more than one-year's growth, otherwise the fire will reduce only the herbaceous vegetation and mowing or spot removal will still be required to eliminate woody plants.

The amount of effort required to control woody and herbaceous weeds is directly proportional to the richness of the soil. Highly fertile, moist organic soils will produce lush growth of desirable and undesirable species. Low-nutrient, drier soils will limit the diversity of desirable species that can be grown but will also reduce the establishment of many weedy species.

There are two broad categories of meadow gardens: those that are comprised primarily or exclusively of broad-leafed perennials and those that are made up primarily of perennial grasses. When sufficient space and sunlight is available, trees and shrubs may also be integrated in meadow gardens.

At their best, meadow gardens provide unique visual and functional elements to gardens that are distinct from layered woodland plantings. When properly managed, meadow gardens add significantly to a landscape's wildlife habitat value.

Especially in larger meadow gardens, matching plants to varied conditions on the site is essential to reduce or eliminate the need for irrigation and to keep maintenance at sustainable levels.

While goldenrods and Joe-Pye weeds are well suited for their functional role in a meadow garden, they also provide food for wildlife.

The presence of birds in meadow gardens requires property managers to carefully think through the best time to mow, if that is part of the maintenance schedule. Eastern meadowlarks, like other grassland birds, nest directly on the ground. Nests escape predation by secrecy and because parents run through vegetation a good distance from the nest before flying rather than flying directly up from or to the nest, which would alert predators to its whereabouts. This predator avoidance behavior restricts meadowlarks to nesting where clump-forming warm-season bunchgrasses and forbs create a maze of escape routes in-between the clumps.

Unlike North American clump-forming species such as Indian grass, broomsedge, little bluestem, big bluestem (*Andropogon gerardii*), switchgrass (*Panicum virgatum*), and prairie dropseed (*Sporobolus heterolepis*), cool season Eurasian grasses that spread by stolons create a continuous cover that is too dense to allow the birds to run through. Areas covered with such grasses are typically rejected as breeding sites. Grassland nesters such as meadowlarks also face danger from mowing during the breeding season.

Ground-nesting birds set up territories and begin breeding in late April depending upon how far north you live. Mowing in May and June should be avoided since this is the time baby birds are most likely to be in ground nests. When possible, it is best to mow in late March or early April and then postpone any future mowings until August.

The meadow in the Robertson garden in Delaware is alive with butterflies, other insects and birds in this mid-August photo. It is planted entirely with sturdy broad-leafed perennial species adapted to the site, including New York ironweed (*Vernonia noveboracensis*), boneset (*Eupatorium perfoliatum*), Joe-Pye weeds (*Eupatorium* species), and goldenrods (*Solidago* species). Mowed grass paths invite strolling through this sunny space edged by woodland.

ABOVE AND OPPOSITE TOP Vegetation in the meadow garden at Longwood Gardens is naturally arranged in accord with moisture conditions. In this view taken in late September in a dry year, a mix of hollowstem Joe-Pye weed (*Eupatorium fistulosum*) and purple-stem aster (*Aster puniceus*) occupies most of the wet area in foreground (above). Grasses including Indian grass (*Sorghastrum nutans*) and little bluestem (*Schizachyrium scoparium*) mix with goldenrods further up the slope where the soil is relatively dry.

Another view in late September, taken in a year with greater rainfall, shows goldenrods still blooming strongly as Joe-Pye weeds, bluestem asters, and New England asters (*Aster novae-angliae*) are about to go to seed in a low relatively moist part of the meadow (top right). The beautiful patterns evident in this image are largely the result of deliberately established plant populations being allowed to self-sow in response to site conditions.

RIGHT In late July, a catbird hunts for meadow insects while clinging to Joe-Pye weed.

FAR RIGHT Anyone who has looked closely at a large population of goldenrods has probably seen one of these galls. The gall is formed in response to the presence of a goldenrod gall fly larva. A downy woodpecker seeks the fat and proteins in this morsel, which are in relatively short supply in winter. Because birds depend upon such stem-boring insects and gall-makers, as well as all the seeds a meadow produces, it is important to allow herbaceous vegetation to remain standing until spring arrives.

AVOVE AND OPPOSITE TOP
Warm-season clump-forming North American grasses including little bluestem (*Schizachyrium scoparium*), broom sedge (*Andropogon virginicus*), and Indian grass (*Sorghastrum nutans*) dominate the meadow garden at Mt. Cuba Center in Delaware in this late-September view . Though a few broad-leafed perennials are interspersed, most of them are planted at the edges where they have a better chance of persisting, removed from direct competition from the grasses (top right).

BOTTOM RIGHT Meadowlark chicks in a prairie-grass planting in Illinois. Just four years earlier, the site had been a cornfield.

This small meadow garden at our Pennsylvania home consists of a matrix of clump-forming native grasses with very sturdy broad-leaved perennials interspersed. These include the bold-textured cup plant (*Silphium perfoliatum*) and heavily rhizomatous common milkweed (*Asclepias syriaca*), both of which are strong enough to persist indefinitely despite competition from the grasses. The milkweed was established by releasing seed into the grass planting. Each year as it reaches its flowering peak in June it is covered with bees and butterflies. Later in the season, it provides food for countless monarch larvae. —RD

LEFT A monarch butterfly larva feeds on milkweed in late August.

ABOVE Pipevine swallowtails and bees take nectar and pollen from swamp thistle (*Cirsium muticum*) in a North Carolina meadow in August. Though this native thistle provides important summer sustenance for the adult swallowtails in summer, the swallowtails would not be present in this landscape if their larval food source, pipevine (*Aristolochia macrophylla*), wasn't present nearby along the meadow's shady woodland edge.

Meadow gardens don't have to be extensive, as demonstrated by this planting around the carport in the Barton garden in Pennsylvania (left). The mix of grasses and broad-leaved perennials provides the perfect textural foil for the mid-century modern architecture and helps connect the interior of the garden to wilder grassy areas at the periphery, as seen in this view from inside the carport (above).

The Tallamys' home habitat in mid-October.

Celebrating Life in a Managed Landscape

Not long ago Cindy and I had a surprise visit from pair of spicebush swallowtails as we tackled our morning pancakes. The swallowtails had decided to mate on a sassafras leaf not 10 inches beyond our window. They rested for a few minutes, and then separated. The male flew off but the female lingered to lay a single green egg on the leaf. The butterflies were beautiful, but I think most of our pleasure came from the element of surprise. We were not expecting to witness spicebush swallowtail reproduction during breakfast; but when we were granted an intimate window to the life of one of the many residents of our landscape, it put a smile on our faces. We could watch our swallowtails during breakfast because we had not pulled the sassafras from our garden when it seeded in as a volunteer six years earlier. It now stands 12 feet high and provides dappled shade for our dining room.

There are two features of our approach to landscaping that we have found enormously entertaining. The first is the element of surprise that Rick describes in the introduction of this chapter and that our swallowtail encounter illustrates so well. When we venture into our yard, we never know what we might find. Our yard is so full of life and

A mating pair of spicebush swallowtails clings to a sassafras branch while the male transfers his nutrient-laden spermatophore to the female.

ABOVE Cindy and I have learned that a mosaic of woodlands, meadow and wetlands produces the highest diversity of life, and since life entertains us, restoring these plant communities has been our goal. Compare the October 2007 aerial view of our property (page 280) with this June 2013 view. We have not allowed the proportion of the landscape in meadow, young trees, and lawn to change in the last 6 years, but note the rate at which the trees are growing. The white oak that we planted as an acorn in our driveway circle 13 years ago is now 20 feet tall and has become a contributing member of the local ecosystem.

RIGHT An indigo bunting clings to a goldenrod while foraging in our meadow area.

wildness that encounters with the unexpected are, in fact, expected: the woodcock that explodes into flight at our feet as we walk along one of our paths in April; the blue jay that streaks by on an October day with its beak and throat stuffed with acorns; the royal walnut moth caterpillar that hangs regally from our fringe tree in July, defying my claim that we will never be lucky enough to find this declining species at our house.

Unexpected encounters in our landscape are exciting, memorable, and just plain fun, and they regularly draw us into our yard to experience them, but equally rewarding is the anticipation created by what we *do* expect to happen each year. So many of the plants and animals that comprise our landscape execute their life histories in such predictable ways that we have come to look forward to these seasonal events as if they were approaching holidays. When will the first American toads sing? When will the juncos and white-throated sparrows arrive from the north in the fall and when will they leave in the spring? What week will the magnolia, black pole, palm, and black-throated green warblers pass through our yard on their way to breed in the northern conifer forests, and when will this year's fox kits first come tumbling out of their den in our front yard? When will the bloodroot, spice-bush, and spring beauties bloom? When will the white oaks that we planted as acorns first produce their own acorns? What year will the zebra swallowtail first discover our pawpaws, and on what day will our bluebirds fledge their first brood of young? Cindy and I find comfort and hope in the dependability of natural cycles; to us they are the fulfilled promises of a vibrant landscape.

Our approach to organizing and managing our property has been guided in part by our goal of restoring ecological function to an exhausted piece of farmland, and in part by our hope to experience the many forms of life such a restoration would attract. We have tried to create a mosaic of meadow, late-successional, and woodland habitats on a site that until recently was mowed for hay.

This meant replacing the less-productive plant species from Asia that dominated our landscape when we moved in with indigenous woody and herbaceous plants that actively contribute to our local food web.

But to experience the ecosystems we were shaping we needed access to our woods, our meadows, our marsh, and our transitional zones. Mowed paths of turf grass have served this purpose well: our paths and the plant communities they traverse are the organic architecture that organize our landscape. With the exception of one rock wall that I occasionally putter with, we have no hardscape at all. The placement of the paths in our landscape has been determined as much by the topography of the land as by our desire to reach particular destinations. Above all, our paths are dynamic. As our plantings have matured, we have not hesitated to move a path from here to there, if for no other reason than to keep the design and the experience fresh.

A bluejay flies with an acorn just plucked from an oak.

We have added many plants to our landscape over the last 12 years, but many more have taken up residence without our help. Each year our squirrels plant new black walnut and hickory trees from nuts they have gathered from three mature trees that once lined a fence on the original farm. Our single patch of mayapples has grown to three widely separated patches, undoubtedly due to the efforts of our seed-dispersing box turtles. Cindy has learned that if she clears Japanese honeysuckle from a small patch of ground in the fall, blue jays will invariably find that patch and use it to store their winter cache of acorns and beechnuts. Since they only recover a fourth of what they cache, blue jays have planted many of our oaks and beeches.

Our kingbirds, mockingbirds and cedar waxwings have spread alternate-leaf dogwoods, eastern red cedars, and black cherries throughout the property, and each spring the March wind covers our land with new sycamore seeds blown in from mature trees nearly a mile away. Even the deer that we fail to discourage pay us back with a few persimmon seedlings each spring. We continue to selectively weed the Asian plants that find their way onto our property, and we occasionally edit a tree that has grown to disrupt the view that we enjoy, but the design, diversity, and abundance of the plants in our landscape are very much the result of a collaboration between the Tallamys and natural processes. **—DT**

LEFT AND ABOVE RIGHT In addition to our small traditional lawn, we use turf grasses in mowed paths that guide us through our landscape. The paths allow us to monitor the progress of our restoration and experience the garden's current inhabitants close at hand. In these late-June photos, dappled sunlight enhances the beauty of the layered vegetation of one of our paths (left), while a daddy long-legs hunts from a leaf of beebalm (*Monarda didyma*) (above right).

RIGHT An orchard oriole finds safety within the dense foliage of an oak we planted to enrich the canopy layer in our landscape.

With visual power to match the most elaborate of designs, this focal point in a New York garden has humble origins. The circle of light (opposite) began as a simple horse trail through the indigenous woods of a working farm. It is still a riding trail. Follow it to the other side and the beech-oak woods opens on salt marsh (above). Look up and you might catch a great egret flying overhead (left). These three images were taken sequentially in early November, attesting to the authenticity and appeal of a landscape that celebrates the cultural layers while preserving functionality and conserving habitat for local flora and fauna. It's an elegant, artful example of a landscape combining beauty, biodiversity, and function: a landscape designed for life.

Landscape and Ecological Functions of Plants for the Mid-Atlantic Including All the Plants Featured in This Book

EXPANDED KEY

COVER FOR WILDLIFE Plant is used by wildlife for shelter and protection.

NEST SITES FOR BIRDS Plant is used by birds for building nests.

POLLEN Plant produces pollen for bees, beetles, flies, and caterpillars.

NECTAR Plant produces nectar for bees, butterflies, and hummingbirds.

WINTERING BIRDS Plant provides nuts, seeds, berries, and other food for wintering birds.

BREEDING BIRDS Plant provides nuts, seeds, berries, and other food for breeding birds.

SPRING MIGRANT BIRDS Plant provides nuts, seeds, berries, and other food for spring migrants.

FALL MIGRANT BIRDS Plant provides nuts, seeds, berries, and other food for fall migrants.

FOOD FOR MAMMALS Plant provides food for a variety of wildlife including squirrels, chipmunks, raccoons, opossums, and foxes.

FOOD FOR CATERPILLARS Plant has foliage that sustains various species of caterpillars.

SEQUESTERS CARBON Tree has potential for absorbing carbon dioxide.

SPRING FLOWERS Plant has *significantly* attractive flowers in spring.

SUMMER FLOWERS Plant has *significantly* attractive flowers in summer.

FALL FLOWERS Plant has *significantly* attractive flowers in fall.

FALL FOLIAGE COLOR Plant foliage turns color in fall and is ornamental.

FRAGRANCE Plant has a noticeable and pleasant fragrance.

EVERGREEN GROUND COVER Plant can be used as evergreen ground cover.

DECIDUOUS GROUND COVER Plant can be used as deciduous ground cover.

SCREENING Plant can be used as evergreen screening.

SHADE/COOLING A shrub or tree that creates significant shade, which can be used to reduce the temperature in the area it covers.

EDIBLE FRUITS FOR HUMAN CONSUMPTION Plant has fruit that is safe (and tasty) for people to consume.

NOTES Includes plant origin if not native to North America and indicates the plant's main ecological or landscape function.

BOTANICAL NAME	COMMON NAME	ECOLOGICAL FUNCTIONS
TREES		
Acer negundo	box elder	🐦 ▣ ❄ 🐦 🦅 🕊 🕊 🌰 🐛
Acer pensylvanicum	striped maple	🐦 ▣ 🐝 🕊
Acer rubrum	red maple	🐦 ▣ 🐝 🕊 🦅 🕊 🕊 🌰 🐛 🌲
Acer saccharum	sugar maple	🐦 ▣ 🐝 🕊 🦅 🕊 🕊 🌰 🐛 🌲
Acer spicatum	mountain maple	🐦 ▣ 🐝 🕊
Amelanchier arborea	downy serviceberry, shadblow serviceberry	🐝 🕊 🦅 🕊 🐛
Amelanchier canadensis	shadbush	🐝 🕊 🦅 🕊 🐛
Amelanchier ×grandiflora	shadbush	🐝 🕊 🦅 🕊 🐛
Amelanchier laevis	smooth serviceberry	🐝 🕊 🦅 🕊 🐛
Betula alleghaniensis	yellow birch	❄ 🦅 🕊 🕊 🕊 🐛
Betula lenta	sweet birch	❄ 🦅 🕊 🕊 🕊 🐛
Betula nigra	river birch	❄ 🐦 🦅 🕊 🐛
Betula populifolia	gray birch	❄ 🐦 🦅 🕊 🐛
Carpinus caroliniana	ironwood	🐦 ▣ 🦅 🕊 🌰 🐛
Carya glabra	pignut hickory	🐦 ▣ 🦅 🕊 🕊 🌰 🐛 🌲
Carya laciniosa	shellbark hickory	🐦 ▣ 🦅 🕊 🕊 🌰 🐛 🌲
Carya ovata	shagbark hickory	🐦 ▣ 🦅 🕊 🕊 🌰 🐛 🌲
Celtis occidentalis	common hackberry	🐝 🕊 ❄ 🦅 🕊 🕊 🐛
Cercidiphyllum japonicum	katsura	🐦 ▣
Cercis canadensis	redbud	🐝 🕊
Chamaecyparis thyoides	Atlantic white cedar	🐦 🌲

LANDSCAPE FUNCTIONS	NOTES
	provides excellent cover and nest sites in riparian corridors
	good understory cover for wildlife
	supports nearly 300 species of caterpillars
	supports 300 species of caterpillars
	good understory cover for wildlife
	first to make fruits in summer; supports 124 species of caterpillars
	first to make fruits in summer; supports 124 species of caterpillars
	first to make fruits in summer; supports 124 species of caterpillars
	first to make fruits in summer; supports 124 species of caterpillars
	supports 411 species of caterpillars; distilled sap used in brewing birch beer
	supports 411 species of caterpillars; distilled sap used in brewing birch beer
	useful along stream banks; supports 411 species of caterpillars
	supports 411 species of caterpillars
	good understory cover; supports 68 species of caterpillars
	produces nutritious nuts for many mammals; supports 235 species of caterpillars
	produces nutritious nuts for many mammals; supports 235 species of caterpillars
	produces nutritious nuts for many mammals; supports 235 species of caterpillars
	several butterfly species develop only on *Celtis*
	native to East Asia; dense foliage shelters nesting birds
	excellent early spring source of pollen and nectar for bees
	useful along streambanks; larval host for rare Hessel's hairstreak

ECOLOGICAL FUNCTIONS

- cover for wildlife
- nest sites for birds
- pollen producer
- nectar producer
- food for wintering birds
- food for breeding birds
- food for spring migrant birds
- food for fall migrant birds
- food for mammals
- food for caterpillars
- sequesters carbon

LANDSCAPE FUNCTIONS

- spring flowers
- summer flowers
- fall flowers
- fall foliage color
- fragrance
- evergreen ground cover
- deciduous ground cover
- screening
- shade and cooling
- edible fruits for humans

BOTANICAL NAME	COMMON NAME	ECOLOGICAL FUNCTIONS
TREES, continued		
Chionanthus virginicus	fringe tree	
Cladrastis kentukea	American yellowwood	
Cornus alternifolia	alternate-leaf dogwood	
Cornus florida	flowering dogwood	
Cotinus obovatus	American smoketree	
Diospyros virginiana	persimmon	
Euonymus atropurpureus	eastern wahoo	
Fagus grandifolia	American beech	
Fraxinus americana	white ash	
Fraxinus pennsylvanica	green ash	
Ginkgo biloba	ginkgo	
Halesia diptera **var.** *magniflora*	large-flowered two-winged silverbell	
Halesia tetraptera	silverbell	
Ilex opaca	American holly	
Juniperus virginiana	eastern red cedar	
Liquidambar styraciflua	sweet gum	
Liriodendron tulipifera	tulip tree	
Magnolia fraseri	Fraser's magnolia	
Magnolia tripetala	umbrella magnolia	
Magnolia virginiana	sweetbay magnolia	
Nyssa sylvatica	black gum	

LANDSCAPE FUNCTIONS	NOTES
	provides good understory shelter
	valuable source of pollen and nectar for bees
	heavy berry producer in midsummer
	nutritious berries are favorites of wintering birds
	seeds are favorites of wintering finches
	fruits feed mammals, turkeys, and many songbirds in the fall
	fruits eaten by many birds
	beechnuts support many mammals and are critical forage for turkeys; foliage supports 125 species of caterpillars
	seeds are favorites of grosbeaks and finches; leaves support 149 species of caterpillars
	seeds are favorites of grosbeaks and finches; leaves support 149 species of caterpillars
	native to China; long-lived, large tree that sequesters tons of carbon; roasted seeds are edible
	blooms are favorites of bumblebees
	blooms are favorites of bumblebees
	red drupes are a staple for many wintering birds
	juniper cones provide important winter food for cedar waxwings; foliage supports many specialist butterflies like the juniper hairstreak; berry-like cones used in flavoring gin
	tiny seeds are favorites of wintering finches; leaves host beauties like the luna moth
	copious seed production supports rodents and ground birds
	seeds eaten by mammals and ground birds
	seeds eaten by mammals and ground birds
	host to sweetbay silk moth
	fruits important for wintering birds

ECOLOGICAL FUNCTIONS

- cover for wildlife
- nest sites for birds
- pollen producer
- nectar producer
- food for wintering birds
- food for breeding birds
- food for spring migrant birds
- food for fall migrant birds
- food for mammals
- food for caterpillars
- sequesters carbon

LANDSCAPE FUNCTIONS

- spring flowers
- summer flowers
- fall flowers
- fall foliage color
- fragrance
- evergreen ground cover
- deciduous ground cover
- screening
- shade and cooling
- edible fruits for humans

BOTANICAL NAME	COMMON NAME	ECOLOGICAL FUNCTIONS
TREES, continued		
Ostrya virginiana	American hop hornbeam	
Oxydendrum arboreum	sourwood	
Pinus rigida	pitch pine	
Pinus strobus	white pine	
Pinus virginiana	Virginia pine	
Platanus occidentalis	American sycamore	
Populus deltoides	eastern cottonwood	
Quercus alba	white oak	
Quercus bicolor	swamp white oak	
Quercus coccinea	scarlet oak	
Quercus falcata	southern red oak	
Quercus macrocarpa	burr oak	
Quercus marilandica	blackjack oak	
Quercus montana	chestnut oak	
Quercus palustris	pin oak	
Quercus phellos	willow oak	
Quercus rubra	red oak	
Quercus velutina	black oak	
Salix nigra	black willow	
Sassafras albidum	sassafras	

LANDSCAPE FUNCTIONS	NOTES
	nutlets support wintering birds and mammals; foliage supports 94 species of caterpillars
	honey produced from sourwood nectar is highly coveted
	seeds provide significant wintering food for many mammals and birds; supports 210 species of caterpillars
	seeds provide significant wintering food for many mammals and birds; supports 210 species of caterpillars
	seeds provide significant wintering food for many mammals and birds; supports 210 species of caterpillars
	useful along stream banks; finches love seeds; hosts 45 species of common caterpillars
	supports 367 caterpillar species
	the best species measured to date in providing caterpillars (557 species) and acorns for mammals and ground birds
	excellent source of caterpillars (557 species) and mast for mammals
	excellent source of caterpillars (557 species) and mast for mammals
	excellent source of caterpillars (557 species) and mast for mammals
	excellent source of caterpillars (557 species) and mast for mammals
	excellent source of caterpillars (557 species) and mast for mammals
	excellent source of caterpillars (557 species) and mast for mammals
	excellent source of caterpillars (557 species) and mast for mammals
	excellent source of caterpillars (557 species) and mast for mammals
	excellent source of caterpillars (557 species) and mast for mammals
	excellent source of caterpillars (557 species) and mast for mammals
	useful along stream banks; excellent source of caterpillars, supporting 455 species
	many birds use fruits in late summer; hosts the spicebush swallowtail larva; pith called file used in thickening gumbo

ECOLOGICAL FUNCTIONS

- cover for wildlife
- nest sites for birds
- pollen producer
- nectar producer
- food for wintering birds
- food for breeding birds
- food for spring migrant birds
- food for fall migrant birds
- food for mammals
- food for caterpillars
- sequesters carbon

LANDSCAPE FUNCTIONS

- spring flowers
- summer flowers
- fall flowers
- fall foliage color
- fragrance
- evergreen ground cover
- deciduous ground cover
- screening
- shade and cooling
- edible fruits for humans

BOTANICAL NAME	COMMON NAME	ECOLOGICAL FUNCTIONS
TREES, continued		
Tilia americana	basswood	
Ulmus americana	American elm (blight-resistant variety)	
Ulmus rubra	slippery elm	
SHRUBS		
Aesculus parviflora	bottlebrush buckeye	
Alnus serrulata	smooth alder	
Amorpha fruticosa	false indigo	
Arctostaphylos uva-ursi	bearberry	
Aronia arbutifolia	red chokeberry	
Aronia melanocarpa	black chokeberry	
Asimina triloba	pawpaw	
Baccharis halimifolia	groundsel bush	
Calycanthus floridus	sweet shrub	
Calycanthus floridus 'Michael Lindsey'	sweet shrub	
Ceanothus americanus	New Jersey tea	
Cephalanthus occidentalis	buttonbush	
Chamaedaphne calyculata	leatherleaf	
Clethra acuminata	cinnamonbark clethra	
Clethra alnifolia	sweet pepper bush	
Comptonia peregrina	sweet fern	
Cornus amomum	silky dogwood	
Cornus racemosa	gray dogwood	

LANDSCAPE FUNCTIONS	NOTES
	supports 149 species of caterpillars
	supports 215 species of caterpillars
	supports 215 species of caterpillars
	superior nectar plant for butterflies
	useful along stream banks; supports 255 species of caterpillars as well as many sawfly larvae
	larval host for several butterfly species; excellent nectar and pollen source for native bees
	dense ground cover that produces berries for wildlife
	good all-around wildlife plant producing cover, fruits, and 29 species of caterpillars for birds
	fruits can be used to make jams and jellies; good all-around wildlife plant producing cover, fruits, and 29 species of caterpillars for birds
	sole larval host for zebra swallowtail
	good late season source of pollen and nectar
	good understory shrub in southern regions
	good understory shrub in southern regions
	supports 43 species of caterpillars
	useful along stream banks; ideal for nectaring butterflies
	supports bumblebee pollinators
	useful along stream banks; ideal for nectaring butterflies
	useful along stream banks; ideal for nectaring butterflies
	supports 64 species of caterpillars including the grey hairstreak
	great resource for pollinators and berry eaters
	great resource for pollinators and berry eaters

ECOLOGICAL FUNCTIONS

- cover for wildlife
- nest sites for birds
- pollen producer
- nectar producer
- food for wintering birds
- food for breeding birds
- food for spring migrant birds
- food for fall migrant birds
- food for mammals
- food for caterpillars
- sequesters carbon

LANDSCAPE FUNCTIONS

- spring flowers
- summer flowers
- fall flowers
- fall foliage color
- fragrance
- evergreen ground cover
- deciduous ground cover
- screening
- shade and cooling
- edible fruits for humans

BOTANICAL NAME	COMMON NAME	ECOLOGICAL FUNCTIONS
SHRUBS, continued		
Cornus sericea	redstem dogwood, red osier dogwood	[bee] [hummingbird] [winter bird] [caterpillar]
Corylus americana	American hazelnut	[ground cover] [small mammal] [nut] [caterpillar]
Dirca palustris	leatherwood	[ground cover] [small mammal] [bee] [hummingbird]
Euonymus americanus	American strawberry bush	[winter bird]
Fothergilla ×intermedia	fothergilla	[bee] [hummingbird]
Gaultheria procumbens	teaberry, wintergreen	[bee] [hummingbird]
Gaylussacia baccata	black huckleberry	[bee] [hummingbird] [bird in flight]
Hamamelis virginiana	witch hazel	[ground cover] [small mammal] [caterpillar]
Hydrangea arborescens	smooth hydrangea	[ground cover] [small mammal] [bee] [hummingbird]
Hydrangea quercifolia	oakleaf hydrangea	[ground cover] [small mammal] [bee] [hummingbird]
Ilex crenata	Japanese holly	[ground cover] [small mammal] [bee] [hummingbird]
Ilex decidua	possum haw	[ground cover] [small mammal] [bee] [hummingbird] [winter bird]
Ilex glabra	inkberry	[ground cover] [small mammal] [bee] [hummingbird] [winter bird]
Ilex glabra 'Densa'		[ground cover] [small mammal] [bee] [hummingbird] [winter bird]
Ilex opaca	American holly	[ground cover] [small mammal] [bee] [hummingbird] [winter bird]
Ilex verticillata	winterberry	[ground cover] [small mammal] [bee] [hummingbird] [winter bird]
Itea virginica	Virginia sweetspire	[bee] [hummingbird]
Kalmia angustifolia	sheep laurel	[bee] [hummingbird]
Kalmia latifolia	mountain laurel	[bee] [hummingbird]
Leucothoë axillaris	coast leucothoe	[bee] [hummingbird]
Leucothoë fontanesiana	drooping leucothoe	[bee] [hummingbird]

LANDSCAPE FUNCTIONS	NOTES
[spring flowers]	bark brightly colored in winter; berries valuable fall/winter bird food
[spring flowers] [fall foliage color] [shade and cooling] [edible fruits]	foliage supports 125 species of caterpillars; nuts valuable forage for mammals and ground birds
[spring flowers] [fall foliage color]	useful source of pollen and nectar along stream banks
[fall foliage color]	fleshy arils eaten by several bird species
[spring flowers] [fall foliage color] [fragrance]	attractive flowers attract many pollinators
[spring flowers] [evergreen ground cover] [edible fruits]	valuable source of pollen and nectar for bumblebees
[spring flowers] [fall foliage color] [deciduous ground cover]	valuable source of pollen, nectar, and fruit
[spring flowers] [fall foliage color] [fragrance] [shade and cooling]	supports 62 species of caterpillars; extracts used medicinally
[spring flowers] [fall flowers]	good source of midsummer pollen and nectar
[spring flowers] [fall flowers] [fall foliage color]	good source of early summer pollen and nectar
[screening]	native to East Asia; dense shrub provides cover
[fall foliage color]	excellent pollen and nectar source for native bees; produces copious berries for winter birds
[screening]	excellent pollen and nectar source for native bees; produces copious berries for winter birds
[screening]	excellent pollen and nectar source for native bees; produces copious berries for winter birds
[screening] [shade and cooling]	excellent pollen and nectar source for native bees; produces copious berries for winter birds
[fall foliage color]	useful along stream banks; colorful berries last through winter, sustaining bluebirds, mockingbirds, hermit thrushes, waxwings, and robins
[spring flowers] [fall foliage color] [fragrance] [deciduous ground cover]	excellent source of pollen and nectar for native bees
[spring flowers] [fall flowers] [evergreen ground cover]	some value for pollinators
[spring flowers] [screening]	some value for pollinators
[spring flowers] [fragrance] [evergreen ground cover]	supports bumblebee pollinators
[spring flowers] [fragrance] [evergreen ground cover]	supports bumblebee pollinators

ECOLOGICAL FUNCTIONS

- cover for wildlife
- nest sites for birds
- pollen producer
- nectar producer
- food for wintering birds
- food for breeding birds
- food for spring migrant birds
- food for fall migrant birds
- food for mammals
- food for caterpillars
- sequesters carbon

LANDSCAPE FUNCTIONS

- spring flowers
- summer flowers
- fall flowers
- fall foliage color
- fragrance
- evergreen ground cover
- deciduous ground cover
- screening
- shade and cooling
- edible fruits for humans

BOTANICAL NAME	COMMON NAME	ECOLOGICAL FUNCTIONS
SHRUBS, continued		
Lindera benzoin	spicebush	
Neviusia alabamensis	Alabama snow wreath	
Physocarpus opulifolius	common ninebark	
Rhododendron arborescens	sweet azalea	
Rhododendron atlanticum	coastal azalea	
Rhododendron austrinum	Florida flame azalea	
Rhododendron calendulaceum	flame azalea	
Rhododendron canescens	Piedmont azalea	
Rhododendron maximum	great laurel, rosebay rhododendron	
Rhododendron periclymenoides	pink azalea, pinxter azalea	
Rhododendron prinophyllum	roseshell azalea	
Rhododendron vaseyi	pinkshell azalea	
Rhododendron viscosum	swamp azalea	
Rhus aromatica	fragrant sumac	
Rhus copallina	winged sumac	
Rhus glabra	smooth sumac	
Rhus typhina	staghorn sumac	
Rosa blanda	meadow rose	
Rosa carolina	Carolina rose	
Rosa palustris	swamp rose	
Rosa setigera	prairie rose	
Rosa virginiana	Virginia rose	
Salix discolor	pussy willow	

LANDSCAPE FUNCTIONS	NOTES
	berries support fall migrants; larval host for spicebush swallowtail
	offers pollen and nectar to pollinators
	supports 50 species of caterpillars
	supports 50 species of caterpillars
	supports 50 species of caterpillars
	supports 50 species of caterpillars
	supports 50 species of caterpillars
	supports 50 species of caterpillars
	valuable cover for wildlife
	supports 50 species of caterpillars
	supports 50 species of caterpillars
	supports 50 species of caterpillars
	supports 50 species of caterpillars
	makes nutritious berries for wintering birds; supports 54 species of caterpillars
	makes nutritious berries for wintering birds; supports 54 species of caterpillars
	makes nutritious berries for wintering birds; supports 54 species of caterpillars
	makes nutritious berries for wintering birds; supports 54 species of caterpillars
	serves as larval host for 135 species of caterpillars
	serves as larval host for 135 species of caterpillars
	serves as larval host for 135 species of caterpillars
	serves as larval host for 135 species of caterpillars
	serves as larval host for 135 species of caterpillars
	useful along stream banks; hosts 455 species of caterpillars

ECOLOGICAL FUNCTIONS

- cover for wildlife
- nest sites for birds
- pollen producer
- nectar producer
- food for wintering birds
- food for breeding birds
- food for spring migrant birds
- food for fall migrant birds
- food for mammals
- food for caterpillars
- sequesters carbon

LANDSCAPE FUNCTIONS

- spring flowers
- summer flowers
- fall flowers
- fall foliage color
- fragrance
- evergreen ground cover
- deciduous ground cover
- screening
- shade and cooling
- edible fruits for humans

BOTANICAL NAME	COMMON NAME	ECOLOGICAL FUNCTIONS
SHRUBS, continued		
Salix sericea	silky willow	
Sambucus canadensis	elderberry	
Spiraea alba	white meadowsweet	
Spiraea tomentosa	steeplebush	
Vaccinium angustifolium	lowbush blueberry	
Vaccinium corymbosum	highbush blueberry	
Viburnum acerifolium	mapleleaf viburnum	
Viburnum dentatum	arrowwood viburnum	
Viburnum nudum	smooth witherod, possumhaw	
Viburnum nudum 'Winterthur'		
Viburnum prunifolium	blackhaw	
Xanthorhiza simplicissima	yellowroot	
Zamia pumila	coontie	
WOODY VINES		
Bignonia capreolata	cross vine	
Campsis radicans	trumpet vine	
Clematis virginiana	virgin's bower	
Lonicera sempervirens	coral honeysuckle	
Parthenocissus quinquefolia	Virginia creeper	
Phoradendron serotinum	mistletoe	
Wisteria frutescens	American wisteria	

LANDSCAPE FUNCTIONS	NOTES
[shade and cooling]	useful along stream banks; hosts 455 species of caterpillars
[spring flowers] [summer flowers] [edible fruits for humans]	fruit can be used in making preserves, jams, and wine; fruits also support fledged birds
[spring flowers] [summer flowers]	useful along stream banks; supports 89 species of caterpillars
[spring flowers]	useful along stream banks; supports 89 species of caterpillars
[summer flowers] [fall foliage color] [deciduous ground cover] [edible fruits for humans]	copious fruits for birds and mammals; hosts 294 species of caterpillars
[summer flowers] [fall foliage color] [edible fruits for humans]	copious fruits for birds and mammals; hosts 294 species of caterpillars
[spring flowers] [fall foliage color]	excellent source of berries and caterpillars for birds
[spring flowers] [fall foliage color]	excellent source of berries and caterpillars for birds
[summer flowers] [fall foliage color]	excellent source of berries and caterpillars for birds
[spring flowers] [fall foliage color]	excellent source of berries and caterpillars for birds
[summer flowers] [fall foliage color]	excellent source of berries and caterpillars for birds
[spring flowers] [fall foliage color] [deciduous ground cover]	good ground cover
[evergreen ground cover]	native to Florida, Cuba, and West Indies; larval host for Atala butterfly
[spring flowers]	excellent source of late summer nectar and pollen for butterflies and bees
[summer flowers]	excellent source of late summer nectar and pollen for butterflies and bees
[fall flowers]	excellent source of late summer nectar and pollen for butterflies and bees
[spring flowers] [fall flowers]	excellent source of late summer nectar and pollen for butterflies and bees
[fall foliage color] [deciduous ground cover]	excellent source of late summer nectar and pollen for butterflies and bees
	excellent source of late summer nectar and pollen for butterflies and bees
[fall flowers]	excellent source of late summer nectar and pollen for butterflies and bees

ECOLOGICAL FUNCTIONS

- cover for wildlife
- nest sites for birds
- pollen producer
- nectar producer
- food for wintering birds
- food for breeding birds
- food for spring migrant birds
- food for fall migrant birds
- food for mammals
- food for caterpillars
- sequesters carbon

LANDSCAPE FUNCTIONS

- spring flowers
- summer flowers
- fall flowers
- fall foliage color
- fragrance
- evergreen ground cover
- deciduous ground cover
- screening
- shade and cooling
- edible fruits for humans

BOTANICAL NAME	COMMON NAME	ECOLOGICAL FUNCTIONS
BROADLEAVED HERBACEOUS PLANTS PLUS BULBS		
Aconitum uncinatum	eastern monkshood	🐝 🐦
Actaea pachypoda	white baneberry	🐝 🐦
Agalinus tenuifolia	slender false-foxglove	🐝 🐦 🐛
Agastache scrophulariifolia	giant purple hyssop	🐝 🐦 ❄ 🐦
Amsonia hubrichtii	threadleaf bluestar	🐝 🐦
Amsonia tabernaemontana	willowleaf bluestar	🐝 🐦
Anemone canadensis	Canada anemone	🌱 🐝 🐦
Antennaria dioica	pussytoes	🐛
Aplectrum hyemale	puttyroot	
Aquilegia canadensis	wild columbine	🐝 🐦
Arisaema triphyllum	Jack-in-the-pulpit	❄ 🐦 🌰
Aristolochia macrophylla	pipevine	🐛
Aruncus dioicus	goat's beard	🐝 🐦
Asarum canadense	wild ginger	🌱
Asclepias incarnata	swamp milkweed	🐝 🐦 🐛
Asclepias syriaca	common milkweed	🐝 🐦 🐛
Asclepias tuberosa	butterfly weed	🐝 🐦 🐛
Aster cordifolius	heart-leaved aster	🐝 🐦 🐛
Aster divaricatus	white wood aster	🐝 🐦 🐛
Aster lateriflorus	calico aster	🐝 🐦 🐛
Aster novae-angliae	New England aster	🐝 🐦 🐛
Aster oblongifolius	aromatic aster	🐝 🐦 🐛
Aster puniceus	purple-stem aster	🐝 🐦 🐛

LANDSCAPE FUNCTIONS	NOTES
	supports native bees
	supports native bees
	excellent late summer source of pollen and nectar for bees and butterflies; larval host for the buckeye
	excellent for pollinators; finches use seeds in winter
	good butterfly nectar plant
	good butterfly nectar plant
	pollinator friendly ground cover
	larval host for the American lady butterfly
	attractive basal leaves persist through winter; not used by wildlife
	excellent hummingbird plant
	seeds dispersed by birds and mammals
	larval host for pipevine swallowtail
	excellent plant for pollinators
	excellent ground cover
	larval host for monarch butterfly
	larval host for monarch butterfly
	larval host for monarch butterfly
	hosts 109 species of caterpillars
	hosts 109 species of caterpillars
	hosts 109 species of caterpillars
	hosts 109 species of caterpillars
	hosts 109 species of caterpillars
	hosts 109 species of caterpillars

ECOLOGICAL FUNCTIONS

- cover for wildlife
- nest sites for birds
- pollen producer
- nectar producer
- food for wintering birds
- food for breeding birds
- food for spring migrant birds
- food for fall migrant birds
- food for mammals
- food for caterpillars
- sequesters carbon

LANDSCAPE FUNCTIONS

- spring flowers
- summer flowers
- fall flowers
- fall foliage color
- fragrance
- evergreen ground cover
- deciduous ground cover
- screening
- shade and cooling
- edible fruits for humans

BOTANICAL NAME	COMMON NAME	ECOLOGICAL FUNCTIONS
BROADLEAVED HERBACEOUS PLANTS PLUS BULBS, continued		
Aster spectabilis	showy aster	🐝 🐦 🐛
Astilbe biternata	American astilbe	🐝 🐦
Baptisia australis	blue false indigo	🐛
Boltonia asteroides	false aster, white doll's daisy	🐝 🐦
Cardamine concatenata	cutleaf toothwort	🐝 🐦
Chamaecrista fasciculata	partridge pea	🦫 🐦 ⊡ 🐝 🐦 ❄ 🐦 🌰 🐛
Chamaelirium luteum	fairy wand	
Chelone glabra	turtlehead	
Chrysogonum virginianum	green and gold	🦫 🐝 🐦
Chrysopis mariana	Maryland golden aster	🐝 🐦
Cimicifuga racemosa	black cohosh	🐝 🐦
Claytonia virginica	spring beauty	🐝 🐦
Coreopsis lanceolata	tickseed	🐝 🐦
Coreopsis rosea	pink coreopsis	🐝 🐦
Coreopsis verticillata	whorled coreopsis	🐝 🐦
Dicentra canadensis	squirrel-corn	🌰
Dicentra cucullaria	Dutchman's breeches	🌰
Dicentra eximia	fringed bleeding heart	🌰
Dioscorea villosa	wild yam	
Echinacea purpurea	purple coneflower	🐝 🐦
Echinacea 'Tomato Soup'		🐝 🐦
Epimedium pinnatum subsp. *colchicum*	barrenwort	
Epimedium ×*versicolor* 'Sulphureum'	barrenwort	

LANDSCAPE FUNCTIONS	NOTES
✾ ▨ (spring flowers, deciduous ground cover)	hosts 109 species of caterpillars
✾ ✾ ▨ (spring flowers, summer flowers, deciduous ground cover)	attracts butterflies
✾ (spring flowers)	larval host for wild indigo duskywing and southern dogface butterflies
✾ (fall flowers)	excellent for fall pollinators
✾ (spring flowers)	spring ephemeral for native bees
✾ ▨ (spring flowers, evergreen ground cover)	provides cover, food for game birds, and larval host for cloudless sulphur
✾ (spring flowers)	not used by wildlife
✾ ✾ (spring flowers, summer flowers)	larval host of the Baltimore checkerspot butterfly
✾ ▨ (spring flowers, evergreen ground cover)	cover and food for early summer pollinators
✾ ✾ (spring flowers, summer flowers)	good for pollinators in sandy soil
✾ 🌹 (spring flowers, fragrance)	excellent source of pollen and nectar in shady conditions
✾ ▨ (spring flowers, deciduous ground cover)	spring ephemeral for native bees
✾ ✾ ▨ (spring flowers, summer flowers, deciduous ground cover)	good spring forage for pollinators
✾ ✾ ▨ (spring flowers, summer flowers, deciduous ground cover)	good spring forage for pollinators
✾ ✾ ▨ (spring flowers, summer flowers, deciduous ground cover)	good spring forage for pollinators
✾ (spring flowers)	rodents love tubers
✾ (summer flowers)	rodents love tubers
✾ ▨ (spring flowers, deciduous ground cover)	rodents love tubers
🍂 (fall foliage color)	attractive seed pods last through winter; little wildlife value
✾ ▨ (spring flowers, deciduous ground cover)	excellent source of midsummer pollen and nectar
✾ (fall flowers)	excellent source of midsummer pollen and nectar
✾ ▪ (spring flowers, evergreen ground cover)	native to China; little wildlife value
✾ ▨ (spring flowers, evergreen ground cover)	native to China; little wildlife value

ECOLOGICAL FUNCTIONS

- cover for wildlife
- nest sites for birds
- pollen producer
- nectar producer
- food for wintering birds
- food for breeding birds
- food for spring migrant birds
- food for fall migrant birds
- food for mammals
- food for caterpillars
- sequesters carbon

LANDSCAPE FUNCTIONS

- spring flowers
- summer flowers
- fall flowers
- fall foliage color
- fragrance
- evergreen ground cover
- deciduous ground cover
- screening
- shade and cooling
- edible fruits for humans

BROADLEAVED HERBACEOUS PLANTS PLUS BULBS, continued

BOTANICAL NAME	COMMON NAME	ECOLOGICAL FUNCTIONS
Erythronium americanum	yellow trout lily	bee, hummingbird
Eupatorium altissimum	tall thoroughwort	bee, hummingbird, caterpillar
Eupatorium coelestinum	mistflower	bee, hummingbird, caterpillar
Eupatorium dubium	Joe-Pye weed	bee, hummingbird, caterpillar
Eupatorium fistulosum	hollowstem Joe-Pye weed	bee, hummingbird, caterpillar
Eupatorium fistulosum 'Bartered Bride'	white-flowered hollowstem Joe-Pye weed	bee, hummingbird, caterpillar
Eupatorium hyssopifolium	hyssopleaf thoroughwort	bee, hummingbird, caterpillar
Eupatorium maculatum	Joe-Pye weed	bee, hummingbird, caterpillar
Eupatorium perfoliatum	boneset	bee, hummingbird, caterpillar
Eupatorium rotundifolium	round-leaved boneset	bee, hummingbird, caterpillar
Eupatorium rugosum	white snakeroot	bee, hummingbird, caterpillar
Eupatorium serotinum	late-blooming thoroughwort	bee, hummingbird, caterpillar
Euphorbia corollata	flowering spurge	bee, hummingbird
Filipendula rubra	queen of the prairie	bee, hummingbird
Fragaria virginiana	common strawberry	ground bird, bee, hummingbird, bird, acorn
Galanthus nivalis	snowdrops	
Geranium maculatum	wild geranium	bee, hummingbird
Helenium autumnale	Helen's flower, sneezeweed	bee, hummingbird
Helianthus angustifolius	swamp sunflower	bee, hummingbird, winter bird, bird, seed, acorn, caterpillar
Helianthus maximiliani	Maximilian sunflower	bee, hummingbird, winter bird, bird, seed, acorn, caterpillar
Heliopsis helianthoides	oxeye	bee, hummingbird, ground bird
Hepatica acutiloba	sharp-lobed hepatica	bee, hummingbird
Hepatica americana	round-lobed hepatica	bee, hummingbird

LANDSCAPE FUNCTIONS	NOTES
	pollinator friendly spring ephemeral
	supports 41 species of caterpillars
	supports 41 species of caterpillars
	supports 41 species of caterpillars
	supports 41 species of caterpillars
	supports 41 species of caterpillars
	supports 41 species of caterpillars
	supports 41 species of caterpillars
	supports 41 species of caterpillars
	supports 41 species of caterpillars
	supports 41 species of caterpillars
	supports 41 species of caterpillars
	adds to the diversity of pollinator friendly plants
	attracts butterflies and hummingbirds
	productive ground cover that supplies food for pollinators, birds, reptiles, and mammals
	little wildlife value
	supports early season native bees
	late summer pollinator plant
	excellent wildlife plant that supports 75 species of caterpillars
	excellent wildlife plant that supports 75 species of caterpillars
	supports pollinators in midsummer
	supports early season native bees
	supports early season native bees

ECOLOGICAL FUNCTIONS

- cover for wildlife
- nest sites for birds
- pollen producer
- nectar producer
- food for wintering birds
- food for breeding birds
- food for spring migrant birds
- food for fall migrant birds
- food for mammals
- food for caterpillars
- sequesters carbon

LANDSCAPE FUNCTIONS

- spring flowers
- summer flowers
- fall flowers
- fall foliage color
- fragrance
- evergreen ground cover
- deciduous ground cover
- screening
- shade and cooling
- edible fruits for humans

BOTANICAL NAME	COMMON NAME	ECOLOGICAL FUNCTIONS
BROADLEAVED HERBACEOUS PLANTS PLUS BULBS, continued		
Heuchera americana	American heuchera, alumroot	🌱
Heuchera macrorhiza	alumroot	🌱
Heuchera villosa	alumroot	🌱
Hibiscus moscheutos	swamp rose-mallow	🐝 🦅 🐛
Houstonia caerulea	bluets	🐝 🦅
Hyacinthoides hispanica	Spanish bluebells	🐝 🦅
Hydrophyllum virginianum	Virginia waterleaf	🐝 🦅
Impatiens capensis	orange jewelweed, touch-me-not	🌱 🐝 🦅
Impatiens pallida	pale jewelweed, touch-me-not	🌱 🐝 🦅
Iris verna	vernal crested iris	🌱
Iris versicolor	blue flag iris	🌱
Jeffersonia diphylla	twinleaf	🌱
Lespedeza virginica	slender bushclover	🌱 🐝 🦅 ❄️ 🐦 🌰 🐛
Liatris spicata	spiked blazing star	🐝 🦅 ❄️ 🐦 🐛
Lilium superbum	Turk's cap lily	🐝 🦅
Lobelia cardinalis	cardinal flower	🐝 🦅
Lobelia siphilitica	great blue lobelia	🐝 🦅
Ludwigia alternifolia	seedbox	🐝 🦅
Lysimachia ciliata	yellow loosestrife	🐝 🦅
Maianthemum canadense	Canada mayflower	🐝 🦅 ❄️🐦
Mertensia virginica	Virginia bluebells	🌱 🐝 🦅
Mimulus ringens	Allegheny monkey flower	🐝 🦅 🐛

LANDSCAPE FUNCTIONS	NOTES
✿ ▨	good ground cover
✿ ✿ ▨	good ground cover; semi-evergreen basal foliage persists through winter
✿ ▨	good ground cover
✿ ▨	larval host for 20 species of caterpillars
✿	green basal rosettes persist through winter; support early season native bees
✿ ▨	native to Europe; provides pollen and nectar for bumblebees
✿ ▨	excellent source of pollen and nectar for early season bees
✿ ▨	provides cover in wet areas; excellent hummingbird plant
✿ ▨	provides cover in wet areas; excellent hummingbird plant
✿ ▨	provides beautiful cover in wet areas
✿ ▨	provides beautiful cover in wet areas
✿ ▨	provides dense ground cover in shade
✿ ▨	good pollinator plant that also serves as larval host for several skippers
✿ ▨	excellent nectar source for butterflies; larval host for camouflaged looper
✿	beautiful butterfly plant
✿ ✿ ▨	one of the best plants for hummingbirds
✿ ✿ ▨	excellent source of nectar for hummingbirds and nocturnal sphinx moths
✿ ▨	adds to the diversity of wetland plants that support pollinators
✿ ▨	shade tolerant pollinator plant
✿ ▨	productive ground cover
✿ ▨	provides cover in wet areas; excellent hummingbird plant
✿ ▨	larval host for the buckeye butterfly

ECOLOGICAL FUNCTIONS

cover for wildlife

nest sites for birds

pollen producer

nectar producer

food for wintering birds

food for breeding birds

food for spring migrant birds

food for fall migrant birds

food for mammals

food for caterpillars

sequesters carbon

LANDSCAPE FUNCTIONS

spring flowers

summer flowers

fall flowers

fall foliage color

fragrance

evergreen ground cover

deciduous ground cover

screening

shade and cooling

edible fruits for humans

BOTANICAL NAME	COMMON NAME	ECOLOGICAL FUNCTIONS
BROADLEAVED HERBACEOUS PLANTS PLUS BULBS, continued		
Mitchella repens	partridgeberry	🐦 🐝 🦋 🐦 🌰
Mitella diphylla	mitrewort, bishop's cap	🐝 🦋
Monarda didyma	beebalm	🐦 ⊕ 🐝 🦋
Nymphaea odorata	fragrant waterlily	🐦
Oenothera fruticosa	sundrops	🐝 🦋 ❄ 🐦
Pachysandra procumbens	Allegheny spurge	🐦 🐝 🦋
Panax trifolius	dwarf ginseng	🐝 🦋
Penstemon digitalis	foxglove beardtongue	🐝 🦋
Phacelia bipinnatifida	fernleaf phacelia	🐝 🦋
Phlox divaricata	woodland phlox, wild blue phlox	🐦 🐝 🦋
Phlox maculata	meadow phlox	🐦 🐝 🦋
Phlox paniculata	summer phlox	🐦 🐝 🦋
Phlox stolonifera	creeping phlox	🐦 🐝 🦋
Podophyllum peltatum	mayapple	🐦 🐝 🦋
Polemonium reptans	creeping Jacob's ladder	🐦 🐝 🦋
Polygonatum commutatum	Solomon's-seal	🐦 🐝 🦋
Potentilla canadensis	dwarf cinquefoil	🐝 🦋 🌰
Potentilla simplex	common cinquefoil	🐝 🦋 🌰
Pycnanthemum muticum	short-toothed mountain mint	🐦 🐝 🦋
Pycnanthemum tenuifolium	narrow-leaved mountain mint	🐦 🐝 🦋
Pycnanthemum virginianum	Virginia mountain mint	🐦 🐝 🦋
Ratibida pinnata	pinnate prairie coneflower	🐝 🦋 ❄ 🐦
Rudbeckia fulgida	orange coneflower	🐝 🦋 ❄ 🐦

LANDSCAPE FUNCTIONS	NOTES
✿ ✤ ▧	ground cover that produces berries used by many birds and mammals
✿ ▧	adds to the diversity of early season pollinator plants
✿ ▧	excellent butterfly and hummingbird plant
✿ ✤	creates good fish habitat
✿ ✤ ▧	valuable plant for native bees
✿ ▧	excellent ground cover with value to early season bees
✿ ▧	adds to the diversity of spring pollinator plants
✿ ✤ ▧	part of the diversity of summer pollinator friendly plants
✿ ▧	adds to the diversity of spring pollinator plants
✿ ▧	provides nectar for the hummingbird sphinx moth
✿ ▧	provides nectar for the hummingbird sphinx moth
✿ ▧	provides nectar for the hummingbird sphinx moth
✿ ▧	provides nectar for the hummingbird sphinx moth
✿ ▧	fruits eaten by box turtles
✿ ▧	adds to the diversity of spring pollinator plants
✿	adds to the diversity of spring pollinator plants
✿ ▧	good early summer source of pollen and nectar
✿ ▧	good early summer source of pollen and nectar
✿ ▧	superior source of pollen and nectar for bees and butterflies
✿ ▧	superior source of pollen and nectar for bees and butterflies
✿ ▧	superior source of pollen and nectar for bees and butterflies
✿	good for pollinators and winter birds
✿ ▧	good for pollinators and winter birds

ECOLOGICAL FUNCTIONS

- 🐛 cover for wildlife
- 🐦 nest sites for birds
- 🐝 pollen producer
- 🐦 nectar producer
- ❄ food for wintering birds
- 🐦 food for breeding birds
- 🕊 food for spring migrant birds
- 🕊 food for fall migrant birds
- 🌰 food for mammals
- 🐛 food for caterpillars
- 🌱 sequesters carbon

LANDSCAPE FUNCTIONS

- ✿ spring flowers
- ✤ summer flowers
- ✿ fall flowers
- 🍁 fall foliage color
- 🌹 fragrance
- ▧ evergreen ground cover
- ▨ deciduous ground cover
- 🎋 screening
- 🌳 shade and cooling
- 🍒 edible fruits for humans

BOTANICAL NAME	COMMON NAME	ECOLOGICAL FUNCTIONS
BROADLEAVED HERBACEOUS PLANTS PLUS BULBS, continued		
Rudbeckia laciniata	cutleaf coneflower	🐝 🦋 ❄ 🐦
Rudbeckia nitida	shining coneflower	🐝 🦋 ❄ 🐦
Salvia lyrata	lyre-leaved sage	🦆 🐝 🦋
Sanguinaria canadensis	bloodroot	🐝 🦋
Sanguinaria canadensis 'Multiplex'	double bloodroot	🐝 🦋
Sedum ternatum	mountain stonecrop	🐝 🦋
Senecio aureus	golden ragwort	🐝 🦋
Senna hebecarpa	wild senna	🐝 🦋 ❄ 🐦 🐛
Silene virginica	fire pink	🐝 🦋 ❄ 🐦
Silphium perfoliatum	cup plant	🦆 🐞 🐝 🦋 ❄ 🐦
Sisyrinchium angustifolium	blue-eyed grass	🦆
Smilacina racemosa	false Solomon's-seal	🐝 🦋 ❄ 🐦 🌰
Solidago caesia	blue-stem goldenrod	🦆 🐞 🐝 🦋 ❄ 🐦 🐛
Solidago canadensis	Canada goldenrod	🦆 🐞 🐝 🦋 ❄ 🐦 🐛
Solidago flexicaulis	zigzag goldenrod	🦆 🐞 🐝 🦋 ❄ 🐦 🐛
Solidago graminifolia	grass-leaved goldenrod	🦆 🐞 🐝 🦋 ❄ 🐦 🐛
Solidago rugosa	rough-stem goldenrod	🦆 🐞 🐝 🦋 ❄ 🐦 🐛
Solidago speciosa	showy goldenrod	🦆 🐞 🐝 🦋 ❄ 🐦 🐛
Spigelia marilandica	pinkroot	🐝 🦋
Stylophorum diphyllum	wood poppy	🐝 🦋 🌰
Symplocarpus foetidus	skunk cabbage	🦆
Tiarella cordifolia	eastern foamflower	🦆 🐝 🦋

LANDSCAPE FUNCTIONS	NOTES
	good for pollinators and winter birds
	good for pollinators and winter birds
	attracts hummingbirds and butterflies
	adds to the diversity of spring pollinator plants; seed elaiosomes support ants
	little wildlife value
	ground cover with some benefits for pollinators
	part of the diversity of summer pollinator friendly plants
	larval host for several species of sulphur butterflies
	seeds support winter birds
	good pollinator plant that provides winter seed for finches
	forms a beautiful, dense groundcover
	adds to the diversity of spring pollinator plants
	excellent meadow plant that supplies cover, seed, pollen, nectar, and food for 115 species of caterpillars
	excellent meadow plant that supplies cover, seed, pollen, nectar, and food for 115 species of caterpillars
	excellent meadow plant that supplies cover, seed, pollen, nectar, and food for 115 species of caterpillars
	excellent meadow plant that supplies cover, seed, pollen, nectar, and food for 115 species of caterpillars
	excellent meadow plant that supplies cover, seed, pollen, nectar, and food for 115 species of caterpillars
	excellent meadow plant that supplies cover, seed, pollen, nectar, and food for 115 species of caterpillars
	attractive hummingbird plant
	adds to diversity of early summer pollinator plants
	provides good cover in wet areas
	excellent ground cover and spring pollinator plant

ECOLOGICAL FUNCTIONS

- cover for wildlife
- nest sites for birds
- pollen producer
- nectar producer
- food for wintering birds
- food for breeding birds
- food for spring migrant birds
- food for fall migrant birds
- food for mammals
- food for caterpillars
- sequesters carbon

LANDSCAPE FUNCTIONS

- spring flowers
- summer flowers
- fall flowers
- fall foliage color
- fragrance
- evergreen ground cover
- deciduous ground cover
- screening
- shade and cooling
- edible fruits for humans

BOTANICAL NAME	COMMON NAME	ECOLOGICAL FUNCTIONS
BROADLEAVED HERBACEOUS PLANTS PLUS BULBS, continued		
Tipularia discolor	cranefly orchid	
Trillium cernuum	nodding trillium	
Trillium flexipes	nodding trillium	
Trillium grandiflorum	showy trillium	
Tulipa sylvestris	wood tulip	
Veratrum viride	green false hellebore	🐝 🦅
Verbena hastata	blue vervain	🐝 🦅
Vernonia noveboracensis	New York ironweed	🐝 🦅 ❄ 🐦
Veronicastrum virginicum	Culver's root	🐝 🦅
Viola blanda	sweet white violet	🐝 🦅
Viola conspersa	dog violet	🐝 🦅
Viola pallens	northern white violet	🐝 🦅
Viola papilionacea	common blue violet	🐝 🦅
Viola pedata	birdsfoot violet	🐝 🦅
Viola pubescens	downy yellow violet	🐝 🦅
Viola septentrionalis	northern blue violet	🐝 🦅
Viola sororia	common blue violet	🐝 🦅
Viola striata	striped cream violet	🐝 🦅
Waldsteinia fragarioides	barren strawberry	🌱 🐝 🦅
Waldsteinia lobata	Piedmont barren strawberry	🌱 🐝 🦅
GRASSES, SEDGES, AND RUSHES		
Andropogon gerardii	big bluestem	🌱 🦋 ❄ 🐦 🐛
Andropogon glomeratus	bushy beardgrass	🌱 🦋 ❄ 🐦 🐛
Andropogon ternarius	splitbeard bluestem	🌱 🦋 ❄ 🐦 🐛

LANDSCAPE FUNCTIONS	NOTES
spring flowers	attractive basal leaves persist through winter; little wildlife value
spring flowers, deciduous ground cover	seed elaiosomes eaten by yellow jackets
spring flowers, deciduous ground cover	seed elaiosomes eaten by yellow jackets
spring flowers, deciduous ground cover	seed elaiosomes eaten by yellow jackets
spring flowers, deciduous ground cover	native to Europe; little wildlife value
spring flowers, summer flowers, deciduous ground cover	adds to the diversity of wetland plants that support pollinators
summer flowers, deciduous ground cover	adds to the diversity of wetland plants that support pollinators
summer flowers, deciduous ground cover	important pollinator plant in damp soils
spring flowers, summer flowers, deciduous ground cover	adds to the diversity of summer pollinator plants
spring flowers, deciduous ground cover	larval host for *Argynnis* and *Speyeria* fritillaries
spring flowers, deciduous ground cover	larval host for *Argynnis* and *Speyeria* fritillaries
spring flowers, deciduous ground cover	larval host for *Argynnis* and *Speyeria* fritillaries
spring flowers, deciduous ground cover	larval host for *Argynnis* and *Speyeria* fritillaries
spring flowers, deciduous ground cover	larval host for *Argynnis* and *Speyeria* fritillaries
spring flowers, deciduous ground cover	larval host for *Argynnis* and *Speyeria* fritillaries
spring flowers, deciduous ground cover	larval host for *Argynnis* and *Speyeria* fritillaries
spring flowers, deciduous ground cover	larval host for *Argynnis* and *Speyeria* fritillaries
spring flowers, deciduous ground cover	larval host for *Argynnis* and *Speyeria* fritillaries
spring flowers, deciduous ground cover	drought-tolerant ground cover
spring flowers, deciduous ground cover	drought-tolerant ground cover
spring flowers, summer flowers, fall foliage color, deciduous ground cover	a bunch grass used by nesting grassland birds
spring flowers, summer flowers, fall foliage color, deciduous ground cover	a bunch grass used by nesting grassland birds
spring flowers, summer flowers, fall foliage color, deciduous ground cover	a bunch grass used by nesting grassland birds

ECOLOGICAL FUNCTIONS

- cover for wildlife
- nest sites for birds
- pollen producer
- nectar producer
- food for wintering birds
- food for breeding birds
- food for spring migrant birds
- food for fall migrant birds
- food for mammals
- food for caterpillars
- sequesters carbon

LANDSCAPE FUNCTIONS

- spring flowers
- summer flowers
- fall flowers
- fall foliage color
- fragrance
- evergreen ground cover
- deciduous ground cover
- screening
- shade and cooling
- edible fruits for humans

BOTANICAL NAME	COMMON NAME	ECOLOGICAL FUNCTIONS
GRASSES, SEDGES, AND RUSHES, continued		
Andropogon virginicus	broomsedge	
Carex flaccosperma	thinfruit sedge	
Carex glaucodea	blue wood sedge	
Carex laxiculmis	spreading sedge	
Carex pensylvanica	Pennsylvania sedge	
Carex plantaginea	plantainleaf sedge	
Carex platyphylla	broadleaf sedge	
Carex stricta	tussock sedge	
Carex vulpinoidea	fox sedge	
Chasmanthium latifolium	river oats	
Elymus canadensis	Canada wild rye	
Elymus hystrix	bottlebrush grass	
Elymus virginicus	Virginia wild rye	
Eragrostis spectabilis	purple lovegrass	
Juncus effusus	common rush	
Panicum virgatum	switchgrass	
Saccharum giganteum	giant plume grass	
Schizachyrium scoparium	little bluestem	
Sorghastrum nutans	Indian grass	
Sporobolus heterolepis	prairie dropseed	
Tripsacum dactyloides	eastern gamagrass	

LANDSCAPE FUNCTIONS	NOTES
	a bunch grass used by nesting grassland birds
	hosts 36 species of caterpillars
	good ground cover that also serves as a larval host for skippers
	hosts 36 species of caterpillars
	good ground cover that also serves as a larval host for skippers; hosts 36 species of caterpillars
	good ground cover that also serves as a larval host for skippers
	good ground cover that also serves as a larval host for skippers
	good ground cover that also serves as a larval host for skippers; hosts 36 species of caterpillars
	hosts 36 species of caterpillars
	provides copious seed for winter birds
	provides copious seed for winter birds
	a bunch grass used by nesting grassland birds
	provides seed for winter birds
	a bunch grass used by nesting grassland birds
	good cover and soil stabilizer in wet areas
	a bunch grass used by nesting grassland birds
	a large bunch grass that may be useful to grassland birds
	a bunch grass used by nesting grassland birds
	good for preventing soil erosion
	a bunch grass used by nesting grassland birds
	a bunch grass used by nesting grassland birds; seed is eaten by wintering birds and mammals

ECOLOGICAL FUNCTIONS

- cover for wildlife
- nest sites for birds
- pollen producer
- nectar producer
- food for wintering birds
- food for breeding birds
- food for spring migrant birds
- food for fall migrant birds
- food for mammals
- food for caterpillars
- sequesters carbon

LANDSCAPE FUNCTIONS

- spring flowers
- summer flowers
- fall flowers
- fall foliage color
- fragrance
- evergreen ground cover
- deciduous ground cover
- screening
- shade and cooling
- edible fruits for humans

BOTANICAL NAME	COMMON NAME	ECOLOGICAL FUNCTIONS
FERNS		
Adiantum pedatum	maidenhair fern	🌿 ▣
Asplenium platyneuron	ebony spleenwort	🌿 ▣
Athyrium filix-femina	lady fern	🌿 ▣
Cystopteris fragilis	brittle bladder fern, fragile fern	🌿 ▣
Dennstaedtia punctilobula	hayscented fern	🌿 ▣
Dryopteris cristata	crested wood fern	🌿 ▣
Dryopteris filix-mas	male fern	🌿 ▣
Dryopteris goldiana	Goldie's fern	🌿 ▣
Dryopteris intermedia	evergreen wood fern	🌿 ▣
Dryopteris marginalis	marginal shield fern	🌿 ▣
Matteuccia struthiopteris var. pensylvanica	ostrich fern	🌿 ▣
Onoclea sensibilis	sensitive fern	🌿 ▣
Osmunda cinnamomea	cinnamon fern	🌿 ▣
Osmunda claytoniana	interrupted fern	🌿 ▣
Osmunda regalis	royal fern	🌿 ▣
Pellaea atropurpurea	purple cliffbrake	🌿
Polypodium virginianum	rock polypody	🌿
Polypodium vulgare	common polypody	🌿
Polystichum acrostichoides	Christmas fern	🌿 ▣
Thelypteris noveboracensis	New York fern	🌿 ▣
Thelypteris palustris	marsh fern	🌿 ▣
Woodwardia areolata	netted chain fern	🌿 ▣
Woodwardia virginica	chain fern	🌿 ▣

LANDSCAPE FUNCTIONS	NOTES
▨	good ground covers, particularly in shady, moist sites
▨	can provide good cover on calciferous soils
▨	good ground covers, particularly in shady, moist sites
	prolific ground covers
▨	excellent ground cover on impoverished, acidic soils
	clumping ferns that provide good cover for ground fauna
▦	clumping ferns that provide good cover for ground fauna
▨	clumping ferns that provide good cover for ground fauna
▦	clumping ferns that provide good cover for ground fauna
▦	clumping ferns that provide good cover for ground fauna
▨	good ground covers, particularly in shady, moist sites
▨	useful for stream and pond edges
▨	useful for stream and pond edges
▨	excellent cover for ground fauna
▨	useful for stream and pond edges
	good in rocky xeric sites
▦	excellent for adding life to rocky surfaces
▦	excellent for adding life to rocky surfaces
▦	excellent cover for ground fauna
▦	excellent cover for ground fauna
▨	excellent cover for wildlife in wet areas
▨	useful for stream and pond edges
▨	good cover in acid bogs

ECOLOGICAL FUNCTIONS

- cover for wildlife
- nest sites for birds
- pollen producer
- nectar producer
- food for wintering birds
- food for breeding birds
- food for spring migrant birds
- food for fall migrant birds
- food for mammals
- food for caterpillars
- sequesters carbon

LANDSCAPE FUNCTIONS

- spring flowers
- summer flowers
- fall flowers
- fall foliage color
- fragrance
- evergreen ground cover
- deciduous ground cover
- screening
- shade and cooling
- edible fruits for humans

Selected Plants for the Southeast, Southwest, Pacific Northwest, Midwest and Mountain States, and New England

EXPANDED KEY

COVER FOR WILDLIFE Plant is used by wildlife for shelter and protection.

NEST SITES FOR BIRDS Plant is used by birds for building nests.

POLLEN AND NECTAR Plant produces pollen and/or nectar for insects and birds.

FOOD FOR BIRDS Plant provides nuts, seeds, berries, and other food for various birds.

FOOD FOR MAMMALS Plant provides food for a variety of wildlife including squirrels, chipmunks, raccoons, opossums, and foxes.

FOOD FOR CATERPILLARS Plant has foliage that sustains various species of caterpillars.

SPRING FLOWERS Plant has *significantly* attractive flowers in spring.

SUMMER FLOWERS Plant has *significantly* attractive flowers in summer.

FALL FLOWERS Plant has *significantly* attractive flowers in fall.

WINTER FLOWERS Plant has *significantly* attractive flowers in winter.

FALL FOLIAGE COLOR Plant foliage turns color in fall and is ornamental.

FRAGRANCE Plant has a noticeable and pleasant fragrance.

EVERGREEN GROUND COVER Plant can be used as evergreen ground cover.

DECIDUOUS GROUND COVER Plant can be used as deciduous ground cover.

SCREENING Plant can be used as evergreen screening.

SHADE/COOLING A shrub or tree that creates significant shade, which can be used to reduce the temperature in the area it covers.

EDIBLE FRUITS FOR HUMAN CONSUMPTION Plant has fruit that is safe (and tasty) for people to consume.

BOTANICAL NAME	COMMON NAME	ECOLOGICAL FUNCTIONS	LANDSCAPE FUNCTIONS
TREES			
Acer barbatum	southern sugar maple		
Acer rubrum	red maple		
Amelanchier arborea	downy serviceberry, shadblow serviceberry		
Asimina triloba	pawpaw		
Betula lenta	black birch, sweet birch		
Betula nigra	river birch		
Carpinus caroliniana	ironwood		
Carya illinoensis	pecan		
Carya ovata	shagbark hickory		
Catalpa bignonioides	catalpa		
Celtis laevigata	Mississippi hackberry		
Cercis canadensis	redbud		
Chionanthus virginicus	fringe tree		
Cladrastis kentukea	yellowwood		
Cornus alternifolia	alternate-leaf dogwood		
Cornus florida	flowering dogwood		
Cotinus obovatus	smoke tree		
Crataegus phaenopyrum	Washington hawthorn		
Crataegus viridis	green hawthorn		
Diospyros virginiana	persimmon		
Fagus grandifolia	American beech		
Fraxinus americana	white ash		
Fraxinus caroliniana	water ash		

BOTANICAL NAME	COMMON NAME	ECOLOGICAL FUNCTIONS	LANDSCAPE FUNCTIONS
TREES, continued			
Gordonia lasianthus	loblolly bay		
Gymnocladus dioicus	Kentucky coffee tree		
Halesia carolina	Carolina silverbell		
Ilex opaca	American holly		
Juglans nigra	black walnut		
Juniperus virginiana	eastern red cedar		
Liquidambar styraciflua	sweet gum		
Liriodendron tulipifera	tulip tree		
Maclura pomifera	osage orange		
Magnolia acuminata	cucumber tree		
Magnolia grandiflora	southern magnolia		
Magnolia macrophylla	large-leaved umbrella tree		
Magnolia virginiana	sweetbay magnolia		
Malus angustifolia	southern crabapple		
Morus rubra	red mulberry		
Osmanthus americanus	devilwood		
Ostrya virginiana	American hop hornbeam		
Oxydendrum arboreum	sourwood		
Persea borbonia	red bay		
Pinus palustris	longleaf pine		
Pinus taeda	loblolly pine		
Pinus virginiana	Virginia pine		
Prunus caroliniana	cherry laurel		
Prunus serotina	black cherry		

BOTANICAL NAME	COMMON NAME	ECOLOGICAL FUNCTIONS	LANDSCAPE FUNCTIONS
TREES, continued			
Quercus alba	white oak	nest sites for birds, pollen and/or nectar producer, food for mammals, food for caterpillars	fall foliage color, shade and cooling
Quercus coccinea	scarlet oak	nest sites for birds, pollen and/or nectar producer, food for mammals, food for caterpillars	fall foliage color, shade and cooling
Quercus palustris	pin oak	nest sites for birds, pollen and/or nectar producer, food for birds, food for mammals, food for caterpillars	fall foliage color, shade and cooling
Quercus phellos	willow oak	nest sites for birds, pollen and/or nectar producer, food for birds, food for mammals, food for caterpillars	fall foliage color, shade and cooling
Quercus rubra	northern red oak	nest sites for birds, pollen and/or nectar producer, food for mammals, food for caterpillars	fall foliage color, shade and cooling
Quercus shumardii	Shumard oak	nest sites for birds, pollen and/or nectar producer, food for mammals, food for caterpillars	fall foliage color, shade and cooling
Quercus virginiana	live oak	cover for wildlife, nest sites for birds, pollen and/or nectar producer, food for birds, food for mammals, food for caterpillars	screening, shade and cooling
Robinia pseudoacacia	black locust	nest sites for birds, pollen and/or nectar producer, food for caterpillars	spring flowers, fragrance
Salix nigra	black willow	nest sites for birds, pollen and/or nectar producer, food for caterpillars	spring flowers, shade and cooling
Sassafras albidum	sassafras	nest sites for birds, pollen and/or nectar producer, food for birds, food for caterpillars	spring flowers, fall foliage color, shade and cooling
Styrax americana	American snowbell	nest sites for birds, pollen and/or nectar producer, food for caterpillars	spring flowers, fall foliage color, shade and cooling
Taxodium ascendens	pond cypress	nest sites for birds, food for caterpillars	fall foliage color
Taxodium distichum	bald cypress	nest sites for birds, food for caterpillars	fall foliage color, shade and cooling
Thuja occidentalis	arborvitae	cover for wildlife, nest sites for birds, food for caterpillars	screening
Tilia americana	basswood	nest sites for birds, pollen and/or nectar producer, food for caterpillars	spring flowers, fragrance, shade and cooling
Tsuga canadensis	Canada hemlock	cover for wildlife, nest sites for birds, food for caterpillars	screening, shade and cooling
Tsuga caroliniana	Carolina hemlock	cover for wildlife, nest sites for birds, food for caterpillars	screening
SHRUBS			
Aesculus pavia	red buckeye	pollen and/or nectar producer, food for mammals, food for caterpillars	spring flowers
Alnus serrulata	smooth alder	nest sites for birds, pollen and/or nectar producer, food for caterpillars	shade and cooling

ECOLOGICAL FUNCTIONS

- cover for wildlife
- nest sites for birds
- pollen and/or nectar producer
- food for birds
- food for mammals
- food for caterpillars

LANDSCAPE FUNCTIONS

- spring flowers
- summer flowers
- fall flowers
- winter flowers
- fall foliage color
- fragrance
- evergreen ground cover
- deciduous ground cover
- screening
- shade and cooling
- edible fruits for humans

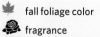

BOTANICAL NAME	COMMON NAME	ECOLOGICAL FUNCTIONS	LANDSCAPE FUNCTIONS
SHRUBS, continued			
Aronia arbutifolia	red chokeberry	🐝🕊️🐛	✿🍁🌳
Aronia melanocarpa	black chokeberry	🐝🕊️🐛	✿🍁🌳
Callicarpa americana	beautyberry	🐝🕊️🐛	✿🍁
Calycanthus floridus	Carolina allspice	🌰🐛	✿🍁🌹
Ceanothus americanus	New Jersey tea	🐝🐛	✿
Cephalanthus occidentalis	buttonbush	🐝🐛	✿🍁🌹
Clethra alnifolia	sweet pepperbush	🐝🐛	✿🍁🌹
Cornus stolonifera	redstem dogwood, red osier dogwood	🐝🕊️🐛	✿🍁
Corylus americana	American hazelnut	🐝🌰🐛	🍒
Cyrilla racemiflora	titi	🦇🐝🐛	✿🍁🌳
Diervilla sessilifolia	southern bush honeysuckle	🐝🐛	✿
Dirca palustris	leatherwood	🕊️🐛	✿🍁
Euonymus americanus	American strawberry bush	🕊️🐛	
Fothergilla gardenii	dwarf fothergilla	🐝🐛	✿🍁🌹
Franklinia alatamaha	Franklin tree	🐝🐛	✿🍁
Hamamelis virginiana	witch hazel	🦇🐛	✿🍁🌳
Hydrangea arborescens	smooth hydrangea	🐝🐛	✿
Hydrangea quercifolia	oakleaf hydrangea	🐝🐛	✿🍁
Hypericum densiflorum	bushy St. John's wort	🐝🐛	✿
Hypericum lloydii	sandhill St. John's wort	🐝🐛	✿▦
Ilex decidua	possumhaw holly	🦇🐝🕊️🐛	🍁🌳
Ilex glabra	inkberry	🐌🐝🕊️🐛	⬛⬛⬛
Ilex verticillata	winterberry	🐝🕊️🐛	🍁🌳
Illicium floridanum	Florida anise	🐌🦇🐛	✿⬛⬛⬛

BOTANICAL NAME	COMMON NAME	ECOLOGICAL FUNCTIONS	LANDSCAPE FUNCTIONS
SHRUBS, continued			
Itea virginica	Virginia sweetspire	🐝🐛	spring flowers, fall foliage
Kalmia latifolia	mountain laurel	cover, nest, 🐝🐛	spring flowers, screening
Leucothoë axillaris	coastal doghobble	cover, 🐝🐛	spring flowers, screening
Leucothoë racemosa	swamp doghobble	🐝	spring flowers, fall foliage
Lindera benzoin	spicebush	nest, 🐝, food for birds, 🐛	spring flowers, fall foliage, shade and cooling
Lyonia lucida	fetterbush	cover, 🐝🐛	spring flowers, screening
Neviusia alabamensis	snow wreath	🐝🐛	spring flowers, fall foliage
Pinckneya pubens	pinkneya	🐝	spring flowers, fall foliage
Physocarpus opulifolius	common ninebark	🐝🐛	spring flowers
Ptelea trifoliata	hoptree	🐝🐛	spring flowers, fragrance
Rhododendron atlanticum	coastal azalea	🐝🐛	spring flowers, fall foliage, fragrance
Rhododendron austrinum	Piedmont flame azalea	🐝🐛	spring flowers, fall foliage
Rhododendron calendulaceum	flame azalea	🐝🐛	spring flowers, fall foliage
Rhododendron canescens	wild azalea	🐝🐛	spring flowers, fall foliage, fragrance
Rhododendron maximum	great laurel, rosebay laurel	cover, 🐝🐛	spring flowers, screening
Rhododendron minus	Carolina rhododendron	cover, 🐝🐛	spring flowers, fall foliage, screening
Rhododendron periclymenoides	pink azalea, pinxter azalea	🐝🐛	spring flowers, fall foliage, fragrance
Rhododendron prunifolium	plumleaf azalea	🐝🐛	spring flowers, fall foliage
Rhododendron viscosum	swamp azalea	🐝🐛	spring flowers, fall foliage, fragrance
Rhus aromatica	fragrant sumac	🐝, food for birds, 🐛	spring flowers, fall foliage

ECOLOGICAL FUNCTIONS

 cover for wildlife

nest sites for birds

 pollen and/or nectar producer

food for birds

food for mammals

food for caterpillars

LANDSCAPE FUNCTIONS

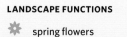 spring flowers

summer flowers

fall flowers

winter flowers

 fall foliage color

fragrance

evergreen ground cover

deciduous ground cover

screening

shade and cooling

edible fruits for humans

BOTANICAL NAME	COMMON NAME	ECOLOGICAL FUNCTIONS	LANDSCAPE FUNCTIONS
SHRUBS, continued			
Robinia hispida	bristly locust		
Rosa carolina	Carolina rose		
Rosa virginiana	Virginia rose		
Sambucus canadensis	elderberry		
Staphylea trifoliata	bladdernut		
Stewartia malacodendron	silky camellia		
Symphoricarpos orbiculatus	coralberry		
Taxus floridana	Florida yew		
Vaccinium ashei	rabbiteye blueberry		
Vaccinium corymbosum	highbush blueberry		
Viburnum acerifolium	mapleleaf viburnum		
Viburnum dentatum	arrowwood viburnum		
Viburnum nudum	smooth witherod, possumhaw		
Viburnum prunifolium	blackhaw		
Xanthorhiza simplicissima	yellowroot		
Zenobia pulverulenta	honeycup		
VINES			
Aristolochia macrophylla	Dutchman's pipe		
Bignonia capreolata	cross vine		
Campsis radicans	trumpet vine		
Clematis virginiana	virgin's bower		
Decumaria barbara	climbing hydrangea		
Gelsemium sempervirens	Carolina jessamine		
Lonicera sempervirens	coral honeysuckle		

BOTANICAL NAME	COMMON NAME	ECOLOGICAL FUNCTIONS	LANDSCAPE FUNCTIONS
VINES, continued			
Parthenocissus quinquefolia	Virginia creeper	pollen/nectar producer, food for birds, food for caterpillars	fall foliage color, deciduous ground cover
Passiflora incarnata	passion vine	pollen/nectar producer, food for mammals, food for caterpillars	summer flowers, fragrance
Smilax smallii	Jackson vine	cover for wildlife, pollen/nectar producer, food for birds, food for caterpillars	screening
Vitis rotundifolia	fox grape, muscadine	pollen/nectar producer, food for birds, food for mammals, food for caterpillars	fall foliage color, edible fruits for humans
Wisteria frutescens	American wisteria	pollen/nectar producer, food for caterpillars	spring flowers, fall foliage color, fragrance
HERBACEOUS PERENNIALS AND BULBS			
Amsonia ciliata	fringed bluestar	pollen/nectar producer, food for caterpillars	spring flowers, fall foliage color
Arisaema triphyllum	Jack-in-the-pulpit	food for birds, food for caterpillars	summer flowers
Asarum canadense	Canada ginger		summer flowers, deciduous ground cover
Asclepias perennis	aquatic milkweed	pollen/nectar producer, food for caterpillars	summer flowers
Asclepias tuberosa	butterfly weed	pollen/nectar producer, food for caterpillars	summer flowers, fall foliage color
Aster dumosus	bushy aster	pollen/nectar producer, food for caterpillars	fall flowers, fragrance
Aster oblongifolius	aromatic aster	pollen/nectar producer, food for caterpillars	fall flowers, fragrance
Baptisia alba	wild white indigo	pollen/nectar producer, food for caterpillars	spring flowers
Chrysogonum virginianum	green and gold	pollen/nectar producer	spring flowers, evergreen ground cover
Conradina canescens	false rosemary	pollen/nectar producer	spring flowers
Crinum americanum	swamp lily	pollen/nectar producer	summer flowers, fragrance
Echinacea purpurea	purple coneflower	pollen/nectar producer, food for birds, food for caterpillars	summer flowers
Eryngium yuccifolium	button snakeroot	pollen/nectar producer, food for caterpillars	summer flowers, evergreen ground cover
Erythrina herbacea	coral bean	pollen/nectar producer, food for birds, food for caterpillars	summer flowers

ECOLOGICAL FUNCTIONS

 cover for wildlife
nest sites for birds
 pollen and/or nectar producer
 food for birds
food for mammals
food for caterpillars

LANDSCAPE FUNCTIONS

 spring flowers
summer flowers
fall flowers
winter flowers

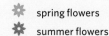 fall foliage color
fragrance
evergreen ground cover
deciduous ground cover

 screening
shade and cooling
edible fruits for humans

BOTANICAL NAME	COMMON NAME	ECOLOGICAL FUNCTIONS	LANDSCAPE FUNCTIONS
HERBACEOUS PERENNIALS AND BULBS, continued			
Eupatorium coelestinum	mistflower	🐝 🐛	✿ 🌹
Eupatorium fistulosum	hollowstem Joe-Pye weed	🐝 🐛	✿ 🌹
Helianthus angustifolius	swamp sunflower	🐝 🐛	✿
Hexastylis arifolia	jug plant		✿ ▦
Hibiscus coccineus	cardinal hibiscus	🐝 🐛	✿ 🍁
Hibiscus moscheutos	swamp rose-mallow	🐝 🐛	✿ 🌹
Impatiens capensis	jewelweed	🐝 🐛	✿
Iris fulva	Louisiana iris	🐝 🐛	✿
Iris virginica	blue-flag iris	🐝 🐛	✿
Liatris elegans	pinkscale blazing star	🐝 🐛	✿
Liatris spicata	spiked blazing star	🐝 🐛	✿
Lobelia cardinalis	cardinal flower	🐝 🐛	✿ ▦
Mitchella repens	partridgeberry	🐝 🐦	✿ ▦
Monarda didyma	beebalm	🐝 🐛	✿ ▦
Nymphaea odorata	white waterlily	🐝 🐦 🐛	✿ 🌹
Pachysandra procumbens	Alleghany spurge	🐝	✿ ▦
Peltandra virginica	arrow arum		✿
Penstemon smallii	Small's beardtongue	🐝 🐛	✿ ▦
Phlox carolina	tall phlox	🐝 🐛	✿ 🌹
Phlox nivalis	trailing phlox	🐝 🐛	✿ 🌹 ▦
Phlox pilosa	downy phlox	🐝 🐛	✿ 🌹
Phlox subulata	moss pink	🐝 🐛	✿ 🌹 ▦
Pontederia cordata	pickerel-weed	▣ 🐝 🐛	✿ 🌹
Rudbeckia hirta	black-eyed Susan	🐝 🐛	✿

BOTANICAL NAME	COMMON NAME	ECOLOGICAL FUNCTIONS	LANDSCAPE FUNCTIONS
HERBACEOUS PERENNIALS AND BULBS, continued			
Ruellia caroliniensis	Carolina wild petunia	pollen/nectar producer, food for caterpillars	summer flowers
Salvia coccinea	scarlet sage	pollen/nectar producer, food for caterpillars	summer flowers
Scutellaria incana	hoary skullcap	pollen/nectar producer, food for caterpillars	summer flowers
Sisyrinchium angustifolium	blue-eyed grass	pollen/nectar producer	spring flowers
Solidago sempervirens	seaside goldenrod	pollen/nectar producer, food for caterpillars	fall flowers, fragrance, deciduous ground cover
Teucrium canadense	wood sage	pollen/nectar producer	summer flowers
Tradescantia ohiensis	spiderwort	pollen/nectar producer, food for caterpillars	spring flowers
Vernonia angustifolia	tall ironweed	pollen/nectar producer, food for caterpillars	summer flowers
GRASSES, SEDGES, AND RUSHES			
Andropogon gerardii	big bluestem	cover for wildlife, pollen/nectar producer, food for caterpillars	summer flowers, fall foliage color
Carex plantaginea	seersucker sedge	food for caterpillars	spring flowers, deciduous ground cover
Chasmanthium latifolium	river oats	cover for wildlife, pollen/nectar producer, food for caterpillars	summer flowers, fall foliage color
Eragrostis spectabilis	purple lovegrass	cover for wildlife, pollen/nectar producer, food for caterpillars	summer flowers, fall foliage color
Juncus effusus	common rush	cover for wildlife, pollen/nectar producer, food for caterpillars	summer flowers, evergreen ground cover
Muhlenbergia capillaris	pink muhly	pollen/nectar producer, food for caterpillars	summer flowers
Panicum virgatum	switchgrass	cover for wildlife, pollen/nectar producer, food for caterpillars	summer flowers
Schizachyrium scoparium	little bluestem	cover for wildlife, pollen/nectar producer	summer flowers
Scirpus cyperinus	bulrush, woolgrass	cover for wildlife, pollen/nectar producer, food for caterpillars	summer flowers
Sorghastrum nutans	Indian grass	pollen/nectar producer, food for caterpillars	summer flowers, fall foliage color
Stenotaphrum secundatum	St. Augustine grass	food for caterpillars	summer flowers, evergreen ground cover

ECOLOGICAL FUNCTIONS

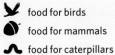

- cover for wildlife
- nest sites for birds
- pollen and/or nectar producer
- food for birds
- food for mammals
- food for caterpillars

LANDSCAPE FUNCTIONS

- spring flowers
- summer flowers
- fall flowers
- winter flowers
- fall foliage color
- fragrance
- evergreen ground cover
- deciduous ground cover
- screening
- shade and cooling
- edible fruits for humans

BOTANICAL NAME	COMMON NAME	ECOLOGICAL FUNCTIONS	LANDSCAPE FUNCTIONS
FERNS			
Adiantum capillus-veneris	southern maidenhair fern		deciduous ground cover
Adiantum pedatum	northern maidenhair fern		deciduous ground cover
Asplenium platyneuron	ebony spleenwort		deciduous ground cover
Athyrium asplenioides	southern lady fern	food for caterpillars	
Dryopteris ×australis	Dixie wood fern	food for caterpillars	evergreen ground cover
Dryopteris ludoviciana	southern wood fern	food for caterpillars	evergreen ground cover
Onoclea sensibilis	sensitive fern	food for caterpillars	deciduous ground cover
Osmunda cinnamomea	cinnamon fern	food for caterpillars	fall foliage color
Osmunda regalis	royal fern	food for caterpillars	fall foliage color
Phegopteris hexagonoptera	broad beech fern		deciduous ground cover
Polystichum acrostichoides	Christmas fern	cover for wildlife, food for caterpillars	evergreen ground cover
Thelypteris kunthii	southern shield fern	food for caterpillars	deciduous ground cover
Thelypteris noveboracensis	New York fern	food for caterpillars	fall foliage color
Woodwardia areolata	netted chain fern		deciduous ground cover
Woodwardia virginica	chain fern	food for caterpillars	

ECOLOGICAL FUNCTIONS

- cover for wildlife
- nest sites for birds
- pollen and/or nectar producer
- food for birds
- food for mammals
- food for caterpillars

LANDSCAPE FUNCTIONS

- spring flowers
- summer flowers
- fall flowers
- winter flowers
- fall foliage color
- fragrance
- evergreen ground cover
- deciduous ground cover
- screening
- shade and cooling
- edible fruits for humans

SELECTED PLANTS FOR THE SOUTHWEST
by **Amy Belk**, design assistant, Zona Gardens, Tucson

BOTANICAL NAME	COMMON NAME	ECOLOGICAL FUNCTIONS	LANDSCAPE FUNCTIONS
TREES			
Abies concolor	white fir		
Acer grandidentatum	bigtooth maple		
Calocedrus decurrens	incense cedar		
Celtis reticulata	netleaf hackberry		
Chilopsis linearis	desert willow		
Cupressus arizonica	Arizona cypress		
Fraxinus velutina	velvet ash		
Juniperus deppeana	alligator juniper		
Juniperus monosperma	one-seed juniper		
Picea pungens	blue spruce		
Pinus aristata	bristlecone pine		
Pinus contorta	lodgepole pine		
Pinus flexilis	limber pine		
Pinus ponderosa	ponderosa pine		
Pinus strobiformis	southwest white pine		
Pseudotsuga menziesii	Douglas fir		
Robinia neomexicana	New Mexico locust		
SHRUBS			
Acacia farnesiana	sweet acacia		
Amorpha canescens	lead plant		
Arctostaphylos uva-ursi	bearberry		
Artemisia cana	silver sage		
Artemisia tridentata	sagebrush		

BOTANICAL NAME	COMMON NAME	ECOLOGICAL FUNCTIONS	LANDSCAPE FUNCTIONS
SHRUBS, continued			
Berberis haematocarpa	desert holly		
Cercocarpus montanus	mountain mahogany		
Chrysothamnus nauseosus	rabbitbrush		
Dendromecon rigida	bush poppy		
Encelia farinosa	brittlebush		
Fendlera rupicola	cliff fendlerbush		
Forestiera neomexicana	New Mexico privet		
Heteromeles arbutifolia	Christmas berry		
Holodiscus dumosus	cliff spirea		
Larrea tridentata	creosote bush		
Philadelphus microphyllus	littleleaf mock orange		
Prunus besseyi	western sand cherry		
Purshia tridentata	antelope bitterbush		
Rhus trilobata	skunkbush sumac		
Ribes aureum	golden currant		
Rosa stellata	desert rose		
Shepherdia argentea	silver buffaloberry		
Yucca baccata	broadleaf yucca		
Yucca glauca	narrowleaf yucca		
VINES			
Clematis columbiana	Rocky Mountain clematis		
Clematis ligusticifolia	western virgin's bower		
Maurandya antirrhiniflora	snapdragon vine		
Vitis arizonica	canyon grape		

BOTANICAL NAME	COMMON NAME	ECOLOGICAL FUNCTIONS	LANDSCAPE FUNCTIONS
HERBACEOUS PERENNIALS AND BULBS			
Agastache cana	wild hyssop	cover for wildlife, pollen/nectar producer, food for birds	spring flowers, summer flowers, fragrance
Allium cernuum	pink nodding onion	pollen/nectar producer, food for mammals, food for caterpillars	spring flowers, summer flowers, fragrance
Aquilegia caerulea	Rocky Mountain columbine	pollen/nectar producer, food for birds, food for caterpillars	spring flowers, summer flowers, fall flowers, fragrance
Aquilegia chrysantha	golden-spurred columbine	cover for wildlife, pollen/nectar producer, food for birds, food for caterpillars	spring flowers, summer flowers, fall flowers, fragrance, deciduous ground cover
Asclepias speciosa	showy milkweed	pollen/nectar producer, food for caterpillars	spring flowers, summer flowers, fragrance
Asclepias tuberosa	butterfly weed	pollen/nectar producer, food for caterpillars	summer flowers, fragrance
Aster bigelovii	purple aster	cover for wildlife, pollen/nectar producer	summer flowers, fall flowers, deciduous ground cover
Baileya multiradiata	desert marigold	cover for wildlife, pollen/nectar producer, food for birds	spring flowers, summer flowers, deciduous ground cover
Berlandiera lyrata	chocolate flower	pollen/nectar producer, food for birds	summer flowers, fragrance, deciduous ground cover
Callirhoe involucrata	wine cup	pollen/nectar producer, food for birds, food for mammals, food for caterpillars	spring flowers, summer flowers, fall flowers, deciduous ground cover
Castilleja integra	Indian paintbrush	pollen/nectar producer, food for birds, food for caterpillars	spring flowers, summer flowers, fall flowers
Cleome serrulata	Rocky Mountain beeplant	cover for wildlife, pollen/nectar producer, food for birds, food for caterpillars	spring flowers, summer flowers, fall flowers, fragrance, edible fruits for humans
Dalea jamesii	James's dalea	cover for wildlife, pollen/nectar producer, food for mammals	spring flowers, summer flowers
Dichelostemma pulchellum	blue dicks	pollen/nectar producer, food for birds, food for mammals	spring flowers, fragrance
Echinacea purpurea	purple coneflower	pollen/nectar producer, food for birds, food for caterpillars	summer flowers, fall flowers, fragrance
Epilobium canum	hummingbird trumpet	cover for wildlife, pollen/nectar producer, food for mammals, food for caterpillars	spring flowers, summer flowers, fall flowers
Eriogonum corymbosum	buckwheatbrush	cover for wildlife, nest sites for birds, pollen/nectar producer, food for birds, food for mammals, food for caterpillars	summer flowers, fall flowers, screening
Eriogonum umbellatum	sulphur-flower buckwheat	cover for wildlife, nest sites for birds, pollen/nectar producer, food for birds, food for mammals, food for caterpillars	spring flowers, summer flowers, evergreen ground cover, screening
Erysimum asperum	western wallflower	pollen/nectar producer, food for birds, food for mammals, food for caterpillars	spring flowers, summer flowers, fall flowers, fragrance
Eschscholzia californica	California poppy	cover for wildlife, pollen/nectar producer, food for caterpillars	spring flowers, fragrance, deciduous ground cover

ECOLOGICAL FUNCTIONS

- cover for wildlife
- nest sites for birds
- pollen and/or nectar producer
- food for birds
- food for mammals
- food for caterpillars

LANDSCAPE FUNCTIONS

- spring flowers
- summer flowers
- fall flowers
- winter flowers
- fall foliage color
- fragrance
- evergreen ground cover
- deciduous ground cover
- screening
- shade and cooling
- edible fruits for humans

BOTANICAL NAME	COMMON NAME	ECOLOGICAL FUNCTIONS	LANDSCAPE FUNCTIONS
HERBACEOUS PERENNIALS AND BULBS, continued			
Helianthus maximiliani	Maximilian sunflower		
Heuchera pulchella	mountain coral bells		
Hymenoxys grandiflora	alpine sunflower		
Ipomoea leptophylla	bush morning glory		
Ipomopsis aggregata	scarlet gilia		
Iris missouriensis	western blue flag		
Liatris punctata	dotted blazing star		
Liatris spicata	spiked blazing star		
Lupinus argenteus	silvery lupine		
Melampodium leucanthum	Blackfoot daisy		
Mirabilis multiflora	desert four o'clock		
Oenothera missouriensis	Missouri evening primrose		
Oenothera speciosa	Mexican evening primrose		
Penstemon barbatus	scarlet bugler		
Penstemon grandiflorus	large-flowered penstemon		
Penstemon secundiflorus	sidebells penstemon		
Polemonium foliosissimum	Jacob's ladder		
Potentilla fruticosa	shrubby cinquefoil		
Ratibida columnifera	Mexican hat		
Rudbeckia hirta	black-eyed Susan		
Salvia azurea	blue sage		
Silene laciniata	Indian pink		
Sphaeralcea ambigua	desert mallow		
Tradescantia occidentalis	western spiderwort		

BOTANICAL NAME	COMMON NAME	ECOLOGICAL FUNCTIONS	LANDSCAPE FUNCTIONS
HERBACEOUS PERENNIALS AND BULBS, continued			
Zinnia grandiflora	prairie zinnia	🐝	✴ ✴ ✴ ▨
GRASSES, SEDGES, AND RUSHES			
Andropogon gerardii	big bluestem	cover, nest, pollen/nectar, food birds, food mammals, caterpillars	spring, summer, fall foliage
Aristida purpurea	purple three awn	cover, nest, pollen/nectar, food birds, food mammals, caterpillars	summer, fall foliage
Bouteloua curtipendula	sideoats grama	cover, nest, pollen/nectar, food birds, food mammals, caterpillars	summer, fall foliage, deciduous ground cover
Bouteloua gracilis	blue gramagrass	cover, nest, pollen/nectar, food birds, food mammals	summer, deciduous ground cover
Buchloe dactyloides	buffalograss	cover, nest, pollen/nectar, food birds, food mammals, caterpillars	spring, summer, fall foliage, deciduous ground cover
Eragrostis intermedia	plains lovegrass	cover, pollen/nectar, food birds, food mammals	summer, fall
Hierochloe odorata	sweetgrass	pollen/nectar, food birds, food mammals	spring, summer, fragrance
Panicum virgatum	switchgrass	cover, nest, pollen/nectar, food birds, food mammals, caterpillars	fall foliage
Schizachyrium scoparium	little bluestem	cover, nest, pollen/nectar, food birds, food mammals, caterpillars	spring, summer, fall foliage, deciduous ground cover
Sorghastrum nutans	Indian grass	cover, nest, pollen/nectar, food birds, food mammals, caterpillars	spring, summer, fall foliage
Sporobolus wrightii	big sacaton	cover, nest, pollen/nectar, food birds, food mammals	spring, summer, fall foliage
Stipa tenuissima	Mexican feathergrass	cover, pollen/nectar, food birds, food mammals	summer, fall, fall foliage
FERNS			
Adiantum capillus-veneris	common maidenhair	cover, nest	deciduous ground cover
Pteridium aquilinum	Western bracken fern	cover	
Woodsia meomexicana	New Mexico cliff fern	cover	

ECOLOGICAL FUNCTIONS

 cover for wildlife   food for birds

nest sites for birds   food for mammals

pollen and/or nectar producer   food for caterpillars

LANDSCAPE FUNCTIONS

 spring flowers   fall foliage color   screening

summer flowers   fragrance   shade and cooling

fall flowers   evergreen ground cover   edible fruits for humans

winter flowers   deciduous ground cover

SELECTED PLANTS FOR THE PACIFIC NORTHWEST

by **Jane Hartline**, founder of Sauvie Island Habitat Partnership

BOTANICAL NAME	COMMON NAME	ECOLOGICAL FUNCTIONS	LANDSCAPE FUNCTIONS
TREES			
Abies amabilis	Pacific silver fir		
Abies concolor	white fir		
Abies grandis	grand fir		
Abies procera	noble fir		
Acer circinatum	vine maple		
Acer macrophyllum	bigleaf maple		
Alnus rubra	red alder		
Arbutus menziesii	Pacific madrone		
Betula occidentalis	water birch		
Betula papyrifera	paper birch		
Calocedrus decurrens	incense cedar		
Chamaecyparis lawsoniana	Port Orford cedar		
Chamaecyparis nootkatensis	yellow cedar		
Chrysolepis chrysophylla	golden chinquapin		
Cornus nuttallii	Pacific dogwood		
Corylus cornuta	beaked hazel		
Crataegus douglasii	Douglas hawthorn		
Frangula purshiana	cascara		
Fraxinus latifolia	Oregon ash		
Larix occidentalis	tamarack		
Lithocarpus densiflorus	tanbark oak		
Malus fusca	Oregon crabapple		
Picea engelmannii	Engelmann spruce		

BOTANICAL NAME	COMMON NAME	ECOLOGICAL FUNCTIONS	LANDSCAPE FUNCTIONS
TREES, continued			
Picea sitchensis	Sitka spruce	cover for wildlife, nest sites for birds, pollen and/or nectar producer	screening, shade and cooling
Pinus contorta	lodgepole pine	cover for wildlife, nest sites for birds, pollen and/or nectar producer	screening, shade and cooling
Pinus lambertiana	sugar pine	cover for wildlife, nest sites for birds, food for mammals, food for caterpillars	screening, shade and cooling
Pinus ponderosa	ponderosa pine	cover for wildlife, nest sites for birds, pollen and/or nectar producer, food for mammals, food for caterpillars	fragrance, screening, shade and cooling
Populus trichocarpa	black cottonwood	cover for wildlife, nest sites for birds, pollen and/or nectar producer, food for birds, food for caterpillars	fragrance, shade and cooling
Pseudotsuga menziesii	Douglas fir	cover for wildlife, nest sites for birds, pollen and/or nectar producer, food for mammals, food for caterpillars	screening, shade and cooling
Quercus chrysolepis	canyon live oak	cover for wildlife, nest sites for birds, pollen and/or nectar producer, food for birds, food for mammals, food for caterpillars	screening, shade and cooling
Quercus garryana	Garry oak	cover for wildlife, nest sites for birds, pollen and/or nectar producer, food for birds, food for mammals, food for caterpillars	shade and cooling
Quercus kelloggii	California black oak	cover for wildlife, nest sites for birds, pollen and/or nectar producer, food for birds, food for mammals, food for caterpillars	fall foliage color, shade and cooling
Quercus vaccinifolia	huckleberry oak	cover for wildlife, nest sites for birds	
Salix scouleriana	Scouler's willow	cover for wildlife, nest sites for birds, pollen and/or nectar producer, food for mammals, food for caterpillars	spring flowers, shade and cooling
Sequoiadendron giganteum	giant sequoia	cover for wildlife, nest sites for birds	screening, shade and cooling
Taxus brevifolia	western yew	cover for wildlife, nest sites for birds	screening, shade and cooling
Thuja plicata	western red cedar	cover for wildlife, nest sites for birds, food for birds, food for mammals, food for caterpillars	fragrance, screening, shade and cooling
Tsuga heterophylla	western hemlock	cover for wildlife, nest sites for birds, food for birds, food for mammals, food for caterpillars	screening, shade and cooling
Umbellularia californica	California bay laurel	cover for wildlife, nest sites for birds, pollen and/or nectar producer, food for birds, food for mammals	spring flowers, fragrance, screening, shade and cooling, edible fruits for humans
SHRUBS			
Amelanchier alnifolia	western serviceberry	cover for wildlife, nest sites for birds, pollen and/or nectar producer, food for birds, food for mammals, food for caterpillars	spring flowers, fall foliage color, shade and cooling, edible fruits for humans
Arctostaphylos columbiana	hairy manzanita	cover for wildlife, nest sites for birds, pollen and/or nectar producer, food for birds, food for mammals, food for caterpillars	spring flowers, fragrance, screening, edible fruits for humans

ECOLOGICAL FUNCTIONS
- cover for wildlife
- nest sites for birds
- pollen and/or nectar producer
- food for birds
- food for mammals
- food for caterpillars

LANDSCAPE FUNCTIONS
- spring flowers
- summer flowers
- fall flowers
- winter flowers
- fall foliage color
- fragrance
- evergreen ground cover
- deciduous ground cover
- screening
- shade and cooling
- edible fruits for humans

BOTANICAL NAME	COMMON NAME	ECOLOGICAL FUNCTIONS	LANDSCAPE FUNCTIONS
SHRUBS, continued			
Arctostaphylos uva-ursi	kinnikinnik		
Ceanothus integerrimus	deerbrush		
Ceanothus prostratus	Mahala mat		
Ceanothus thyrsiflorus	blueblossum		
Cercocarpus montanus	mountain mahogany		
Chrysolepis sempervirens	bush chinquapin		
Cornus sericea	redstem dogwood, red osier dogwood		
Empetrum nigrum	crowberry		
Euonymus occidentalis	western wahoo		
Garrya elliptica	silk-tassel bush		
Gaultheria ovatifolia	Oregon wintergreen		
Gaultheria shallon	salal		
Holodiscus discolor	oceanspray		
Kalmia microphylla	bog laurel		
Kalmiopsis leachiana	kalmiopsis		
Ledum glandulosum	trapper's tea		
Ledum groenlandicum	Labrador tea		
Leucothoë davisiae	western leucothoe		
Lithocarpus densiflorus var. echinoides	tanbark oak		
Lonicera involucrata	twinberry		
Mahonia aquifolium	Oregon grape		
Mahonia nervosa	low Oregon grape		
Myrica californica	California wax myrtle		

SHRUBS, continued

BOTANICAL NAME	COMMON NAME	ECOLOGICAL FUNCTIONS	LANDSCAPE FUNCTIONS
Myrica gale	sweetgale	cover for wildlife, pollen/nectar producer	winter flowers
Paxistima myrsinites	Oregon box	cover for wildlife, nest sites for birds	winter flowers
Penstemon fruticosus	shrubby penstemon	cover for wildlife, nest sites for birds, pollen/nectar producer	spring flowers, summer flowers
Philadelphus lewisii	mock orange	cover for wildlife, nest sites for birds, pollen/nectar producer, food for caterpillars	spring flowers, summer flowers, fragrance
Physocarpus capitatus	Pacific ninebark	cover for wildlife, nest sites for birds, pollen/nectar producer, food for mammals, food for caterpillars	spring flowers
Potentilla fruticosa	shrubby cinquefoil	cover for wildlife, nest sites for birds, pollen/nectar producer	summer flowers, fall flowers
Rhododendron macrophyllum	Pacific rhododendron	cover for wildlife, nest sites for birds, pollen/nectar producer, food for mammals, food for caterpillars	spring flowers, summer flowers
Rhododendron occidentale	western azalea	cover for wildlife, nest sites for birds, pollen/nectar producer, food for mammals	spring flowers, summer flowers, fragrance
Rhus glabra	smooth sumac	cover for wildlife, nest sites for birds, pollen/nectar producer, food for birds, food for mammals, food for caterpillars	spring flowers, summer flowers, fall foliage color
Ribes sanguineum	red-flowering currant	cover for wildlife, nest sites for birds, pollen/nectar producer, food for birds, food for mammals, food for caterpillars	spring flowers, edible fruits for humans
Rosa nutkana	Nootka rose	cover for wildlife, nest sites for birds, pollen/nectar producer, food for birds, food for mammals, food for caterpillars	spring flowers, fragrance
Rubus parviflorus	thimbleberry	cover for wildlife, pollen/nectar producer, food for mammals	spring flowers, edible fruits for humans
Rubus spectabilis	salmonberry	cover for wildlife, nest sites for birds, pollen/nectar producer, food for birds, food for mammals	spring flowers, edible fruits for humans
Sambucus cerulea	blue elderberry	cover for wildlife, nest sites for birds, pollen/nectar producer, food for birds, food for mammals, food for caterpillars	spring flowers, edible fruits for humans
Sorbus sitchensis	Sitka mountain ash	cover for wildlife, nest sites for birds, pollen/nectar producer, food for birds, food for mammals	spring flowers, fall foliage color
Spiraea douglasii	rose spirea	cover for wildlife, nest sites for birds, pollen/nectar producer, food for caterpillars	spring flowers
Symphoricarpos albus	snowberry	cover for wildlife, nest sites for birds, pollen/nectar producer, food for birds, food for mammals, food for caterpillars	
Vaccinium ovatum	evergreen huckleberry	cover for wildlife, nest sites for birds, pollen/nectar producer, food for birds, food for mammals, food for caterpillars	spring flowers, screening, edible fruits for humans
Vaccinium oxycoccus	cranberry	cover for wildlife, pollen/nectar producer	edible fruits for humans
Vaccinium parvifolium	red huckleberry	cover for wildlife, nest sites for birds, pollen/nectar producer, food for birds, food for mammals, food for caterpillars	spring flowers, fall foliage color, edible fruits for humans

ECOLOGICAL FUNCTIONS

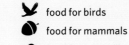

- cover for wildlife
- nest sites for birds
- pollen and/or nectar producer
- food for birds
- food for mammals
- food for caterpillars

LANDSCAPE FUNCTIONS

- spring flowers
- summer flowers
- fall flowers
- winter flowers

- fall foliage color
- fragrance
- evergreen ground cover
- deciduous ground cover
- screening
- shade and cooling
- edible fruits for humans

BOTANICAL NAME	COMMON NAME	ECOLOGICAL FUNCTIONS	LANDSCAPE FUNCTIONS
SHRUBS, continued			
Viburnum edule	moosewood viburnum		
VINES			
Lonicera ciliosa	trumpet honeysuckle		
Lonicera hispidula	hairy honeysuckle		
Vitis californica	western wild grape		
HERBACEOUS PERENNIALS AND BULBS			
Achlys triphylla	vanilla leaf		
Aconitum columbianum	Columbian monkshood		
Alchillea millefolium	yarrow		
Aquilegia formosa	red columbine		
Aralia californica	western aralia		
Aruncus dioicus	goat's beard		
Asarum caudatum	long-tailed wild ginger		
Aster subspicata	Douglas aster		
Campanula rotundifolia	harebell		
Clematis hirsutissima	hairy clematis		
Clinopodium douglasii	yerba buena		
Cornus canadensis	bunchberry		
Corydalis scouleri	corydalis		
Darmera peltatum	umbrella plant		
Dicentra formosa	western bleeding heart		
Eriophyllum lanatum	Oregon sunshine		
Erythronium oreganum	fawn lily		
Fragaria chiloensis	coastal strawberry		
Fragaria virginiana	wild strawberry		

HERBACEOUS PERENNIALS AND BULBS, continued

BOTANICAL NAME	COMMON NAME	ECOLOGICAL FUNCTIONS	LANDSCAPE FUNCTIONS
Geranium oreganum	Oregon geranium	cover for wildlife, pollen/nectar producer, food for mammals, food for caterpillars	spring flowers, deciduous ground cover
Geranium viscosissimum	sticky purple geranium	pollen/nectar producer	spring flowers
Heuchera micrantha	small-flowered alumroot	pollen/nectar producer	spring flowers
Iliamna rivularis	streambank wild hollyhock	cover for wildlife	spring flowers, deciduous ground cover
Iris tenax	Oregon iris	pollen/nectar producer	spring flowers
Lilium columbianum	tiger lily	pollen/nectar producer	summer flowers
Linnaea borealis	twinflower	food for birds	spring flowers, fragrance, evergreen ground cover
Lupinus polyphyllus	bigleaf lupine	pollen/nectar producer	spring flowers, fragrance
Maianthemum dilatatum	false lily-of-the-valley	cover for wildlife, pollen/nectar producer	spring flowers, deciduous ground cover
Maianthemum racemosum	false Solomon's-seal	pollen/nectar producer, food for caterpillars	spring flowers, fragrance
Mertensia paniculata	tall bluebells		spring flowers, fall foliage color
Mimulus guttatus	monkey flower	pollen/nectar producer	summer flowers
Oenothera biennis	evening primrose	pollen/nectar producer	summer flowers
Oxalis oregana	redwood sorrel	pollen/nectar producer, food for birds, food for mammals	spring flowers
Penstemon serrulatus	Cascade penstemon	pollen/nectar producer, food for caterpillars	summer flowers
Sedum spathulifolium	common stonecrop	pollen/nectar producer, food for caterpillars	summer flowers, evergreen ground cover
Sidalcea campestris	meadow checkermallow	pollen/nectar producer, food for caterpillars	summer flowers
Sisyrinchium bellum	western blue-eyed grass	pollen/nectar producer	spring flowers
Solidago canadensis	Canada goldenrod	pollen/nectar producer, food for birds, food for caterpillars	fall flowers
Tellima grandiflora	fringecup	cover for wildlife, pollen/nectar producer, food for caterpillars	spring flowers, summer flowers, fragrance

ECOLOGICAL FUNCTIONS

- cover for wildlife
- nest sites for birds
- pollen and/or nectar producer
- food for birds
- food for mammals
- food for caterpillars

LANDSCAPE FUNCTIONS

- spring flowers
- summer flowers
- fall flowers
- winter flowers
- fall foliage color
- fragrance
- evergreen ground cover
- deciduous ground cover
- screening
- shade and cooling
- edible fruits for humans

BOTANICAL NAME	COMMON NAME	ECOLOGICAL FUNCTIONS	LANDSCAPE FUNCTIONS
HERBACEOUS PERENNIALS AND BULBS, continued			
Thermopsis montana	golden pea		
Tiarella trifoliata	threeleaf foamflower		
Trientalis arctica	northern starflower		
Trillium ovatum	Western white		
Vancouveria hexandra	vancouveria		
Viola glabella	stream violet		
Zigadenus elegans	mountain death camas		
GRASSES, SEDGES, AND RUSHES			
Carex obnupta	slough sedge		
Carex praegracilis	clustered field sedge		
Danthonia californica	California oatgrass		
Deschampsia cespitosa	tufted hairgrass		
Festuca roemeri	Roemer's fescue		
Juncus patens	spreading rush		
Koeleria macrantha	prairie June grass		
FERNS			
Adiantum pedatum	maidenhair fern		
Asplenium trichomanes	spleenwort, maidenhair spleenwort		
Athyrium filix-femina	lady fern		
Blechnum spicant	deer fern		
Gymnocarpium dryopteris	oak fern		
Pellaea atropurpurea	purple cliffbrake		
Polypodium glycyrrhiza	licorice fern		
Polystichum munitum	sword fern		
Woodwardia fimbriata	giant chain fern		

SELECTED PLANTS FOR THE MIDWEST AND MOUNTAIN STATES
by **Jim McCormac**, author of *Birds of Ohio*

BOTANICAL NAME	COMMON NAME	ECOLOGICAL FUNCTIONS	LANDSCAPE FUNCTIONS
TREES			
Abies balsamea	balsam fir		
Acer pensylvanicum	striped maple		
Acer rubrum	red maple		
Acer saccharum	sugar maple		
Acer saccharinum	silver maple		
Alnus incana	gray alder		
Alnus viridis	mountain alder		
Amelanchier arborea	downy serviceberry, shadblow serviceberry		
Betula alleghaniensis	yellow birch		
Betula nigra	river birch		
Betula papyrifera	paper birch		
Carpinus caroliniana	ironwood		
Carya cordiformis	bitternut hickory		
Carya ovata	shagbark hickory		
Celtis occidentalis	common hackberry		
Cercis canadensis	redbud		
Cornus alternifolia	alternate-leaf dogwood		
Crataegus crus-galli	cockspur hawthorn		

ECOLOGICAL FUNCTIONS
- cover for wildlife
- nest sites for birds
- pollen and/or nectar producer
- food for birds
- food for mammals
- food for caterpillars

LANDSCAPE FUNCTIONS
- spring flowers
- summer flowers
- fall flowers
- winter flowers
- fall foliage color
- fragrance
- evergreen ground cover
- deciduous ground cover
- screening
- shade and cooling
- edible fruits for humans

BOTANICAL NAME	COMMON NAME	ECOLOGICAL FUNCTIONS	LANDSCAPE FUNCTIONS
TREES, continued			
Diospyros virginiana	persimmon		
Euonymus atropurpureus	eastern wahoo, burning bush		
Fagus grandifolia	American beech		
Fraxinus americana	white ash		
Fraxinus nigra	black ash		
Gleditsia triacanthos	honey locust		
Gymnocladus dioicus	Kentucky coffee tree		
Juglans cinerea	butternut		
Juglans nigra	black walnut		
Juniperus virginiana	red cedar		
Larix laricina	tamarack		
Liriodendron tulipifera	tulip tree		
Malus ioensis	wild crabapple		
Morus rubra	red mulberry		
Nyssa sylvatica	black gum		
Ostrya virginiana	American hop hornbeam		
Picea glauca	white spruce		
Picea mariana	black spruce		
Pinus banksiana	Jack pine		
Pinus resinosa	red pine		
Pinus rigida	pitch pine		
Pinus strobus	white pine		
Platanus occidentalis	American sycamore		
Populus deltoides	eastern cottonwood		

BOTANICAL NAME	COMMON NAME	ECOLOGICAL FUNCTIONS	LANDSCAPE FUNCTIONS
TREES, continued			
Populus tremuloides	quaking aspen	cover for wildlife, nest sites for birds, food for birds, food for mammals, food for caterpillars	spring flowers, fall foliage color, shade and cooling
Prunus americana	American plum	cover for wildlife, nest sites for birds, pollen/nectar, food for birds, food for mammals, food for caterpillars	spring flowers, fall foliage color, shade and cooling, edible fruits for humans
Prunus serotina	black cherry	cover for wildlife, nest sites for birds, pollen/nectar, food for birds, food for mammals, food for caterpillars	spring flowers, fall foliage color, shade and cooling, edible fruits for humans
Prunus virginiana	chokecherry	cover for wildlife, nest sites for birds, pollen/nectar, food for birds, food for mammals, food for caterpillars	spring flowers, fall foliage color, shade and cooling, edible fruits for humans
Ptelea trifoliata	hoptree	cover for wildlife, nest sites for birds, pollen/nectar, food for caterpillars	spring flowers, fall foliage color, shade and cooling
Quercus alba	white oak	cover for wildlife, nest sites for birds, pollen/nectar, food for birds, food for mammals, food for caterpillars	spring flowers, fall foliage color, shade and cooling
Quercus macrocarpa	burr oak	cover for wildlife, nest sites for birds, pollen/nectar, food for birds, food for mammals, food for caterpillars	spring flowers, fall foliage color, shade and cooling
Quercus muehlenbergii	chinkapin oak	cover for wildlife, nest sites for birds, pollen/nectar, food for birds, food for mammals, food for caterpillars	spring flowers, fall foliage color, shade and cooling
Quercus palustris	pin oak	cover for wildlife, nest sites for birds, pollen/nectar, food for birds, food for mammals, food for caterpillars	spring flowers, fall foliage color, shade and cooling
Quercus prinoides	dwarf chinkapin oak	cover for wildlife, nest sites for birds, pollen/nectar, food for birds, food for mammals, food for caterpillars	spring flowers, fall foliage color
Quercus rubra	red oak	cover for wildlife, nest sites for birds, pollen/nectar, food for birds, food for mammals, food for caterpillars	spring flowers, fall foliage color, shade and cooling
Quercus velutina	black oak	cover for wildlife, nest sites for birds, pollen/nectar, food for birds, food for mammals, food for caterpillars	spring flowers, fall foliage color, shade and cooling
Robinia pseudoacacia	black locust	cover for wildlife, nest sites for birds, pollen/nectar, food for mammals, food for caterpillars	spring flowers, fall foliage color, fragrance, shade and cooling
Salix nigra	black willow	cover for wildlife, nest sites for birds, pollen/nectar, food for caterpillars	spring flowers, fall foliage color, shade and cooling
Sassafras albidum	sassafras	cover for wildlife, nest sites for birds, pollen/nectar, food for birds, food for mammals, food for caterpillars	spring flowers, fall foliage color, shade and cooling
Sorbus americana	mountain ash	cover for wildlife, nest sites for birds, pollen/nectar, food for birds, food for mammals, food for caterpillars	spring flowers, fall foliage color, shade and cooling
Thuja occidentalis	northern white cedar	cover for wildlife, nest sites for birds, food for birds, food for mammals, food for caterpillars	spring flowers, screening, shade and cooling
Tilia americana	basswood	cover for wildlife, nest sites for birds, pollen/nectar, food for birds, food for mammals, food for caterpillars	spring flowers, fall foliage color, shade and cooling
Ulmus americana	American elm (blight-resistant variety)	cover for wildlife, nest sites for birds, food for birds, food for mammals, food for caterpillars	spring flowers, fall foliage color, shade and cooling
Zanthoxylum americanum	prickly ash	cover for wildlife, nest sites for birds, pollen/nectar, food for caterpillars	spring flowers, shade and cooling

ECOLOGICAL FUNCTIONS

- cover for wildlife
- nest sites for birds
- pollen and/or nectar producer
- food for birds
- food for mammals
- food for caterpillars

LANDSCAPE FUNCTIONS

- spring flowers
- summer flowers
- fall flowers
- winter flowers
- fall foliage color
- fragrance
- evergreen ground cover
- deciduous ground cover
- screening
- shade and cooling
- edible fruits for humans

BOTANICAL NAME	COMMON NAME	ECOLOGICAL FUNCTIONS	LANDSCAPE FUNCTIONS
SHRUBS			
Aesculus glabra	Ohio buckeye		
Amorpha canescens	lead plant		
Amorpha fruticosa	false indigo		
Aronia melanocarpa	black chokeberry		
Asimina triloba	pawpaw		
Atriplex canescens	four-winged saltbrush		
Betula pumila	bog birch		
Ceanothus americanus	New Jersey tea		
Cephalanthus occidentalis	buttonbush		
Chamaedaphne calyculata	leatherleaf		
Cornus amomum	silky dogwood		
Cornus canadensis	bunchberry		
Cornus racemosa	gray dogwood		
Cornus sericea	redtwig dogwood		
Corylus americana	American hazelnut		
Crataegus mollis	downy hawthorn		
Diervilla lonicera	bush honeysuckle		
Dirca palustris	leatherwood		
Gaylussacia baccata	black huckleberry		
Hamamelis virginiana	witch hazel		
Ilex glabra	inkberry		
Ilex mucronata	American mountain holly		
Ilex opaca	American holly		
Ilex verticillata	winterberry		

BOTANICAL NAME	COMMON NAME	ECOLOGICAL FUNCTIONS	LANDSCAPE FUNCTIONS
SHRUBS, continued			
Juniperus communis	common juniper	cover for wildlife, nest sites for birds, food for birds, food for mammals, food for caterpillars	spring flowers, screening
Juniperus horizontalis	horizontal juniper	cover for wildlife, nest sites for birds, food for birds, food for mammals, food for caterpillars	summer flowers, evergreen ground cover
Kalmia latifolia	mountain laurel	cover for wildlife, nest sites for birds, pollen and/or nectar producer	summer flowers, shade and cooling
Lindera benzoin	spicebush	cover for wildlife, nest sites for birds, pollen and/or nectar producer, food for birds, food for mammals, food for caterpillars	spring flowers, fall foliage color, shade and cooling
Myrica pensylvanica	northern bayberry	cover for wildlife, nest sites for birds, pollen and/or nectar producer, food for birds, food for mammals, food for caterpillars	spring flowers, shade and cooling
Physocarpus opulifolius	common ninebark	cover for wildlife, nest sites for birds, pollen and/or nectar producer, food for birds, food for mammals, food for caterpillars	summer flowers, shade and cooling
Rhamnus lanceolata	lanceleaf buckthorn	cover for wildlife, nest sites for birds, pollen and/or nectar producer, food for birds, food for caterpillars	summer flowers, fall foliage color, shade and cooling
Rhus aromatica	fragrant sumac	cover for wildlife, nest sites for birds, pollen and/or nectar producer, food for birds, food for mammals, food for caterpillars	spring flowers, fall foliage color, deciduous ground cover, shade and cooling
Rhus copallina	winged sumac	cover for wildlife, nest sites for birds, pollen and/or nectar producer, food for birds, food for mammals, food for caterpillars	summer flowers, fall foliage color, shade and cooling
Rhus glabra	smooth sumac	cover for wildlife, nest sites for birds, pollen and/or nectar producer, food for birds, food for mammals, food for caterpillars	summer flowers, fall foliage color, shade and cooling
Rhus typhina	staghorn sumac	cover for wildlife, nest sites for birds, pollen and/or nectar producer, food for birds, food for mammals, food for caterpillars	summer flowers, fall foliage color, shade and cooling
Ribes americanum	wild black currant	pollen and/or nectar producer, food for mammals	spring flowers, edible fruits for humans
Ribes missouriense	Missouri gooseberry	pollen and/or nectar producer, food for mammals	summer flowers, edible fruits for humans
Rosa acicularis	prickly rose	pollen and/or nectar producer, food for birds, food for mammals	summer flowers, fragrance
Rosa arkansana	Arkansas rose	pollen and/or nectar producer, food for birds, food for mammals	summer flowers
Rosa blanda	meadow rose	pollen and/or nectar producer, food for birds, food for mammals	summer flowers
Rosa setigera	prairie rose	pollen and/or nectar producer, food for birds, food for mammals	summer flowers
Rubus flagellaris	northern dewberry	pollen and/or nectar producer, food for birds, food for mammals, food for caterpillars	summer flowers
Rubus idaeus	red raspberry	cover for wildlife, nest sites for birds, pollen and/or nectar producer, food for birds, food for mammals, food for caterpillars	summer flowers, edible fruits for humans
Rubus occidentalis	black raspberry	cover for wildlife, nest sites for birds, pollen and/or nectar producer, food for birds, food for mammals, food for caterpillars	summer flowers, edible fruits for humans

ECOLOGICAL FUNCTIONS

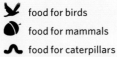

- cover for wildlife
- nest sites for birds
- pollen and/or nectar producer
- food for birds
- food for mammals
- food for caterpillars

LANDSCAPE FUNCTIONS

- spring flowers
- summer flowers
- fall flowers
- winter flowers
- fall foliage color
- fragrance
- evergreen ground cover
- deciduous ground cover
- screening
- shade and cooling
- edible fruits for humans

BOTANICAL NAME	COMMON NAME	ECOLOGICAL FUNCTIONS	LANDSCAPE FUNCTIONS
SHRUBS, continued			
Salix amygdaloides	peachleaf willow		
Salix discolor	pussy willow		
Salix eriocephala	Missouri River willow		
Salix humilis	prairie willow		
Salix interior	sandbar willow		
Salix petiolaris	meadow willow		
Sambucus canadensis	elderberry		
Shepherdia argentea	silver buffaloberry		
Shepherdia canadensis	russet buffaloberry		
Spiraea alba	white meadowsweet		
Spiraea tomentosa	steeplebush		
Staphylea trifolia	bladdernut		
Symphoricarpos albus	snowberry		
Symphoricarpos orbiculatus	coralberry		
Taxus canadensis	Canada yew		
Vaccinium angustifolium	low sweet blueberry		
Vaccinium corymbosum	highbush blueberry		
Vaccinium vitis-idaea	mountain cranberry		
Viburnum acerifolium	mapleleaf viburnum		
Viburnum cassinoides	smooth witherod, possumhaw		
Viburnum dentatum	arrowwood		
Viburnum lentago	nannyberry		
Viburnum prunifolium	blackhaw		

BOTANICAL NAME	COMMON NAME	ECOLOGICAL FUNCTIONS	LANDSCAPE FUNCTIONS
VINES			
Ampelopsis cordata	raccoon grape	cover for wildlife, pollen/nectar producer, food for birds, food for mammals, food for caterpillars	summer flowers
Celastrus scandens	American bittersweet	cover for wildlife, pollen/nectar producer, food for birds, food for mammals, food for caterpillars	summer flowers, fall foliage color
Lonicera dioica	limber honeysuckle	pollen/nectar producer, food for caterpillars	summer flowers
Menispermum canadense	moonseed	pollen/nectar producer, food for caterpillars	summer flowers
Parthenocissus quinquefolia	Virginia creeper	pollen/nectar producer, food for birds, food for mammals, food for caterpillars	summer flowers, fall foliage color
Parthenocissus vitacea	woodbine	cover for wildlife, pollen/nectar producer, food for birds, food for mammals, food for caterpillars	summer flowers, fall foliage color, deciduous ground cover
Vitis cinerea	winter grape	cover for wildlife, nest sites for birds, pollen/nectar producer, food for birds, food for mammals, food for caterpillars	summer flowers
Vitis riparia	riverbank grape	cover for wildlife, nest sites for birds, pollen/nectar producer, food for birds, food for mammals, food for caterpillars	summer flowers
Vitis vulpina	frost grape	cover for wildlife, nest sites for birds, pollen/nectar producer, food for birds, food for mammals, food for caterpillars	summer flowers
HERBACEOUS PERENNIALS AND BULBS			
Actaea racemosa	black cohosh	pollen/nectar producer, food for caterpillars	summer flowers
Actaea rubra	red baneberry	pollen/nectar producer	summer flowers
Ageratina altissima	white snakeroot	pollen/nectar producer	fall flowers
Anemone canadensis	Canada anemone	pollen/nectar producer	summer flowers
Anemone quinquefolia	wood anemone	pollen/nectar producer	spring flowers
Aquilegia canadensis	wild columbine	pollen/nectar producer	spring flowers
Arisaema triphyllum	Jack-in-the-pulpit	pollen/nectar producer	spring flowers
Asarum canadense	wild ginger	pollen/nectar producer, food for caterpillars	spring flowers, deciduous ground cover
Asclepias incarnata	swamp milkweed	pollen/nectar producer, food for caterpillars	summer flowers, fragrance
Asclepias syriaca	common milkweed	pollen/nectar producer, food for caterpillars	summer flowers, fragrance

ECOLOGICAL FUNCTIONS

cover for wildlife

nest sites for birds

pollen and/or nectar producer

food for birds

food for mammals

food for caterpillars

LANDSCAPE FUNCTIONS

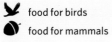

spring flowers

summer flowers

fall flowers

winter flowers

fall foliage color

fragrance

evergreen ground cover

deciduous ground cover

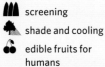

screening

shade and cooling

edible fruits for humans

351

HERBACEOUS PERENNIALS AND BULBS, continued

BOTANICAL NAME	COMMON NAME	ECOLOGICAL FUNCTIONS	LANDSCAPE FUNCTIONS
Asclepias tuberosa	butterfly weed	(bee) (caterpillar)	(flower)
Aster ericoides	white heath aster	(bee) (bird) (caterpillar)	(flower)
Aster novae-angliae	New England aster	(bee) (bird) (caterpillar)	(flower)
Baptisia alba	wild white indigo	(bee) (caterpillar)	(flower)
Baptisia australis	blue false indigo	(bee) (caterpillar)	(flower)
Boltonia asteroides	false aster, white doll's daisy	(bee) (bird) (caterpillar)	(flower)
Calla palustris	water arum	(bee)	(flower)
Caltha palustris	marsh marigold	(bee)	(flower)
Campanula rotundifolia	harebell	(bee)	(flower)
Caulophyllum thalictroides	blue cohosh	(bee)	(flower)
Chelone glabra	turtlehead	(bee) (caterpillar)	(flower)
Cimicifuga racemosa	black cohosh	(bee) (caterpillar)	(flower)
Clintonia borealis	blue bead lily	(bee)	(flower) (hatched)
Coreopsis lanceolata	tickseed	(bee) (bird) (caterpillar)	(flower)
Coreopsis rosea	pink coreopsis	(bee) (bird) (caterpillar)	(flower)
Delphinium tricorne	dwarf larkspur	(bee)	(flower)
Dicentra canadensis	squirrel-corn	(bee)	(flower)
Dicentra cucullaria	Dutchman's breeches	(bee)	(flower)
Dodecatheon meadia	shooting star	(bee)	(flower)
Echinacea purpurea	purple coneflower	(bee) (bird) (caterpillar)	(flower)
Erythronium americanum	yellow trout lily	(bee)	(flower) (hatched)
Eutrochium maculatum	spotted Joe-Pye weed	(bee) (bird) (caterpillar)	(flower)
Eupatorium perfoliatum	boneset	(bee) (bird) (caterpillar)	(flower)
Filipendula rubra	queen of the prairie	(bee) (bird) (caterpillar)	(flower)

BOTANICAL NAME	COMMON NAME	ECOLOGICAL FUNCTIONS	LANDSCAPE FUNCTIONS
HERBACEOUS PERENNIALS AND BULBS, continued			
Gaultheria procumbens	teaberry	pollen/nectar producer	spring flowers; evergreen ground cover
Gaylussacia brachycera	box huckleberry	pollen/nectar producer; food for birds; food for caterpillars	spring flowers; fall foliage color; evergreen ground cover; edible fruits for humans
Gentiana clausa	closed gentian	pollen/nectar producer	fall flowers
Geranium maculatum	wild geranium	pollen/nectar producer	spring flowers
Geum triflorum	prairie smoke	pollen/nectar producer	spring flowers
Helenium autumnale	Helen's flower, sneezeweed	pollen/nectar producer; food for birds; food for caterpillars	fall flowers
Heliopsis helianthoides	oxeye	pollen/nectar producer; food for birds; food for caterpillars	summer flowers
Hepatica acutiloba	sharp-lobed hepatica	pollen/nectar producer	spring flowers
Hepatica americana	round-lobed hepatica	pollen/nectar producer	spring flowers
Heuchera americana	alumroot, coral bells	pollen/nectar producer	spring flowers; deciduous ground cover
Hibiscus moscheutos	rose-mallow	pollen/nectar producer; food for caterpillars	summer flowers
Houstonia caerulea	bluets	pollen/nectar producer	spring flowers
Hydrastis canadensis	goldenseal	pollen/nectar producer	spring flowers
Iris cristata	crested iris	pollen/nectar producer	spring flowers; deciduous ground cover
Iris versicolor	blue flag iris	pollen/nectar producer	summer flowers
Jeffersonia diphylla	twinleaf	pollen/nectar producer	spring flowers; deciduous ground cover
Liatris spicata	spiked blazing star	pollen/nectar producer; food for birds	summer flowers
Lilium philadelphicum	wood lily	pollen/nectar producer	summer flowers
Lobelia cardinalis	cardinal flower	pollen/nectar producer	summer flowers
Lobelia siphilitica	great blue lobelia	pollen/nectar producer	fall flowers

ECOLOGICAL FUNCTIONS

 cover for wildlife
nest sites for birds
 pollen and/or nectar producer

food for birds
food for mammals
 food for caterpillars

LANDSCAPE FUNCTIONS

spring flowers
summer flowers
fall flowers
winter flowers

 fall foliage color
fragrance
evergreen ground cover
deciduous ground cover

screening
shade and cooling
edible fruits for humans

HERBACEOUS PERENNIALS AND BULBS, continued

BOTANICAL NAME	COMMON NAME	ECOLOGICAL FUNCTIONS	LANDSCAPE FUNCTIONS
Lupinus perennis	blue lupine	(bee, caterpillar)	(flower, hatch)
Mahonia repens	creeping mahonia	(beaver, butterfly, bee, bird, caterpillar)	(flower, leaf, hatch, cherry)
Maianthemum canadense	Canada mayflower	(bee)	(flower, hatch)
Maianthemum racemosum	false Solomon's-seal	(bee)	(flower)
Mertensia virginica	Virginia bluebells	(bee)	(flower, hatch)
Mitchella repens	partridgeberry	(bee, bird, acorn)	(flower, hatch)
Mitella diphylla	miterwort	(bee)	(flower)
Monarda didyma	beebalm	(bee)	(flower)
Monarda fistulosa	wild bergamot	(bee)	(flower)
Oenothera fruticosa	sundrops	(bee, caterpillar)	(flower)
Opuntia humifusa	eastern prickly pear	(bee)	(flower, hatch, cherry)
Panax quinquefolius	ginseng	(bee)	(flower)
Penstemon digitalis	foxglove beardtongue	(bee)	(flower)
Penstemon hirsutus	hairy beardtongue	(bee)	(flower)
Phlox divaricata	wild blue phlox	(bee)	(flower)
Phlox maculata	wild sweet William	(bee)	(flower)
Phlox subulata	moss pink	(bee)	(flower, hatch)
Physostegia virginiana	false dragonhead	(bee)	(flower)
Podophyllum peltatum	mayapple	(bee, caterpillar)	(flower, hatch)
Polemonium reptans	creeping Jacob's ladder	(bee)	(flower)
Polygonatum biflorum	Solomon's-seal	(bee)	(flower)
Potentilla tridentata	shrubby fivefingers	(bee)	(flower, hatch)
Ratibida pinnata	pinnate prairie coneflower	(bee, bird, caterpillar)	(flower)
Rudbeckia fulgida	orange coneflower	(bee, bird, caterpillar)	(flower)

BOTANICAL NAME	COMMON NAME	ECOLOGICAL FUNCTIONS	LANDSCAPE FUNCTIONS
HERBACEOUS PERENNIALS AND BULBS, continued			
Rudbeckia hirta	black-eyed Susan	pollen/nectar producer, food for birds, food for caterpillars	summer flowers
Rudbeckia laciniata	cutleaf coneflower	pollen/nectar producer, food for birds, food for caterpillars	summer flowers
Sanguinaria canadensis	bloodroot	pollen/nectar producer	spring flowers
Senecio aureus	golden ragwort	pollen/nectar producer, food for birds, food for caterpillars	spring flowers, deciduous ground cover
Sisyrinchium angustifolium	blue-eyed grass	pollen/nectar producer	summer flowers
Solidago caesia	blue-stem goldenrod	pollen/nectar producer	fall flowers
Solidago rugosa	rough-stem goldenrod	pollen/nectar producer, food for birds, food for caterpillars	fall flowers
Solidago speciosa	showy goldenrod	pollen/nectar producer, food for birds, food for caterpillars	fall flowers
Stylophorum diphyllum	wood poppy	pollen/nectar producer	spring flowers
Teucrium canadense	wood sage	pollen/nectar producer	summer flowers
Thalictrum dasycarpum	purple meadow rue	pollen/nectar producer	summer flowers
Thalictrum pubescens	tall meadow rue	pollen/nectar producer	summer flowers
Tiarella cordifolia	eastern foamflower	pollen/nectar producer	spring flowers, deciduous ground cover
Tradescantia ohiensis	spiderwort	pollen/nectar producer	summer flowers
Tradescantia virginiana	Virginia spiderwort	pollen/nectar producer	spring flowers
Trientalis borealis	starflower	pollen/nectar producer	spring flowers
Trillium flexipes	bent trillium	pollen/nectar producer	spring flowers
Trillium grandiflorum	white trillium	pollen/nectar producer	spring flowers
Trillium sessile	red trillium	pollen/nectar producer	spring flowers
Uvularia grandiflora	large-flowered bellwort	pollen/nectar producer	spring flowers

ECOLOGICAL FUNCTIONS

 cover for wildlife
nest sites for birds
pollen and/or nectar producer

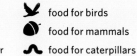 food for birds
food for mammals
food for caterpillars

LANDSCAPE FUNCTIONS

spring flowers
summer flowers
fall flowers
winter flowers

 fall foliage color
fragrance
evergreen ground cover
deciduous ground cover

screening
shade and cooling
edible fruits for humans

BOTANICAL NAME	COMMON NAME	ECOLOGICAL FUNCTIONS	LANDSCAPE FUNCTIONS
HERBACEOUS PERENNIALS AND BULBS, continued			
Veronicastrum virginicum	Culver's root	🐝	✳
Viola cucullata	marsh blue violet	🐝	✳
Viola pedata	birdsfoot violet	🐝 〰	✳
Viola pubescens	yellow violet	🐝 〰	✳
Viola sororia	hooded violet	🐝 〰	✳
Waldsteinia fragarioides	barren strawberry	🐝 🦅 🌰	✳ ▦
Zizia aurea	golden Alexanders	🐝	✳
GRASSES, SEDGES, AND RUSHES			
Acorus americanus	sweetflag	🐝	✳
Andropogon gerardii	big bluestem	🌱 🕷 🦅 🌰 〰	✳
Andropogon virginicus	broomsedge	🌱 🕷 🦅 🌰 〰	✳
Aristida purpurea	purple three awn	🌱 🕷 🦅 🌰 〰	✳
Bouteloua gracilis	blue gramagrass	🌱 🕷 🦅 🌰 〰	✳
Buchloe dactyloides	buffalograss	🌱 🕷 🦅 🌰 〰	✳
Carex muskingumensis	palm sedge	〰	✳
Carex pensylvanica	Pennsylvania sedge	〰	✳
Carex plantaginea	plantain sedge	🌱	✳
Carex platyphylla	broadleaf sedge	🌱	✳
Chasmanthium latifolium	river oats	〰	✳
Deschampsia cespitosa	tufted hairgrass	🌱 🕷	✳
Elymus glaucus	blue wild rye	〰	✳
Eragrostis spectabilis	purple lovegrass	🦅	✳
Juncus effusus	common rush	🌱	✳
Panicum virgatum	switchgrass	🌱 🕷 🦅 〰	✳

BOTANICAL NAME	COMMON NAME	ECOLOGICAL FUNCTIONS	LANDSCAPE FUNCTIONS
GRASSES, SEDGES, AND RUSHES, continued			
Schizachyrium scoparium	little bluestem	cover for wildlife, nest sites for birds, food for birds, food for caterpillars	fall flowers, fall foliage color, deciduous ground cover
Scirpus cyperinus	bulrush, woolgrass	cover for wildlife, food for birds	fall flowers
Sorghastrum nutans	Indian grass	cover for wildlife, nest sites for birds, food for birds, food for caterpillars	fall flowers
Spartina pectinata	prairie cord-grass	cover for wildlife, nest sites for birds, food for birds, food for caterpillars	fall flowers
Sporobolus heterolepis	prairie dropseed	cover for wildlife, nest sites for birds, food for birds, food for caterpillars	fall flowers
Tridens flavus	purpletop	food for caterpillars	fall flowers
Typha latifolia	broadleaf cattail	cover for wildlife, nest sites for birds, food for birds, food for mammals	fall flowers, shade and cooling
FERNS			
Adiantum pedatum	maidenhair fern	cover for wildlife, nest sites for birds	deciduous ground cover
Asplenium trichomanes	spleenwort, maidenhair spleenwort	cover for wildlife, nest sites for birds	
Athyrium filix-femina	lady fern	cover for wildlife, nest sites for birds	deciduous ground cover
Botrychium virginianum	rattlesnake fern	cover for wildlife, nest sites for birds	
Cryptogramma stelleri	slender rock brake	cover for wildlife, nest sites for birds	
Cystopteris fragilis	brittle bladder fern, fragile fern	cover for wildlife, nest sites for birds	
Dennstaedtia punctilobula	hayscented fern	cover for wildlife, nest sites for birds	deciduous ground cover
Dryopteris cristata	crested wood fern	cover for wildlife, nest sites for birds	deciduous ground cover
Dryopteris filix-mas	male fern	cover for wildlife, nest sites for birds	deciduous ground cover
Dryopteris goldiana	Goldie's fern	cover for wildlife, nest sites for birds	deciduous ground cover
Dryopteris intermedia	evergreen wood fern	cover for wildlife, nest sites for birds	deciduous ground cover
Dryopteris marginalis	marginal shield fern	cover for wildlife, nest sites for birds	deciduous ground cover

ECOLOGICAL FUNCTIONS

- cover for wildlife
- nest sites for birds
- pollen and/or nectar producer
- food for birds
- food for mammals
- food for caterpillars

LANDSCAPE FUNCTIONS

- spring flowers
- summer flowers
- fall flowers
- winter flowers
- fall foliage color
- fragrance
- evergreen ground cover
- deciduous ground cover
- screening
- shade and cooling
- edible fruits for humans

BOTANICAL NAME	COMMON NAME	ECOLOGICAL FUNCTIONS	LANDSCAPE FUNCTIONS
FERNS, continued			
Gymnocarpium dryopteris	oak fern	cover for wildlife, nest sites for birds	deciduous ground cover
Matteuccia struthiopteris	ostrich fern	cover for wildlife, nest sites for birds	deciduous ground cover
Onoclea sensibilis	sensitive fern	cover for wildlife, nest sites for birds	deciduous ground cover
Osmunda cinnamomea	cinnamon fern	cover for wildlife, nest sites for birds, food for caterpillars	deciduous ground cover
Osmunda claytoniana	interrupted fern	cover for wildlife, nest sites for birds	deciduous ground cover
Osmunda regalis	royal fern	cover for wildlife, nest sites for birds	deciduous ground cover
Pellaea atropurpurea	purple cliffbrake	cover for wildlife	
Phegopteris hexagonoptera	broad beech fern	cover for wildlife	
Polypodium virginianum	rock polypody	cover for wildlife	evergreen ground cover
Polystichum acrostichoides	Christmas fern	cover for wildlife, nest sites for birds	evergreen ground cover
Polystichum braunii	Braun's holly fern	cover for wildlife, nest sites for birds	evergreen ground cover
Pteridium aquilinum	bracken fern	food for caterpillars	
Thelypteris palustris	marsh fern	cover for wildlife, nest sites for birds, food for caterpillars	deciduous ground cover
Woodsia obtusa	blunt-lobed woodsia	cover for wildlife	
Woodwardia virginica	chain fern	cover for wildlife, nest sites for birds	deciduous ground cover

ECOLOGICAL FUNCTIONS

- cover for wildlife
- nest sites for birds
- pollen and/or nectar producer
- food for birds
- food for mammals
- food for caterpillars

LANDSCAPE FUNCTIONS

- spring flowers
- summer flowers
- fall flowers
- winter flowers
- fall foliage color
- fragrance
- evergreen ground cover
- deciduous ground cover
- screening
- shade and cooling
- edible fruits for humans

SELECTED PLANTS FOR NEW ENGLAND

by **Chris Schorn**, New England Wild Flower Society

BOTANICAL NAME	COMMON NAME	ECOLOGICAL FUNCTIONS	LANDSCAPE FUNCTIONS
TREES			
Abies balsamea	balsam fir		
Acer rubrum	red maple		
Acer penslyvanicum	striped maple		
Acer saccharum	sugar maple		
Amelanchier arborea	shadblow serviceberry		
Betula alleghaniensis	yellow birch		
Betula lenta	sweet birch		
Betula nigra	river birch		
Betula papyrifera	paper birch		
Carya ovata	shagbark hickory		
Celtis occidentalis	common hackberry		
Cercis canadensis	redbud		
Cornus florida	flowering dogwood		
Fagus grandifolia	American beech		
Fraxinus americana	white ash		
Juglans nigra	black walnut		
Juniperus virginiana	red cedar		
Larix laricina	tamarack		
Liquidambar styraciflua	sweet gum		
Liriodendron tulipifera	tulip tree		
Nyssa sylvatica	black gum		
Ostrya virginiana	American hop hornbeam		
Picea glauca	white spruce		

BOTANICAL NAME	COMMON NAME	ECOLOGICAL FUNCTIONS	LANDSCAPE FUNCTIONS
TREES, continued			
Pinus banksiana	Jack pine		
Pinus rigida	pitch pine		
Pinus strobus	white pine		
Prunus serotina	black cherry		
Quercus alba	white oak		
Quercus palustris	pin oak		
Quercus prinus	chestnut oak		
Quercus rubra	red oak		
Salix nigra	black willow		
Sassafras albidum	sassafras		
Sorbus americana	American mountain ash		
Thuja occidentalis	arborvitae, northern white cedar		
Tilia americana	basswood		
Zanthoxylum americanum	prickly ash		
SHRUBS			
Alnus incana	gray alder		
Alnus viridis	mountain alder		
Aronia arbutifolia	red chokeberry		
Ceanothus americanus	New Jersey tea		
Cephalanthus occidentalis	buttonbush		
Chamaedaphne calyculata	leatherleaf		
Clethra alnifolia	sweet pepperbush		
Cornus amomum	silky dogwood		
Corylus americana	American hazelnut		

BOTANICAL NAME	COMMON NAME	ECOLOGICAL FUNCTIONS	LANDSCAPE FUNCTIONS
SHRUBS, continued			
Diervilla lonicera	northern bush honeysuckle	cover for wildlife; pollen and/or nectar producer; food for birds	spring flowers; fall foliage color; fragrance; shade and cooling
Dirca palustris	leatherwood	pollen and/or nectar producer	spring flowers; fall foliage color; shade and cooling
Epigaea repens	trailing arbutus	pollen and/or nectar producer; food for birds; food for mammals; food for caterpillars	spring flowers; fragrance; deciduous ground cover
Gaultheria procumbens	teaberry, wintergreen	food for birds; food for mammals	spring flowers; fragrance; evergreen ground cover
Gaylussacia baccata	black huckleberry	cover for wildlife; pollen and/or nectar producer; food for birds; food for mammals	spring flowers; fall foliage color; shade and cooling; edible fruits for humans
Gaylussacia brachycera	box huckleberry	cover for wildlife; food for birds; food for mammals; food for caterpillars	spring flowers; deciduous ground cover; edible fruits for humans
Hamamelis virginiana	witch hazel	nest sites for birds; pollen and/or nectar producer; food for birds	spring flowers; fall foliage color; fragrance; shade and cooling
Ilex glabra	inkberry	cover for wildlife; nest sites for birds; pollen and/or nectar producer; food for birds	spring flowers; fall foliage color; shade and cooling
Ilex opaca	American holly	cover for wildlife; nest sites for birds; pollen and/or nectar producer; food for birds	spring flowers; screening; shade and cooling
Ilex verticillata	winterberry	cover for wildlife; nest sites for birds; pollen and/or nectar producer; food for birds; food for caterpillars	spring flowers; fall foliage color; shade and cooling
Juniperus horizontalis	horizontal juniper	cover for wildlife	fragrance; evergreen ground cover
Kalmia latifolia	mountain laurel	cover for wildlife; nest sites for birds; pollen and/or nectar producer; food for caterpillars	spring flowers; fragrance; screening; shade and cooling
Lindera benzoin	spicebush	cover for wildlife; nest sites for birds; pollen and/or nectar producer; food for birds; food for caterpillars	spring flowers; fall foliage color; fragrance; shade and cooling
Myrica pensylvanica	northern bayberry	cover for wildlife; nest sites for birds; pollen and/or nectar producer; food for birds; food for mammals	fall foliage color; fragrance; shade and cooling
Rhododendron canadense	rhodora	cover for wildlife; nest sites for birds; pollen and/or nectar producer; food for caterpillars	spring flowers; fragrance; shade and cooling
Rhododendron maximum	great laurel, rosebay rhododendron	cover for wildlife; nest sites for birds; pollen and/or nectar producer; food for caterpillars	spring flowers; fragrance; screening; shade and cooling
Rhus aromatica	fragrant sumac	cover for wildlife; pollen and/or nectar producer; food for birds; food for mammals; food for caterpillars	spring flowers; fall foliage color; fragrance; shade and cooling
Rhus copallina	winged sumac	cover for wildlife; pollen and/or nectar producer; food for birds; food for mammals; food for caterpillars	spring flowers; fall foliage color; shade and cooling
Rhus glabra	smooth sumac	cover for wildlife; pollen and/or nectar producer; food for birds; food for mammals; food for caterpillars	spring flowers; fall foliage color; shade and cooling
Rhus typhina	staghorn sumac	cover for wildlife; pollen and/or nectar producer; food for birds; food for mammals; food for caterpillars	spring flowers; fall foliage color; shade and cooling

ECOLOGICAL FUNCTIONS

- cover for wildlife
- nest sites for birds
- pollen and/or nectar producer
- food for birds
- food for mammals
- food for caterpillars

LANDSCAPE FUNCTIONS

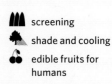

- spring flowers
- summer flowers
- fall flowers
- winter flowers
- fall foliage color
- fragrance
- evergreen ground cover
- deciduous ground cover
- screening
- shade and cooling
- edible fruits for humans

BOTANICAL NAME	COMMON NAME	ECOLOGICAL FUNCTIONS	LANDSCAPE FUNCTIONS
SHRUBS, continued			
Rosa virginiana	Virginia rose		
Rubus idaeus	red raspberry		
Rubus odoratus	flowering raspberry		
Salix discolor	pussy willow		
Sambucus canadensis	elderberry		
Spiraea alba	white meadowsweet		
Symphoricarpos albus	snowberry		
Taxus canadensis	Canada yew		
Vaccinium angustifolium	lowbush blueberry		
Vaccinium corymbosum	highbush blueberry		
Vaccinium vitis-idaea	mountain cranberry		
Viburnum acerifolium	mapleleaf viburnum		
Viburnum dentatum	arrowwood		
Viburnum lentago	nannyberry		
Viburnum nudum	smooth witherod, possumhaw		
VINES			
Celastrus scandens	American bittersweet		
Lonicera dioica	limber honeysuckle		
Parthenocissus quinquefolia	Virginia creeper		
Parthenocissus vitacea	woodbine		
Vitis aestivalis	summer grape		
Vitis labrusca	fox grape		
Vitis riparia	riverbank grape		

BOTANICAL NAME	COMMON NAME	ECOLOGICAL FUNCTIONS	LANDSCAPE FUNCTIONS
HERBACEOUS PERENNIALS AND BULBS			
Actaea rubra	red baneberry	pollen/nectar producer, food for birds, food for mammals, food for caterpillars	summer flowers, fragrance
Anemone quinquefolia	wood anemone	pollen/nectar producer, food for caterpillars	spring flowers, deciduous ground cover
Aquilegia canadensis	wild columbine	pollen/nectar producer, food for birds, food for caterpillars	spring flowers
Arisaema triphyllum	Jack-in-the-pulpit	pollen/nectar producer, food for birds, food for mammals, food for caterpillars	spring flowers
Asclepias syriaca	common milkweed	pollen/nectar producer, food for caterpillars	summer flowers, fragrance
Asclepias tuberosa	butterfly weed	pollen/nectar producer, food for caterpillars	summer flowers, fragrance
Aster divaricatus	white wood aster	pollen/nectar producer, food for caterpillars	fall flowers
Aster ericoides	white heath aster	pollen/nectar producer, food for caterpillars	fall flowers
Aster novae-angliae	New England aster	pollen/nectar producer, food for caterpillars	fall flowers
Aster novi-belgii	New York aster	pollen/nectar producer, food for caterpillars	fall flowers
Calla palustris	water arum	cover for wildlife	summer flowers
Caulophyllum thalictroides	blue cohosh	pollen/nectar producer, food for birds	spring flowers
Chelone glabra	turtlehead	cover for wildlife, nest sites for birds, pollen/nectar producer, food for caterpillars	summer flowers, deciduous ground cover
Cimicifuga racemosa	black cohosh	pollen/nectar producer, food for caterpillars	summer flowers
Clintonia borealis	blue bead lily	pollen/nectar producer, food for birds, food for mammals	spring flowers
Coreopsis rosea	pink coreopsis	pollen/nectar producer, food for birds, food for caterpillars	summer flowers
Dicentra canadensis	squirrel-corn	pollen/nectar producer, food for mammals	spring flowers
Eupatorium maculatum	spotted Joe-Pye weed	pollen/nectar producer, food for caterpillars	summer flowers, fragrance
Eupatorium rugosum	white snakeroot	pollen/nectar producer, food for caterpillars	fall flowers
Gentiana clausa	closed gentian	pollen/nectar producer	fall flowers

ECOLOGICAL FUNCTIONS

- cover for wildlife
- nest sites for birds
- pollen and/or nectar producer
- food for birds
- food for mammals
- food for caterpillars

LANDSCAPE FUNCTIONS

- spring flowers
- summer flowers
- fall flowers
- winter flowers
- fall foliage color
- fragrance
- evergreen ground cover
- deciduous ground cover
- screening
- shade and cooling
- edible fruits for humans

BOTANICAL NAME	COMMON NAME	ECOLOGICAL FUNCTIONS	LANDSCAPE FUNCTIONS
HERBACEOUS PERENNIALS AND BULBS, continued			
Geranium maculatum	wild geranium	🐝 🐦 🌰 🐛	✿
Hedyotis caerulea	bluets	🐝	✿
Heliopsis helianthoides	oxeye	🐝 🐛	✿
Hepatica acutiloba	sharp-lobed hepatica	🐝 🐛	✿
Hibiscus moscheutos	swamp rose-mallow	🦋 🐝	✿
Iris versicolor	blue flag iris	🐢 🐝	✿
Lilium canadense	Canada lily	🐝	✿
Lilium philadelphicum	wood lily	🐝 🐛	✿ 🌹
Lobelia cardinalis	cardinal flower	🐝 🐛	✿
Lobelia siphilitica	great blue lobelia	🐝	✿
Lupinus perennis	blue lupine	🐢 🐝 🐦 🐛	✿ 🌹
Mitchella repens	partridgeberry	🐦 🌰	✿ 🌹 ▨
Monarda didyma	beebalm	🐢 🐝 🐦 🐛	✿ 🌹
Panax quinquefolius	ginseng	🐝 🐦 🌰 🐛	✿ 🌹
Penstemon digitalis	foxglove beardtongue	🐢 🦋 🐝 🐛	✿
Phlox divaricata	woodland phlox, wild blue phlox	🐝 🐛	✿ 🌹 ▨
Phlox subulata	moss pink	🐛	✿ ▨
Podophyllum peltatum	mayapple	🐦 🌰 🐛	✿ ▨ 🍒
Polygonatum commutatum	Solomon's-seal	🐢 🐝 🐦 🌰 🐛	✿ 🌹 ▨
Potentilla tridentata	shrubby fivefingers		✿ ▨
Rudbeckia hirta	black-eyed Susan	🐝 🐛	✿
Sanguinaria canadensis	bloodroot	🐝 🐛	✿
Smilacina racemosa	false Solomon's-seal	🐝 🐦 🌰 🐛	✿ 🌹 🍒

BOTANICAL NAME	COMMON NAME	ECOLOGICAL FUNCTIONS	LANDSCAPE FUNCTIONS
HERBACEOUS PERENNIALS AND BULBS, continued			
Solidago caesia	blue-stem goldenrod	pollen/nectar, caterpillars	fall flowers
Solidago rugosa	rough-stem goldenrod	pollen/nectar, caterpillars	fall flowers
Teucrium canadense	wood sage	pollen/nectar, caterpillars	fall flowers
Tiarella cordifolia	eastern foamflower	pollen/nectar	spring flowers
Trillium erectum	purple trillium	pollen/nectar, food for birds, food for mammals, caterpillars	spring flowers
Trillium grandiflorum	white trillium	pollen/nectar, food for birds, food for mammals, caterpillars	spring flowers
Viola cucullata	marsh blue violet	pollen/nectar, food for birds, caterpillars	spring flowers, deciduous ground cover
Viola pedata	birdsfoot violet	pollen/nectar, food for birds, caterpillars	spring flowers
Viola pubescens	yellow violet	pollen/nectar, food for birds, caterpillars	spring flowers, deciduous ground cover
Zizia aurea	golden Alexanders	pollen/nectar, caterpillars	fall flowers
GRASSES, SEDGES, AND RUSHES			
Andropogon gerardii	big bluestem	cover for wildlife, nest sites for birds, food for birds	deciduous ground cover
Andropogon virginicus	broomsedge	cover for wildlife, nest sites for birds, food for birds	deciduous ground cover
Carex pensylvanica	Pennsylvania sedge	cover for wildlife, nest sites for birds, food for birds, food for mammals	deciduous ground cover
Deschampsia cespitosa	tufted hairgrass	cover for wildlife, nest sites for birds, food for birds, food for mammals, caterpillars	deciduous ground cover
Eragrostis spectabilis	purple lovegrass	cover for wildlife, nest sites for birds, food for birds, caterpillars	deciduous ground cover
Juncus effusus	common rush	cover for wildlife, nest sites for birds, food for birds, food for mammals	deciduous ground cover
Panicum virgatum	switchgrass	cover for wildlife, nest sites for birds, food for birds, food for mammals, caterpillars	deciduous ground cover
Scirpus cyperinus	bulrush, woolgrass	cover for wildlife, nest sites for birds, food for birds, caterpillars	deciduous ground cover
Schizachyrium scoparium	little bluestem	cover for wildlife, nest sites for birds, food for birds, caterpillars	deciduous ground cover

ECOLOGICAL FUNCTIONS

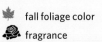

- cover for wildlife
- nest sites for birds
- pollen and/or nectar producer
- food for birds
- food for mammals
- food for caterpillars

LANDSCAPE FUNCTIONS

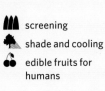

- spring flowers
- summer flowers
- fall flowers
- winter flowers
- fall foliage color
- fragrance
- evergreen ground cover
- deciduous ground cover
- screening
- shade and cooling
- edible fruits for humans

BOTANICAL NAME	COMMON NAME	ECOLOGICAL FUNCTIONS	LANDSCAPE FUNCTIONS
GRASSES, SEDGES, AND RUSHES, continued			
Spartina pectinata	prairie cord-grass	cover for wildlife, nest sites for birds, food for birds	deciduous ground cover
Sporobolus heterolepis	prairie dropseed	cover for wildlife, nest sites for birds, pollen/nectar producer, food for birds	deciduous ground cover
Tridens flavus	purpletop, redtop	cover for wildlife, nest sites for birds, food for birds, food for mammals, food for caterpillars	deciduous ground cover
Typha angustifolia	narrowleaf cattail	nest sites for birds, food for birds, food for mammals, food for caterpillars	deciduous ground cover
FERNS			
Athyrium filix-femina	lady fern	cover for wildlife, nest sites for birds, food for caterpillars	deciduous ground cover
Dennstaedtia punctilobula	hayscented fern	cover for wildlife, nest sites for birds, food for caterpillars	deciduous ground cover
Dryopteris intermedia	evergreen wood fern	cover for wildlife, nest sites for birds, food for caterpillars	evergreen ground cover
Matteuccia struthiopteris	ostrich fern	cover for wildlife, nest sites for birds, food for mammals, food for caterpillars	deciduous ground cover
Onoclea sensibilis	sensitive fern	cover for wildlife, nest sites for birds, food for caterpillars	deciduous ground cover
Osmunda cinnamomea	cinnamon fern	cover for wildlife, nest sites for birds, food for caterpillars	deciduous ground cover
Osmunda regalis	royal fern	cover for wildlife, nest sites for birds, food for caterpillars	deciduous ground cover
Phegopteris hexagonoptera	broad beech fern	cover for wildlife, food for caterpillars	deciduous ground cover
Polystichum acrostichoides	Christmas fern	cover for wildlife, nest sites for birds, food for caterpillars	evergreen ground cover
Thelypteris noveboracensis	New York fern	cover for wildlife, nest sites for birds, food for caterpillars	deciduous ground cover

ECOLOGICAL FUNCTIONS

- cover for wildlife
- nest sites for birds
- pollen and/or nectar producer
- food for birds
- food for mammals
- food for caterpillars

LANDSCAPE FUNCTIONS

- spring flowers
- summer flowers
- fall flowers
- winter flowers
- fall foliage color
- fragrance
- evergreen ground cover
- deciduous ground cover
- screening
- shade and cooling
- edible fruits for humans

References

Brewer, R. 1961. Comparative notes on the life history of the Carolina chickadee. *Wilson Bulletin* 73: 348–373.

Burghardt, K. T., and D. W. Tallamy. 2013. Plant origin asymmetrically impacts feeding guilds and drives community structure of herbivorous arthropods. *Diversity and Distributions* 19: 1553–1556.

Burghardt, K. T., D. W. Tallamy, C. Philips, and K. J. Shropshire. 2010. Non-native plants reduce abundance, richness, and host specialization in lepidopteran communities. *Ecosphere* 1: art11. doi:10.1890/ES10-00032.1.

Burghardt, K. T., D. W. Tallamy, and W. G. Shriver. 2008. The impact of native plants on biodiversity in suburban landscapes. *Conservation Biology* 23: 219–244.

Burke, D. M., and E. Nol. 1998. Influence of food abundance, nest-site habitat, and forest fragmentation on breeding ovenbirds. *The Auk* 115: 96–104.

Coder, K. D. 1993. Quantifiable urban forest benefits and costs: current findings and future research. In a white paper titled *Consolidating and Communicating Urban Forest Benefits*. Kent, Ohio: Davey Resource Group.

Cody, M. L. 1974. *Competition and the Structure of Bird Communities*. Princeton, New Jersey: Princeton University Press. Princeton.

Costanza, R., R. d'Arge, R. de Groot, S. Farber, M. Grasso, B. Hannon, K. Limburg, S. Naeem, R. V. O'Neill, J. Paruelo, R. G. Raskin, P. Sutton, and M. van den Belt. 1997. The value of the world's ecosystem services and natural capital. *Nature* 387: 253–260.

Costello, S. L., P. D. Pratt, M. B. Rayamajhi, and T. D. Center. 2003. Arthropods associated with aboveground portions of the invasive tree, *Melaleuca quinquenervia*, in South Florida, USA. *The Florida Entomologist* 86: 300–322.

Dickinson, M. B., ed. 1999. *Field Guide to the Birds of North America*. 3rd ed. Washington, D.C.: National Geographic Society.

Emerson, R. W. (1836) 2009. Nature. In *Nature and Other Essays*. Reprint, Mineola, New York: Dover Publications.

Erhlich, P. R., and A. H. Erhlich. 1981. *Extinction: The Causes and Consequences of the Disappearance of Species*. New York: Random House.

Forister, M. L., L. A. Dyer, M. S. Singer, J. O. Stireman, and J. T. Lill. 2012. Revisiting the evolution of ecological specialization, with emphasis on insect-plant interactions. *Ecology* 93: 981–991.

Grinnell, J. 1917. The niche-relationships of the California thrasher. *The Auk* 34: 427–433.

Hobbs, R. J., E. Higgs, and J. A. Harris. 2009. Novel ecosystems: implications for conservation and restoration. *Trends in Ecology and Evolution* 24: 599–605.

Hutchinson, G. E. 1957. Concluding remarks. Cold Spring Harbor Symposia on Quantitative Biology 22: 415–427.

MacArthur, R. 1955. Fluctuations of animal populations and a measure of community stability. *Ecology* 36: 533–536.

MacArthur, R., H. Recher, and M. Cody. 1966. On the relation between habitat selection and species diversity. *American Naturalist* 100: 319–332.

Maestre F. T., J. L. Quero, N. J. Gotelli, A. Escudero, V. Ochoa, et al. 2012. Plant species richness and ecosystem multifunctionality in global drylands. *Science* 335: 214–218.

Marra, P. P., K. A. Hobson, and R. T. Holmes. 1998. Linking winter and summer events in a migratory bird by using stable-carbon isotopes. *Science* 282: 1884–1886.

McCann, K. S. 2011. *Food Webs*. Princeton: New Jersey: Princeton University Press.

Millennium Ecosystem Assessment. 2005. *Ecosystems and Human Well-Being. Synthesis 1*. Washington, D.C.: Island Press.

Naeem, S., J. E. Duffy, and E. Zavaleta. 2012. The functions of biological diversity in an age of extinction. *Science* 336: 1401–1406.

Perry, D. A., R. Oren, and S. C. Hart. 2008. *Forest Ecosystems.* 2nd ed. Baltimore, Maryland: Johns Hopkins University Press.

Powell, K. I., J. M. Chase, and T. M. Knight. 2011. A synthesis of plant invasion effects on biodiversity across spatial scales. *American Journal of Botany* 98: 539–548.

Powell, K. I., J. M. Chase, and T. M. Knight. 2013. Invasive plants have scale-dependent effects on diversity by altering species-area relationships. *Science* 339: 316–318.

Reed, S. 2010. *Energy-Wise Landscape Design: A New Approach for Your Home and Garden.* Gabriola, British Columbia: New Society Publishers.

Reich, P. B., D. Tilman, F. Isbell, K. Mueller, S. E. Hobbie, D. Flynn, and N. Eisenhauer. 2012. Impacts of biodiversity loss escalate through time as redundancy fades. *Science* 336: 589–592.

Richards, O. W., and R. G. Davies. 1977. *Imm's General Textbook of Entomology.* 10th edition. *Vol. 1: Structure, Physiology, and Development.* New York: John Wiley.

Robinson, W. D. 1999. Long-term changes in the avifauna of Barro Colorado Island, Panama: A tropical forest Isolate. *Conservation Biology* 13: 85–97.

Rosenzweig, M. L. 2003. *Win-Win Ecology: How the Earth's Species Can Survive in the Midst of Human Enterprise.* New York: Oxford University Press.

Sheil, D., and D. Murdiyarso. 2009. How forests attract rain: an examination of a new hypothesis. *BioScience* 59: 341–347.

Shrewsbury, P. M., and M. J. Raupp. 2000. Evaluation of components of vegetational texture for predicting azalea lace bug, *Stephanitis pyrioides* (Heteroptera: Tingidae), abundance in managed landscapes. *Environmental Entomology* 29: 919–926.

Smith, A. D. M., C. J. Brown, C. M. Bulman, E. A. Fulton, P. Johnson, I. C. Kaplan, H. Lozano-Montes, S. Mackinson, M. Marzloff, L. J. Shannon, Y.-J.Shin, and J. Tam. 2011. Impacts of fishing low-trophic level species on marine ecosystems. *Science* 333: 1147–1150.

Stanford, J. A., C. A. Frissell, and C. C. Coutant. 2006. The status of habitats. In *Return to the River: Restoring Salmon to the Columbia River.* Ed. R. N. Williams. San Diego, California: Elsevier Press. 173–248.

Strong, D. R., J. H. Lawton, and R. Southwood. 1984. *Insects on Plants: Community Patterns and Mechanisms.* Cambridge: Harvard University Press.

Tallamy, D. W. 2004. Do alien plants reduce insect biomass? *Conservation Biology* 18: 1689–1692.

Tallamy, D. W., and K. J. Shropshire. 2009. Ranking lepidopteran use of native versus introduced plants. *Conservation Biology* 23: 941–947.

Tallamy, D. W., J. Bruck, S. Walker, K. Pippins, S. Shpak, and A. Lucey. Submitted. The abundance, diversity, and geographic origin of suburban landscape plantings. *Arboriculture and Urban Forestry.*

Tewksbury, L., R. Casagrande, B. Blossey, P. Häfliger, and M. Schwarzländer. 2002. Potential for biological control of *Phragmites australis* in north America. *Biological Control* 23: 191–212.

Urquhart, F. A. 1976. Found at last: the monarch's winter home. *National Geographic* 150:160–173.

U.S. Census Bureau. 2010. http://www.census.gov/prod/2011pubs/h150-09.pdf.

U.S. EPA. 2009. Trees and vegetation. In *Reducing Urban Heat Islands: Compendium of Strategies.* http://epa.gov/heatisland/mitigation/trees.htm.

Verhoeven, K. J., A. Biere, J. A. Harvey, and W. H. van der Putten. 2009. Plant invaders and their novel natural enemies: who is naïve? *Ecology Letters* 12: 107–117.

Wright, F. L. 1954. *The Natural House.* New York: Bramhall House.

Zanette, L., P. Doyle, and S. M. Trémont. 2000. Food shortage in small fragments: evidence from an area-sensitive passerine. *Ecology* 81: 1654–1666.

Acknowledgments

The authors thank the following people and institutions who contributed information, photography, and/or opened their gardens to us in the production of this book: Sue and Doug Barton, Bok Tower Gardens, Cole Burrell, James and Claire Cecchi, Abby Coffin, John Cram, Jerry and Diane Darke, Angie Dunson, Governor and Mrs. Pierre S. du Pont, Mr. and Mrs. William H. Frederick, Jr., Leonard J. Buck Garden, Longwood Gardens, Mt. Cuba Center, Robert Reimer, Mike Riska, Cindy Tallamy, Patricia and Charles Robertson, The University of Delwaware Botanic Garden, John van Neil, Meg and Adam Waldron, Jim White, Philip Williams, Winterthur Museum, Garden and Library, and Melinda Zoehrer.

Photo Credits

All photographs by Rick Darke except for the following:

Jay Cossey, page 29 zebra swallowtail larva on pawpaw leaf.

Jerry Darke, pages 51 pileated woodpecker at bottom right, 225 barred owl.

Doug Tallamy, pages 8 all, 22 all, 23 eastern gray squirrel, 32 woodthrush on nest, 35 spicebush swallowtail larva, adult spicebush swallowtail, 49 land snail, salamander, ant carrying bloodroot seed, 55 Baltimore oriole with nest, 73 all, 74 all, 75 all, 76 all, 77 all, 78 all, 79 all, 94 all, 95 all, 96 all, 97 all, 98 all, 99 all, 100 all, 104 all, 110 all, 115 all, 119 all, 125 all, 128 all, 129 all, 141 all, 142 colletid bee emerging from nest, andrenid bee on woodland phlox, 143 baby turtle in hand, 148 hover fly on bluet, 153 click beetle, 186 red-banded hairstreak on arrowwood viburnum, 189 zebra swallowtail on sweet pepperbush, 194 young mantids hatching from egg case, 222 all, 223 all, 242 ruby-throated hummingbird on trumpet honeysuckle, 246 pipevine swallowtail eggs, pipevine swallowtail with chrysalis, 273 catbird, downy woodpecker with gall, 275 meadowlark chicks, 280 all, 281 all, 282 indigo bunting, 283 all, 285 orchard oriole in oak.

John van Neil, page 49 springtails on leaf.

Jim White, page 67 spring peeper.

Melinda Zoehrer, pages 62 ebony jewelwing, 245 pipevine flower, 277 monarch butterfly larva.

Index

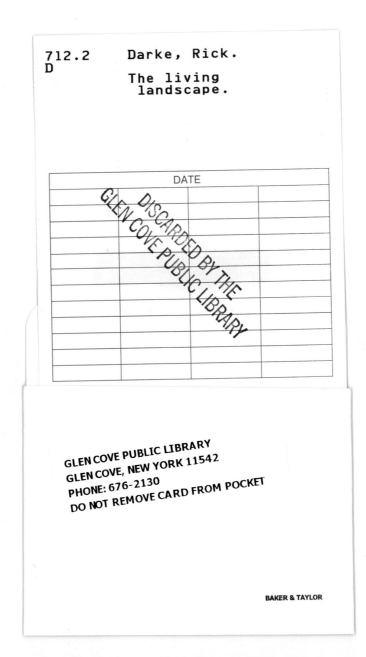